GLOBAL POLICY STUDIES

International Interaction toward Improving Public Policy

POLICY STUDIES ORGANIZATION SERIES

General Editor: Stuart S. Nagel, Professor of Political Science, University of Illinois at Urbana-Champaign

Naomi Carmon (*editor*)
NEIGHBOURHOOD POLICY AND PROGRAMMES: Past and Present

David Louis Cingranelli (*editor*)
HUMAN RIGHTS: Theory and Measurement

Sheldon H. Danziger and Kent E. Portney (*editors*)
THE DISTRIBUTIONAL IMPACTS OF PUBLIC POLICIES

Don F. Hadwiger and William P. Browne (*editors*)
PUBLIC POLICY AND AGRICULTURAL TECHNOLOGY: Adversity despite Achievement

Richard C. Hula (*editor*)
MARKET-BASED PUBLIC POLICY

Rita Mae Kelly (*editor*)
PROMOTING PRODUCTIVITY IN THE PUBLIC SECTOR: Problems, Strategies and Prospects

Fred Lazin, Samuel Aroni and Yehuda Gradus (*editors*)
THE POLICY IMPACT OF UNIVERSITIES IN DEVELOPING REGIONS

Stuart S. Nagel
DECISION-AIDING SOFTWARE: Skills, Obstacles and Applications

Stuart S. Nagel (*editor*)
GLOBAL POLICY STUDIES: International Interaction toward Improving Public Policy

J. David Roessner (*editor*)
GOVERNMENT INNOVATION POLICY: Design, Implementation, Evaluation

Global Policy Studies

International Interaction toward Improving Public Policy

Edited by
Stuart S. Nagel
Professor of Political Science
University of Illinois at Urbana-Champaign

MACMILLAN

in association with the
POLICY STUDIES
ORGANIZATION

First published 1991

Published by
MACMILLAN ACADEMIC AND PROFESSIONAL LTD
Houndmills, Basingstoke, Hampshire RG21 2XS
and London
Companies and representatives
throughout the world

Typeset by Latimer Trend & Company Ltd
Printed in Hong Kong

British Library Cataloguing in Publication Data
Nagel, Stuart S. *1934–*
Global policy studies: international interaction toward
improving public policy.—(Policy Studies Organization
series)
1. International relations. Policies of governments
I. Nagel, Stuart, Stuart S.
303.482
ISBN 0–333–52600–7

Dedicated to improving public policy
across and within multiple nations

Contents

viii *Contents*

List of Figures

List of Tables

Notes on the Contributors

Jonathan F. Galloway is Professor of Politics, Irwin D. & Fern D. Young Presidential chair, International Relations Chairperson, Lake Forest College, Illinois. Elected member of the International Institute of Space Law and the American Astronautical Society. Author of *The Politics and Technology of Satellite Communications* (1972) and a number of articles on law and policy *vis-à-vis* outer space, e.g. 'International Law and the Protection of the Ozone Layer'. Member of the International Studies Association and The American Political Science Association and author of a number of articles on multinational corporations, e.g. 'Multinational Enterprises as Worldwide Interest Groups'. Member of the North American Society of Social Philosophy and author of several articles, e.g. 'Human Rights and U.S. Foreign Policy'.

Scott McKinney is Associate Professor of Economics at Hobart and William Smith Colleges, Geneva, New York. He received his Ph.D. from Indiana University-Bloomington, where he specialized in public finance and urban economics. He has published articles on various aspects of US metropolitan areas – interjurisdictional externalities, residential segregation, and the efficient provision of public goods and services – and is now doing research on economic aspects of international cooperation in drug control.

Longin Pastusiak is Professor in the Polish Institute of International Affairs in Warsaw. Author of more than 500 scholarly publications including 40 books. 1985–8 President of the Polish Political Science Association. Since 1988 member of Executive Committee of IPSA.

Andrew M. Scott, after serving as a Navy pilot in the Second World War, graduated from Dartmouth and took his Ph.D. at Harvard. He worked for foreign affairs agencies in Washington, DC for several years before moving into academic life. Professor Scott has taught courses in international politics and American foreign policy at the University of North Carolina-Chapel Hill, and has written a number of books including *The Revolution in Statecraft*; *The Functioning of the International Political System*, and *The Dynamics of Interdependence*.

Marvin S. Soroos is Professor and head of the Department of Political Science at North Carolina State University. His books include *The Global Predicament: Ecological Perspectives on World Order* (1979), *Environment and the Global Arena: Actors, Values, Policies, and Futures* (1985), and *Beyond Sovereignty: the Challenge of Global Policy* (1986).

Arild Underdal (b. 1946) is Professor of Political Science at the University of Oslo, Norway. His major research interests are the study of negotiation, international cooperation, and resource management. His publications include *The Politics of International Fisheries Management* (1980), and a forthcoming book (co-authored, in Norwegian) on wage negotiations in the public sector.

Inés Vargas was educated as a jurist (University of Chile), Professor in Labour Law and Social Security, University of Chile (1970–3). Vice-Minister of Justice in the Allende's government, Chile (1972–3); Researcher at the International Peace Research Institute, Oslo, PRIO (1980–7) and at the Norwegian Institute of Human Rights (1988–90).

Louise G. White is Associate Professor in the Department of Public Affairs at George Mason University. She has written in the general area of development management, including *Creating Opportunities for Change: Approaches for Managing Development Programs*, and *Managing Development in the Third World* (with Coralie Bryant). She also wrote *Political Analysis: Technique and Practice* and has published articles on institutional analysis and design.

James E. Winkates is Research Professor of International Affairs, Air War College, Maxwell AFB, Montgomery. Dr Winkates co-edited 'Terrorism: War By Another Name?', a special theme issue of the *Quarterly Journal of Ideology* (Spring 1988), and is the author of many articles, monographs, reports, and reviews since coming to the Air War College in 1976. He received the AWC Faculty Research Award for both 1988 and 1989.

Introduction to Global Policy Studies

The purpose of this symposium of research papers is to summarize and stimulate new ideas in the new field of global policy studies.

WHAT THE FIELD INCLUDES

The field of global policy studies can be **defined** as the study of international interactions designed to deal with shared public policy problems.

Such **policy problems** can include:

1. **Trans-boundary problems** like people, pollution, or goods literally going across international boundaries.
2. **Common property problems** like the oceans, Antarctica, or the atmosphere, which nobody owns but which are a kind of common good that needs to be regulated, expanded, or substituted, or else (like the tragedy of the commons) they will be devoured to the mutual detriment of the nations of the world.
3. **Simultaneous problems** like health, education, and welfare, about which all countries can learn from each other.

HOW THE FIELD DIFFERS FROM RELATED AREAS

Global policy studies is related to **international relations**, comparative government, and public policy studies. None of those three political science fields alone, however, can adequately study the subject of global policy studies. International relations concentrates on relations among countries that relate to diplomacy, alliances, and the resolution of disputes that might otherwise result in war. There are international institutions concerned with public policy studies, such as the specialized agencies of the United Nations, but they are not part of the mainstream of the study of international relations. One might also note that important international interactions associated with global policy studies may not be institutionalized, such as the economic summit meetings, or other even less formal meetings among government officials of various countries designed to deal with shared policy problems.

The field of **comparative** public policy is cross-national in the sense of dealing with a multiplicity of countries. The analysis, however, tends to be of one country at a time. Sometimes comparisons are made across countries with an attempt to explain and evaluate differences and similarities. The element of **international interaction** is, however, missing, which is essential to global policy studies. 'Global' does not mean that all countries of the world interact simultaneously, but rather that all countries of the world do share the policy problems under consideration, or at least potentially share them.

The field of **policy studies** tends to concentrate on the single country of the political or social scientist who is working in the field. Some policy studies scholars do look to other countries, but mainly for the purpose of getting ideas that have predictive or prescriptive power within their own countries. They seldom look to international interaction, although they may look at the interaction that occurs between states, provinces, cities, or other sub-national units within their own countries. If each country seeks to maximize its own quality of life without cooperative interaction, the countries in general may suffer important **opportunity costs** as in other sub-optimizing situations. The classical example is each country trying to produce whatever goods it produces best; as a result, the world winds up with surpluses and shortages on all goods. It should, however, be noted that in the absence of world government, it will be necessary for individual countries working together by formal or informal agreement to make use of the positive and negative incentives which they have available for encouraging internationally desired behavior.

THE ORGANIZATION OF THIS BOOK

Cross-cutting Issues and Processes

The chapters in this book are organized in two parts. Part I deals with cross-cutting issues and processes. The basic concepts in the field, as developed by Marvin Soroos (Chapter 1), refer to such matters as:

1. The **definition** of global policy studies.
2. How the field **relates to other fields**.

3. The nature of global policy **problems**.
4. States in the global policy **process**.
5. Global **policy making arenas**.
6. Relevant **participants**.
7. **Diverse forms of global policies**.

The basic methods, as developed by Stuart Nagel (Chapter 2), refer to such matters as how to systematically process a set of:

1. Global policy **goals**.
2. **Alternatives** available for achieving them.
3. **Relations** between goals and alternatives.
4. Choosing or explaining the best alternative, combination, allocation, or predictive **decision-rule**.

Chapter 2 also emphasizes the importance of such substance issues as:

1. **Technology policy**, such as deciding among alternative energy sources or deciding among alternative ways of reducing pollution.
2. **Economic policy**, such as how to reduce unemployment and inflation or deciding on the appropriate division of labor between the public sector and the private sector.
3. **Social policy**, such as deciding how to reduce ethnic discrimination.
4. **Political policy**, including alternative ways of handling freedom of speech.

Another cross-cutting issue relates to the role of the nation state in dealing with global policy problems. That issue is discussed by Louise White (Chapter 3), viewing the nation state from the three perspectives of being:

1. Sometimes a **hindrance** to dealing with global policy problems.
2. Sometimes **irrelevant**.
3. Sometimes a **resource** for economic development as well as a **custodian** of multiple policy values.

The chapter by Arild Underdal on the art and science of international cooperation (Chapter 4) discusses such issues as:

1. **Diagnosing** collective problems.
2. Noting where **policy coordination** can make a difference.
3. Going **from diagnosis to cure**.
4. Arranging for **international cooperation**.
5. Designing **politically feasible solutions**.

6.   The role of **process engineering** in global policy problems.

Andrew Scott (Chapter 5) does a comparative study of global policy problems which is especially directed at answering such questions as:

1.   What **is** a problem?
2.   What **caused** the problem?
3.   When did **significant changes** occur?
4.   What is the **extent** of the problem?
5.   What are the **trends**?
6.   Does the problem link up with **other problems**?
7.   Should there be an attempt at **intervening**?
8.   What is the **aggregate impact** of the related problems?
9.   How might **remote sensing and systematic monitoring** help, especially as developed by intelligence-gathering agencies?

Chapter 6 by Longin Pastusiak on 'Eastern Europe and Global Issues' is especially timely. Professor Pastusiak is the president of the Polish Political Science Association and a recent candidate for the Polish Parliament. His chapter was written both before and after changes in Eastern Europe. He thereby bridges the old socialism and the new pragmatism from revolutionary internationalism toward regional and world trade. He also bridges verbal and quantitative analysis.

Specific Policy Problems

Part II of the book deals with specific policy problems, including those that are economic, technological, and political. The first such problem is the economic problem of international trade union solidarity actions, as discussed by Inés Vargas (Chapter 7). She is especially concerned with the Coca Cola case and the case of ships flying flags of convenience. She also draws broader legal, economic, and cross-national implications.

This is followed by Jonathan Galloway on global telecommunications policy (Chapter 8). As with all these specific policy problems, global telecommunications requires **cooperative interaction** among countries in order to have a meaningful world-wide telecommunications system, especially with regard to the use of communication satellites.

The next policy problem involves the atmosphere, including problems that relate to the greenhouse or world-warming effect, the disappearing ozone layer, and acid rain, as discussed by Marvin Soroos (Chapter 9). Each of these problems if not handled cooperatively can have highly adverse effects on agriculture, human cancers, and the destruction of fish as a source of food. As with most of these specific policy problems, the international interaction takes the form of bilateral and multilateral agreements among countries, regional associations like the European Community (EC), and United Nations agencies like the Food and Agricultural Organization (FAO).

Terrorism can be classified as a political policy problem. The study on that subject by James Winkates (Chapter 10) discusses the role of the group of seven industrialized countries (G-7) who originally met mainly to discuss international trade matters, but who have become a good example of semi-formal interaction to deal with global policy problems.

The last study, by Scott McKinney (Chapter 11), is on international crime policy and efficient resource allocation. It deals with such specific policy problems as how to deal with the drug cartel, the extradition of fugitives from justice who are not necessarily involved in drugs, and various kinds of smuggling including illegal ivory which has recently become an international crime problem. This chapter is a fitting one for ending the book because it develops the broader implications of anti-crime allocation, discussing ideas that apply to who gets and should get what, when, how, and why regarding the allocation of public policy resources in general. That is a fundamental part of political science and public policy studies.

Additional papers dealing with the cross-cutting issues of global policy studies and specific global policy problems will be available in a 1990 issue of the *International Political Science Review*. There is no overlap between the longer, more in-depth chapters in this volume and the articles in that journal issue, although they both have similar introductory material. The journal issue, under cross-cutting issues, includes an article on 'The Moral and Value Foundations of Multilateralism' by Klaus Hufner and Jens Naumann. Under specific policy problems, the journal issue includes 'Global Policy, Employment, and Human Rights' by Richard Siegel, 'Managing the World Economy' by Aaron Segal, 'Global Environmental Degradation and International Organizations' by Mukund Untawale, and 'Educational Policy and Development' by Benjamin Levin.

BALANCE ON MULTIPLE DIMENSIONS

This symposium volume and experience in the field provide good balance on a number of dimensions – theoretical, geographical, purposive, disciplinary, ideological, and methodological.

1. Balance between cross-cutting **theoretical matters** and those that are more specific in nature. The theoretical orientation, however, is not overly abstract, and the discussion of the specific policy problems does not emphasize anecdotal case studies.

2. Balance among various **parts of the world** is represented by the authors including political and social scientists from England, Germany, Poland, India, Spain, the Philippines, and the United States. There is even better balance in terms of the countries that are referred to in the contributions, which include all major parts of the world.

3. Balance between prescriptive or **evaluative** analysis and predictive or **explanatory** analysis. The field is thus concerned with both (1) explaining variations in the occurrence of international interaction for dealing with shared policy problems and (2) prescribing how such international interaction can be improved and made more effective, efficient, and equitable in achieving its goals.

4. Balance across **disciplinary** perspectives. The authors in this symposium are primarily political scientists, but they recognize that one cannot deal adequately with policy problems without bringing in the perspectives of other social sciences and other fields of knowledge, such as economics, sociology, psychology, and natural science.

5. Balance across **ideological** perspectives. The authors come from a variety of ideological backgrounds in terms of how government should relate to the economy or to the people, and how government should be organized. There may, however, be an underlying pragmatism that is especially associated with policy studies as contrasted to political theory, and a searching for solutions to global policy problems that will be recognized as desirable regardless of ideology. There may also be an underlying virtual unanimity in favor of an expansion of the elements of democracy that are conducive to academic creativity and interaction, as contrasted to balancing democracy and dictatorship.

6. Balance across **methodological** orientations. This includes studies that emphasize verbal analysis or quantitative analysis. There may,

however, be a tendency to get away from unstructured verbal description and make more use of systematic analytic frameworks such as talking in terms of multi-criteria decision-making. Doing so involves analyzing a set of goals to be achieved, alternatives available for achieving them, and relations between goals and alternatives in order to choose or explain the best alternative, combination, allocation, or predictive decision-rule. There may also be a tendency to get away from unthinking cross-national quantitative description that involves correlating policy-irrelevant or policy-relevant variables against other variables or each other for 160 members of the United Nations.

CURRENT DEVELOPMENTS

It is difficult to say when the study of international interaction to deal with shared policy problems first began. One landmark book in the field is Marvin Soroos (1986). Before that, there have been studies of specialized agencies within the United Nations and the League of Nations, including the International Labor Organization, the World Health Organization, and other international agencies concerned with specific policy problems. That earlier literature tended to focus on those semi-governmental institutions rather than on more informal types of interaction. A key volume in the earlier literature is Keohane and Nye (1977).

A key event since the Soroos book was published is the development of the beginnings of a Study Group on 'Global Policy Studies' within the International Political Science Association (IPSA). That Study Group arose as a result of the enthusiasm shown at the 1988 IPSA triannual meeting in Washington, DC in the global policy studies panels, which also resulted in the preparation of the papers included in this symposium volume.

References

Keohane, R. and Nye, J. (1977)   *Power and Independence: World Politics in Transition* (Boston: Little, Brown).
Soroos, M. (1986)   *Beyond Sovereignty: The Challenge of Global Policy* (Columbia, SC: University of South Carolina Press).

Part I
Cross-cutting Issues

1 A Theoretical Framework for Global Policy Studies

Marvin S. Soroos

INTRODUCTION

It is not only appropriate, but also of critical importance, that the theoretical approach of policy studies be extended to the global sphere of human activity. Mankind faces numerous challenges which cannot be effectively addressed by nation-states acting on their own, several of which are avoiding war, constraining arms races, managing the world economy, reducing the prevalence of poverty and hunger, promoting the observance of human rights, preventing the spread of contagious diseases, refereeing competing uses of the oceans and outer space, and preserving the natural environment. Policy studies offer a theoretical framework for analyzing and evaluating the collective efforts of both governmental and non-governmental actors to address these and many other global problems within the context of international institutions, such as the United Nations and its affiliated specialized agencies.

The field of policy studies has grown and developed rapidly in recent decades as a multidisciplinary approach to inquiry into societal problems and the strategies adopted by governments to address them.[1] With a few exceptions, however, the scope of policy studies has been limited to the efforts of national governments or their sub-units to address the particular problems of their constituent populations, such as their needs for health care, education, employment, transportation, and security. Policy studies specialists have been reluctant to apply their perspective and method beyond the domain of nation-states to the problem-solving efforts at the international and global levels of political organization. One apparent reason is the common conception of a 'policy' as being the product of a type of governmental structure that does not exist in the anarchic international political order.

By contrast, the perspective taken in this chapter presumes that forms of international governance have evolved through which public policies are formulated and implemented to address global problems. These efforts have been adapted to the horizontal structure of the international order in which states are generally bound only by rules and obligations they have agreed to accept in contrast to vertically organized political systems within states, which empower governments to impose and enforce regulations on the citizenry without their individual consent. Despite the absence of a central world government, there are numerous circumstances in which states have seen it in their interest to accept constraints on their behavior in order to contribute to a coordinated international effort to come to grips with the larger problems faced by the world community.

This chapter illustrates the applicability of the theoretical perspective of policy studies to the enterprise of global problem-solving by addressing three questions. First, what **types of policy problems exist** that are of global concern? Second, how are **public policies made** at the global level? In responding to this question, specific attention is given to the stages in global policy processes, the arenas in which they take place, and the participating actors. Third, what is the **nature of the resulting policies**, and how are they **implemented**?

GLOBAL POLICY PROBLEMS

A **policy problem** is a set of circumstances that can potentially be improved upon by purposeful action. These circumstances may be an actual condition, such as the plight of as many as 500 million people worldwide that the Food and Agriculture Organization (FAO) identifies as being undernourished, or a future possibility, such as a cataclysmic nuclear war (FAO, 1987). A state of affairs that is not subject to human intervention, such as the occurrence of an earthquake, is not properly classified as a policy problem, although the challenge of minimizing the damage resulting from an earthquake, such as by emergency planning and reinforced structures, fulfills the criterion of a policy problem.

Global policy problems can be distinguished from those that are merely national, or from the larger category of international policy problems, on the basis of two criteria, which normally go hand in hand. First, the problem has aroused concern **throughout much of the world**. Second, it has been, or can be expected to be, taken up by one or more **international institutions** that are universal in the sense of being open to the membership of most if not all states, such as the United Nations. The agenda for the annual sessions of the General Assembly, which in 1987 included 143 items, offers an overview of the leading contemporary global policy problems (*UN Chronicle*, March 1988: 8). To fulfill these two criteria, it is not necessary that a problem be planetary in scope, as with the prospect of global climate change caused by the buildup of carbon dioxide or other 'greenhouse' gases in the atmosphere. Regional trouble spots, such as the armed conflicts in the Persian Gulf area, and even happenings within states, such as South Africa's apartheid system, have been subjects of global concern and have appeared on the agenda of General Assembly.[2]

Most global policy problems fall into one of three categories. **Transboundary** problems originate in one state but have ramifications for others. Economic policies adopted by one state to curb inflation or protect jobs threatened by imports can reverberate through the economies of others. Similarly, pollutants released into rivers or the atmosphere damage the environment of neighboring states. Large numbers of refugees fleeing oppressive political or economic circumstances migrate across international boundaries pose an additional burden for their new hosts. A second group of problems involves conflicting uses of **international commons**, including the oceans and seabed, outer space, the atmosphere, the electromagnetic spectrum, and Antarctica. Third, problems that are essentially **internal** to states appear on international agendas either because they are common to many states, such as illiteracy, rapid urbanization, and excessive population growth, or because what occurs within a given state is of concern to the outside world, examples being the flagrant abuse of human rights or the destruction of the habitat of endangered species that are unique to that country.[3]

STAGES IN THE GLOBAL POLICY PROCESS

In analyzing a policy process, it is useful to break the endeavor into a series of stages, beginning with the **identification** of a policy problem and proceeding to the **development** and **implementation** of a policy, and finally to a **review** and **decision** on whether to continue the policy. A more detailed list of steps in a rational policy process is presented in Table 1.1. In actual practice, policy-making at all levels is normally a much less orderly and logical process. Nevertheless, the rational policy model serves as a useful framework for sorting out and analyzing the components of the process.

Some if not all of these steps in the model policy process can be identified in international efforts to deal with specific global problems.

Table 1.1   Stages in a rational policy process

1. **Recognition** of a policy problem
2. **Specification** of procedures
3. Understanding on **goals** and **principles**
4. **Formulation** of **policy alternatives**
5. **Consideration** of **policy alternatives**
6. **Decision** on a policy
7. **Implementation** of the policy
8. **Review** and **evaluation** of the policy
9. Decision on the **future** of the policy

Certain global policy problems, such as war and poverty, are all too obvious from the events of the day and appear on the agendas of international institutions without any procedural fanfare. Other problems are not so apparent to the casual observer and become issues only after a concerted effort has been made to publicize them. Meetings of scientists, such as the Biosphere Conference sponsored by UNESCO in 1968 and the International Climate Conference convened by the World Meteorological Conference in 1979, may be a critical step in drawing worldwide attention to emerging policy problems.

Procedural issues can have a significant impact on the outcome of international policy processes. Policy deliberations may take place in established bodies such as the Security Council that have well defined procedures. In other contexts, the procedural questions become a key part of the negotiations because of their symbolic importance or how they affect the voting strength of conflicting blocs of states. Procedures were important for the Third United Nations Conference on the Law of the Sea (UNCLOS III) in which the objective was to craft a package agreement on 25 groupings of issues that could be accepted unanimously by the 150 participating states. The 'global negotiations' on reforming the international economic system that were to be held in the 1980s have been put off indefinitely for lack of agreement on procedures, in particular on a forum with voting rules acceptable to both the North and South.

Goals can be thought of as objectives that policy-makers seek to achieve, whereas principles are ground rules that are not to be violated or compromised in pursuit of the goals. Extensive listings of global goals and principles are listed in the preambles to charters of international institutions and in the numerous treaties and resolutions that are adopted each year. These goals and principles are commonly stated in abstract platitudes such as peace, security, economic growth, human dignity, sovereignty, equity, and good neighborliness, and thus are subject to competing interpretations. Goals can be quite specific, however, and unrealistic as well. For example, the goal of International Drinking Water Supply and Sanitation Decade which began in 1980 has been that all people will have access to safe water and adequate sanitation by 1990. Goals and principles on a particular issue are occasionally the subject of considerable discussion before being set forth in an official resolution, a notable example being the General Assembly's Declaration of Principles Governing the Seabed . . . Beyond the Limits of National Jurisdiction of 1970, which established the basis for negotiations at UNCLOS III.

The heart of any policy process is 4–6 in Table 1.1, of first formulating and then considering policy alternatives, and finally reaching a decision on the policy to pursue. Most global policy problems can be addressed in a variety of ways. For example, international fishery commissions confronted with the need to reduce annual catches to preserve a fishery consider options that include reducing the length of 'open' fishing season, specifying rules on the equipment such as the size of the mesh of nets, assigning a quota for the catch of each country, and setting limits on the size of each country's fleet.[4] Proposals for global policies may be introduced by individual states or larger blocs of them. The Group of 77, a coalition of Third World countries, put forward a major package of proposals for a 'new international economic order' and a 'new world communications and information order'.

Policy options at the international level become a subject of negotiation that can be both intensive and contentious. Discussions leading to compromises in international bodies may refer to a single 'negotiating text' which undergoes considerable revision and refinement before the document is put to a vote or signature by the participating states. This stage in the policy process can drag on for years and even decades. Agreement was not reached until 1966 on two conventions elaborating the human rights which were initially spelled out in the Universal Declaration of Human Rights of 1948. The new law of the sea convention was adopted in 1982 after twelve intensive negotiating sessions that comprised UNCLOS III, which were held over nine years. By contrast, within four months of the Chernobyl disaster in 1986, members of the International Atomic Energy Agency (IAEA) had agreed to conventions on the early notification of nuclear accidents and on assistance in the case of a nuclear accident or radiological emergency.

Ideally, decisions on global policies are reached by consensus because states cannot be compelled to comply with documents they do not accept. It may be necessary, however, to revert to voting procedures if unanimity cannot be accomplished, as was ultimately the case with UNCLOS III when the United States held out on the section pertaining to deep seabed mining. In most international bodies, voting is conducted according to a 'one-nation, one-vote' rule, with a one-half or two-thirds majority being sufficient to pass a measure. Larger states have argued that this voting arrangement is grossly unfair because a majority of votes can be cast by small states that together account for only about 1 per cent of the world's population. The World Bank and International Monetary Fund are examples of the relatively few international institutions that weight votes according to the size of state's financial contribution to the organization. Accordingly, the veto power in the Security Council is a concession to the role the five permanent members were expected to play in maintaining world peace.

The sharpest contrast between international and national policy processes is perhaps in the implementation stage. The international level has no analogue for national law enforcement and criminal justice agencies. International institutions generally have neither the authority nor the means to enforce regulations, although the United Nations Charter has an unimplemented provision for a multinational military force to be available to confront aggression. Rather it is presumed that governments of states will take steps in good faith to ensure that not only they, but also actors under their legal jurisdiction, comply with the commitments made to international policies. States are also the primary source of pressure on other states to conform to international rules of conduct, which can be brought to bear by complaints, accusations, trade sanctions, and occasionally military intervention. International agencies can, however, play other roles in implementing global policies. For example, the United Nations Environment Programme (UNEP) coordinates the extensive Global Environmental Monitoring System, which monitors the condition of the natural environment by compiling worldwide data on variables such as the level of atmospheric and marine pollutants and the extent of forest destruction. The United Nations Commission on Human Rights investigates allegations of abuses of civil and political rights and issues reports on the most flagrant violators, which may prompt other states to apply sanctions on the guilty governments.

Policy reviews and evaluations leading to a decision to continue, modify, or replace a policy can be as important a part of the global policy process as they are with domestic policies. Reviews of the adequacy and effectiveness of international development policies were undertaken by commissions led by Lester Pearson and Sir Robert Jackson in 1969–70 and by Willy Brandt in 1978–9, which informed the development strategies for the Second and Third United Nations Development Decades proclaimed for the 1970s and 1980s.[5] The Non-Proliferation Treaty (NPT) of 1968 has been reviewed every fifth year in conferences attended by its ratifiers, as provided for in the treaty. Despite the contentiousness of these sessions, the NPT remains in effect in its original form. The International Telecommunications Union holds a major World Administrative Radio Conference, known as a general WARC, every twentieth year to assess and modify allocations of radio frequencies, the most recent having been convened in Geneva in 1979.

Global policy-solving is often a messy, drawn out process that does not conform very closely to the series of steps that has just been outlined, but this is also the case with policy-making at other levels. Moreover, conflicts can delay or stymie the process at any phase, or make it necessary to cycle back to an earlier stage to address an unresolved issue that poses an obstacle to further agreements. Nevertheless, global policies are adopted and implemented on numerous issues that have been successful to varying degrees in responding to the problems that they were designed to address.

GLOBAL POLICY-MAKING ARENAS

Global policies are made in a plethora of deliberative bodies that are part of 33 international governmental organizations that are universal in the sense of being open to all states (Union of International Associations, 1987/88, Appendix 7).[6] Among these are the principal organs of the United Nations system, in particular the General Assembly, Security Council, and Economic and Social Council (ECO-SOC); the nineteen specialized agencies loosely overseen by ECOSOC; and a variety of other organs, programs and special bodies reporting to the General Assembly or ECOSOC, a few examples of which are the United Nations Conference on Trade and Development, the United Nations Fund for Population Activities, and the World Food Council.[7] Most of these institutions have multiple bodies that are involved at some stage in the policy process, including assemblies, councils, standing or ad hoc committees, commission, sub-commissions, and working groups.

The crowded agendas for regular sessions of key international bodies, in particular the General Assembly, have prompted the convening of special sessions or ad hoc world conferences to discuss more fully and to act on specific global policy problems. Special sessions of the General Assembly have dealt with problems such as raw materials and development (1974), development and international cooperation (1975), disarmament (1978, 1982, and 1988), international economic cooperation (1980), and the critical economic situation in Africa (1986). In addition, 'emergency special sessions' of the General Assembly can be convened within 24 hours if a veto prevents the Security Council from taking action on an immediate threat to international peace and security, as provided for under terms of the Uniting for Peace Resolution adopted by the Assembly in 1950.

Major ad hoc world conferences sponsored by the United Nations have been an important setting for global policy-making during the 1970s and 1980s. The first of these so-called 'global town meetings' was the United Nations Conference on the Human Environment held in Stockholm in 1972, which led to the establishment of the United Nations Environment Programme. The conference was attended not only by most member states of the United Nations, but also by representatives of international governmental organizations with environmentally related functions and more than 500 non-governmental organizations with concerns about international environmental issues. The success of the Stockholm conference in laying the groundwork for a worldwide response to a growing agenda of environmental problems was made possible by four years of preparatory meetings that resolved most of the issues that could have stymied agreements at the conference.[8] Major conferences have been held on numerous other issues, such as population (1974, 1984), food (1974), the status of women (1975, 1980, 1985), human settlements (1976), water (1977), desertification (1977), science and technology for development (1979), new and renewable sources of energy (1981), outer space (1982), peaceful uses of nuclear energy (1987), drug abuse and illicit trafficking (1987), and AIDS (1988).[9]

Efforts to address any particular global problem move through a succession of these policy-making and implementing arenas. One possible sequence is illustrated in Figure 1.1. In Figure 1.1, the seriousness of a problem and the need for an international response has been documented in exploratory meetings, such as an international

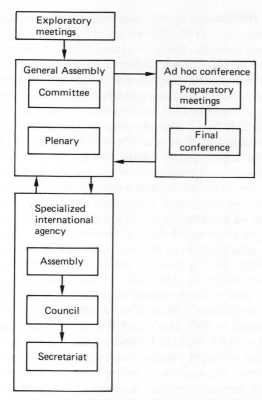

Figure 1.1 Typical sequence of arenas in the global policy process

conference of leading scientists. Then it is brought to the attention of the General Assembly where it is assigned to one of its seven standing committees for more detailed investigation and discussion. If the problem is deemed to be a significant and timely one that requires more attention than can be given during the regular sessions of the Assembly, a special session or an ad hoc world conference may be convened to allow sufficient time for preparatory meetings. Thus, when the special conference takes place, usually for no longer than a few weeks, relatively little remains to be done except to hold concluding discussions on the final documents, typically a statement of principles and a plan of action, before approving them as recommendations to the General Assembly to put into effect.

The long-term implementation of policies may be transferred to a specialized international agency that was either previously existing or has been created to carry out the policy at hand. Once in the domain of the specialized agencies, the issue is first taken up by an assembly, in which all member states are represented, for decisions on general policy guidelines. These guidelines are then forwarded to the agency's council, a smaller body comprizing representatives of an elected group of states, to work out a more detailed implementation strategy. Most of these more manageably sized councils meet one or more times a year in contrast to assemblies, most of which have regularly scheduled sessions at intervals of several years. Finally, the policy is turned over to the executive director and secretariat of the agency for actual implementation. A review of the policy and a decision on its continuation might take place in the specialized agency, or alternatively in the General Assembly, an ad hoc conference, or a specially appointed commission.

It should be emphasized that this progression of arenas is only an illustration, which relates to the way some policy problems have been addressed better than it does for others. It corresponds quite well to international efforts to deal with global environmental problems generally, as well as some specific ones such as water, desertification, and human settlements. The most recent efforts to develop a law of the sea, which began in 1967, also match the model fairly closely, although the outcome of the UNCLOS III process was a treaty that was opened for ratification without further action by the General Assembly. Many policy problems are dealt with entirely by the specialized agencies, especially on technical matters such as those pertaining to health, meteorology, and telecommunications. On major, long-standing issues, such as peacekeeping and economic development, the sequence of arenas is much more complicated than in Figure 1.1.

PARTICIPANTS IN THE GLOBAL POLICY PROCESS

Global policy is the product of the interaction of various types of interacting actors, the principal ones being the governments of states, along with both governmental and non-governmental types of international organizations. States continue to be the key decision-makers on global problems and have the primary responsibility for implementing them, despite the view in some circles that they are a form of political organization ill-suited for an era of heightened interdependence.[10]

How states are represented in international organizations is an important factor in the deliberations on global policies. In the more central, general purpose international bodies, such as the General Assembly, member states are typically represented by diplomats or political appointees, and on special occasions by heads of state or foreign ministers. In the specialized, functional agencies, delegates are drawn more frequently from the corresponding national ministries; thus, an environmental minister may head a national delegation to a conference convened by the United Nations Environment Programme. Alternatively, private individuals who have a specific type of expertise may be tapped to provide representation when governmental officials with the requisite expertise are not available. The amount of discretion that governments allow their delegations varies considerably from one country to another, and for any given country depending upon the international deliberative body in which policies are being developed as well as the type of issue under consideration. The less the delegations are supervised, the greater are the possibilities for working out compromises on global policies, but the less likely is it that a resulting treaty will be accepted and vigorously implemented by the home government (Jacobson, 1984: 100–15).

States are not unitary actors but complex networks of actors, which commonly have different objectives and may even work at cross-purposes. In democratic countries, national legislatures may play an independent role in global policy processes by virtue of their constitutionally mandated responsibilities that typically include ratification of treaties negotiated by the executive branch and the adoption of measures necessary to implement their provisions. Likewise, national high courts occasionally resolve conflicts arising between national laws and international obligations. The responsiveness of the various branches of governments to the nationalistic outlook of their political constituencies is one of the principal obstacles to international collaboration in addressing major global problems.

International governmental organizations (IGOs) are created by states not only to provide arenas in which international policies can be addressed but also, through their directors and secretariats, to play an active part in the evolution of international public policies. These roles may include setting agendas, preparing negotiating texts, conducting or coordinating background studies, serving as repositories and clearing houses of information, publicizing global problems and encouraging appropriate responses by states, managing special funds created to finance international programs, and coordinating technical assistance. A few IGOs are assigned the politically sensitive task of monitoring compliance with international regulations and issuing reports on persistent violators, notable examples being the United Nations Commission on Human Rights, which scrutinizes performance of states in upholding international human rights standards, and the International Atomic Energy Agency (IAEA), which inspects nuclear facilities to detect the diversion of fissionable materials to the production of bombs. In carrying out these responsibilities, IGOs such as the IAEA may become official parties to multilateral treaties. Furthermore, IGOs often establish working relationships with one another when their functional responsibilities overlap, although it is also not uncommon for them to work at cross-purposes.

Non-governmental organizations (NGOs) are a polyglot group of international actors, more than 4000 of which draw their membership from at least two countries (Union of International Associations, 1987/88, Appendix 7). Some NGOs play significant roles in global policy processes, but most are merely peripheral participants, if they are involved at all. Several international institutions acknowledge the special interests and potential contributions of certain NGOs by conferring 'consultative status', which allows them more access to the workings of the institution (Willetts, 1982: 11–17). The involvement of the NGO community is largely in identifying problems and in advocating global policies, but some are looked upon to play a more substantial role. The International Council of Scientific Unions (ICSU) is frequently called upon by international agencies to provide objective scientific expertise which has informed global policies on a variety of subjects, especially in the environmental realm. The ICSU sponsored the International Geophysical Year (1957–8) and is currently organizing the International Geosphere–Biosphere Programme, an even more ambitious global scientific effort for the 1990s (see Malone, 1986). Amnesty International is the most prominent among a group of IGOs, sometimes known as the 'human rights industry', which investigates alleged human rights violations and submits reports to intergovernmental commissions through formally established procedures. The International Committee of the Red Cross is one of several NGOs that carries out emergency relief programs sponsored by IGOs.

Not all participants in the policy process fit neatly into one of the categories described above. A pivotal role is occasionally played by a commission of internationally eminent persons, appointed to act more as individuals than as representatives of a state or an international organization in studying and reporting on a significant policy problem. An example is the Group of High-Level Intergovernmental Experts, otherwise known as the 'Committee of 18', which was charged with proposing administrative and financial reforms for the beleaguered United Nations system. Another is the World Commission on Environment and Development, chaired by Prime Minister Gro Harlem Brundtland of Norway, which released an influential report entitled *Our Common Future* (1987). The prominence of a commission's leaders and members can draw more attention to such a report than is given to the multitude of other United Nations reports. It should also be acknowledged that certain individuals have transcended their formal roles to become especially influential actors, such as Raul Preblisch of Argentina on international development policies, Arvid Pardo of Malta on the law of the sea, and Maurice Strong of Canada on the global environment.

THE FORM OF GLOBAL POLICIES

Most global policies can be categorized either as regulations that define the limits of permissible behavior for national governments and those under their jurisdictions or, alternatively, as programs administered by international agencies. Regulations may be **prohibitions**, such as the ban on testing nuclear bombs in the atmosphere, oceans, or outer space in the Limited Test-Ban Treaty of 1963, or **limits**, such as the quotas assigned by fishery commissions based upon calculations of maximum sustainable yield. Some are **obligations**, such as promptly to report outbreaks of certain contagious diseases to the World Health Organization (WHO), or **standards**, such as the requirement for segregated ballast tanks on oil tankers contained in a convention adopted by the International Maritime Organization in 1973. Regulations may also spell out **privileges**, such as the right to position satellites in a prescribed position in the geostationary orbit as provided for by the allocation plans adopted in the International Telecommunications Union.

Many varied programs have been set up to provide services at the international level, funded in some instances by assessments that are assigned to states, but now more often by whatever contributions states elect to pledge. The scattered peace-keeping operations of the Security Council and General Assembly, the humanitarian relief to refugees from the UN High Commissioner for Refugees, the technical assistance programs coordinated by the United Nations Development Programme, the loans of the International Monetary Fund (IMF) and World Bank, and the information available from the International

Registry of Potentially Toxic Substances of the United Nations Environment Programme are examples of global programs.

International regulations may be found in several basic forms of international law. The more traditional form is **customary law**, which is comprised of the norms of behavior observed by most nations over an extended, but not specifically defined, period of time. These norms are considered to be binding on all states, the only exception being those that consistently refused to acknowledge them as they became the customary behavior for other states.[11] An example is the freedom of the seas beyond the narrow band of territorial waters off the coast of states, which in modern times dates back to the seventeenth century writings of Dutch jurist Hugo Grotius (see Anand, 1983). While customary law does not originate with a written document, efforts have been made to codify it to diminish its ambiguity, most notably by the United Nations International Law Commission.

It could be argued that customary norms of behavior are not in fact policies because their origins are independent of the international policy processes described in the previous section and thus are not part of a planned strategy for addressing a problem. Nevertheless, this traditional form of international law does offer guides for behavior which, if they continue to be observed by most states, can ameliorate many international problems, as in delineating the responsibilities of states in regard to operations within their jurisdiction that damage the environment beyond their borders (see Schneider, 1979). Because of its inherent vagueness, however, customary law has not proved to be an adequate guide for behavior in an increasingly complex and interdependent world.

There has thus been a trend in recent decades to state more international regulations in the explicit wording of treaties, which are negotiated, adopted, and implemented more in accordance with the model global policy process described above. The word 'treaty' is a generic term for international agreements than can involve as few as two states or, at the other extreme, all of the more than 160 states currently existing. Treaties open to adoption by large numbers of states are often labelled conventions; those that are the constitutions for international institutions are usually referred to as charters or covenants. In contrast to customary international law, which is binding on all states, only those states that formally file papers indicating their acceptance of a treaty are obligated to comply with its provisions. A treaty is thus in effect a contrast between ratifying states that provides for reciprocating restraints and obligations. In order to take advantage of the explicitness, specificity, and flexibility of the treaty form of international law, some codifications of customary norms have been offered as drafts of multilateral conventions that can be revised through negotiation before being opened for ratification. This procedure was followed with the International Law Commission's efforts to codify the customary law of the sea, which led to four treaties that were discussed and eventually adopted at the first United Nations Conference on the Law of the Sea held in 1958.

Resolutions are considered and voted upon by states in international deliberative bodies, and thus bear some similarity to national legislation. They may set forth goals and principles, regulations or the framework for international programs. Major resolutions, especially those that set forth a majority view on basic principles, are sometimes labeled declarations to lend them greater solemnity, an example being the Universal Declaration of Human Rights (1948). Resolutions are being used increasingly as instruments of global policies because they can be adopted quickly without drawn out negotiations and the lengthy lapse in time between adoption and ratification that are often the bane of the treaty process. Furthermore, as with treaties, resolutions can be an instrument for changing the behavior of states in response to new problems, in contrast to customary law which presumes a continuity of behavior.

The primary drawback of resolutions is that they are generally not binding, even on the states which voted for them. Thus, resolutions are commonly perceived to offer little more than a reading of the opinion of governments on a given issue, and are clearly beyond the domain of international law. Some resolutions, however, have proved to be significant statements of international public policy. Resolution 242 adopted by the Security Council in the aftermath of the Six Day War of 1967 is still a widely acknowledged cornerstone of international policy on the Arab–Israeli conflict. Furthermore, it can be argued that a vote approaching unanimity can be evidence that a resolution contains norms of behavior that are universally accepted and, thus, are arguably expressions of international customary law (see D'Amato, 1971). Some of these resolutions are frequently cited in international litigation, which is another indication that they have achieved the stature of international law, as has been the case with the declaration on environmental principles adopted at Stockholm in 1972. It is also strongly presumed that the rules contained in the resolutions of certain international organizations, such as the World Health Organization, will be complied with by member states by virtue of commitments made in ratifying the organization's charter.

ASSESSMENT

How adequate have global policy mechanisms been in addressing the many challenges that confront the world community? The record thus far is clearly mixed, as it is with problem-solving endeavors at national and sub-national levels. More accomplishments can be expected when policy decisions are made on technical criteria, as has generally been the case for the uniform specifications of the International Telecommunications Union and the International Civil Aviation Organization, or when the benefits of international cooperation outweigh the costs for most states, as has been true of the rules of the World Health Organization. Less progress has been made on more politicized matters, such as the protection of human rights, or issues that have implications for military security, including most of those in the field of arms control. Agreements on global policies can be stymied by the divergent interests of states, as has been the case with establishing rules for mining the deep seabed and reforming the international economic order. Some imperatives are more readily dealt with than others even within the same general grouping of issues. For example, it has been much easier for the membership of the United Nations Environment Programme and the World Meteorological Organization to begin addressing the ozone-depletion problem by mandating percentage cutbacks in production of CFCs, for which other chemicals will be feasible substitutes, than to come to grips with the 'global warming' phenomenon, which will require fundamental changes in the production and use of energy.

The institutional mechanisms for global problem-solving have undergone considerable growth and refinement over the past several decades, as has the body of international public policies. This is not to say, however, that the existing system, even operating at peak effectiveness, is adequate to the tasks at hand. Moreover, momentum has diminished during the 1980s as both the industrialized and Third World members have become disillusioned with the United Nations framework and, in a more general way, the whole enterprise of multilateral problem-solving. The larger financial supporters of the United Nations have been dissatisfied with the disproportionate voting strength of the numerous small states under the one-nation, one-vote system in most international bodies, a tendency that became more pronounced with the dismantling of the colonial empires during the 1950s and 1960s. Conversely, the optimism of the Third World that international institutions could be used as vehicles of change and reform that could significantly improve their condition has waned due to the reluctance of the developed countries to make substantial contributions toward this end. A growing tendency to withhold payment of assessments, most notably by the United States, has brought about a financial crisis for the United Nations, which has forced deep cutbacks in its programmes and demoralized its staff. Nonetheless, despite much publicized difficulties of the United Nations system as a whole, efforts at global problem-solving continue on many fronts, especially on the more technical and less politicized subjects. Furthermore, it is possible that the current tribulations of the United Nations are leading to both structural and behavior reforms that will increase its effectiveness, stimulated by the growing recognition of the imperative to address the increasingly serious agenda of economic and environmental problems at the global level.

Notes

1. For overviews of the field of policy studies, see Lindblom (1980), Nagel (1984), and Hilsman (1987).
2. Overviews of the policy problems facing the United Nations are presented in an annual series sponsored by the United Nations Association of the United States of America, the most recent being Tessitore and Woolfson (1989).
3. For a fuller explanation of these types of policy problems, see Soroos (1986: 64–70).
4. See Young (1977) for an analysis of the regulations of international fishery commissions in the North Pacific region.
5. See the reports of the Pearson Commission (1969); Jackson Commission (1969); and Brandt Commission (1980, 1983).
6. Using a criteria for defining IGOs that includes organizations created by other IGOs, Jacobson (1984) compiled a list of 621 IGOs in existence in 1980, of which 75 were potentially universal in membership.
7. For a comprehensive listing of UN organs, agencies, committees, etc., see Tessitore and Woolfson (1989, Appendix). For a recent description and assessment of the United Nations specialized agencies, see Williams (1987).
8. A description of the Stockholm conference from a policy perspective is presented by Handelman, Shapiro, and Vasquez (1974).

9.   The role of world conferences in global policy-making is discussed by Bennett (1988: 293–324).
10. Among those taking this position is Falk (1975).
11. For a discussion of customary law and other sources of international law, see Akehurst (1982) and Von Glahn (1986).

References

Akehurst, M. (1982)   *A Modern Introduction to International Law* (London: George Allen & Unwin) 4th edn.

Anand, R. P. (1983)   *Origin and Development of the Law of the Sea: History of International Law Revisited* (The Hague: Martinus Nijhoff).

Bennett, A. L. (1988)   *International Organizations: Principles and Issues* (Englewood Cliffs, NJ: Prentice-Hall) 4th edn.

Brandt Commission (Independent Commission on Development Issues) (1980)   *North–South: A Program for Survival* (Cambridge, Mass.: MIT Press).

Brandt Commission (Independent Commission on Development Issues) (1983)   *Common Crisis North–South: Cooperation for World Recovery* (Cambridge, Mass.: MIT Press).

Brundtland Commission (World Commission on Environment and Development) (1987)   *Our Common Future* (New York: Oxford University Press).

D'Amato, A. A. (1971)   *The Concept of Custom in International Law* (Ithica, NY: Cornell University Press).

Falk, R. A. (1975)   *A Study of Future Worlds* (New York: Free Press).

Food and Agriculture Organization (FAO) (1987)   *Fifth World Food Survey* (Rome: FAO).

Handelman, J. R., Shapiro, H. B., and Vasquez, J. A. (1974)   *Introductory Case Studies for International Relations: Vietnam/The Middle East/Environmental Crisis* (Chicago: Rand McNalley).

Hilsman, R. (1987)   *The Politics of Policy Making in Defense and Foreign Affairs: Conceptual Models and Bureaucratic Politics* (Englewood Cliffs, NJ: Prentice-Hall).

Jacobson, H. K. (1984)   *Networks of Interdependence: International Organizations and the Global Political System* (New York: Alfred A. Knopf, 1984) 2nd edn.

Jackson Commission (1969)   *A Study of the Capacity of the United Nations Development System* (Geneva: United Nations, 1969).

Lindblom, C. E. (1980)   *The Policy Making Process* (Englewood Cliffs, NJ: Prentice-Hall) 2nd edn.

Malone, T. F. (1986)   'Mission to Planet Earth: Integrating Studies of Global Change', *Environment*, **28**(1): 6–11, 39–42.

Nagel, S. S. (1984)   *Public Policy: Goals, Means, and Methods* (New York: St Martin's Press).

Pearson Commission (Commission on International Development) (1969)   *Partners in Development* (New York: Praeger).

Schneider, J. (1979)   *World Public Order of the Environment: Towards an*

International Ecological Law and Organization (Toronto: University of Toronto Press).

Soroos, M. S. (1986) *Beyond Sovereignty: the Challenge of Global Policy* (Columbia, SC: University of South Carolina Press).

Tessitore, J., Woolfson, S. (eds) (1989) *Issues Before the 43rd General Assembly of the United Nations* (Lexington, Mass.: Lexington Books).

Union of International Associations (eds) (1987/88) *Yearbook of International Organizations, 1987/1988*, vol. 1.

Von Glahn, G. (1986) *Law Among Nations: An Introduction to Public International Law* (New York: Macmillan, 1986) 4th edn.

Willetts, P. (1982) 'Pressure Groups as Transnational Actors', in Willetts, P. (ed.), *Pressure Groups in the Global System*: 1–27 (London: Frances Pinter).

Williams, D. (1987) *The Specialized Agencies and the United Nations: the System in Crisis* (New York: St Martin's Press).

Young, O. R. (1977) *Resource Management at the International Level* (New York: Nichols Publishing Co.).

2 Super-optimizing Analysis and Developmental Policy

Stuart S. Nagel

The purpose of this chapter is to discuss how super-optimum solutions (SOS) can be applied to developmental policy. SOS analysis involves arriving at solutions to policy problems whereby both liberals and conservatives can come out ahead of their initial best expectations. Developmental policy includes basically the same set of policy problems that developed countries have, except they involve a different context. The policy problems which this chapter uses for illustrative purposes include labor management, transportation, agriculture, education, immigration and military bases.[1]

BASIC SOS CONCEPTS USING MINIMUM WAGE POLICY

Table 2.1 presents the Philippine minimum wage problem in the context of an SOS framework, table, matrix, chart, spreadsheet, or other synonym for a set of rows and columns. An SOS table shows the goals to be achieved on the columns, the policy alternatives available on the rows, the relations between alternatives and goals in the cells, various overall totals for the alternatives at the far right, and a capability of determining what it would take to bring a second-place or other-place alternative up to first place.

To be an SOS table rather than just an ordinary decision-analysis table, it is necessary that there be **at least one conservative, liberal, and SOS alternative**. The conservative alternative can generally be considered as representing the best expectations of the conservatives, although their best expectations may be better expressed in terms of the degree of goal achievement they might best expect. The liberal alternative generally reflects the best expectations of the liberals. The SOS alternative (if it really is an SOS alternative) is capable of **exceeding both the conservative and liberal best expectations** in terms of their respective alternatives and/or goals.

Table 2.1 The Philippine minimum wage problem

Alternatives / Criteria	L goal Decent wages	C goal – Overpayment	N total (Neutral weights)	L total (Liberal weights)	C total (Conservative weights)
C Alternative 90 per day	2	4	12	10	14*
L Alternative 100 per day	4	2	12	14*	10
N Alternative 95 per day	3	3	12	12	12
SOS Alternative 101 to worker, 89 from employer, 12 wage supplement	5	5	20	20**	20**

The Inputs

In the context of the Philippine minimum wage problem as of January 1990, the conservatives would like to keep the minimum wage down to about 90 pesos per day. The liberals would like to get the minimum wage up to about 100 pesos per day. The neutral alternative usually splits the difference between the conservative and liberal alternative, or takes a little of each. In this context, the neutral or compromise alternative is 95 pesos per day.

The goals of both the conservatives and liberals are to pay decent wages but to avoid overpayment. The important thing in this context is not determining exactly what a decent wage is, but the relativistic idea that **100 pesos scores better on achieving a decent wage than 90 pesos does**. Likewise, 90 pesos scores better on avoiding overpayment than 100 pesos does.

Instead of (or in addition to) expressing those relations in words, we can summarize them by using relativistic numbers on a 1–5 scale. On such a scale, a **5** means that the alternative is highly conducive to the goal relative to the other alternatives. A **4** means mildly conducive; a **3** means neither conducive nor adverse; a **2** means mildly adverse; and a **1** means the alternative is highly adverse to the goal.

In the context of the Philippine minimum wage problem, one could give the liberal alternative a 4 on decent wages, the conservative alternative a 2, and the neutral alternative a 3. (Those are just relative numbers; it would be just as meaningful to use the numbers 400, 200, and 300, or 12, 6, and 9.) The important characteristic is the **rank order**, and to a lesser extent the **relative distances**. Rank order is especially important and also relative distance, because the bottom line in policy evaluation is determining which alternative ranks **first and best**.

Likewise on avoiding overpayment, the conservative alternative receives a 4, the liberal alternative a 2, and the neutral alternative a 3. We are temporarily not mentioning the exact nature of the SOS alternative; we need to first clarify the analysis working with the more traditional alternatives to the minimum wage problem, or whatever the policy problem might be.

After determining the basic alternatives, goals, and relations, the next step in an SOS analysis is to discuss the **relative weights of the goals**. A 1–3 scale is a simple and common way of measuring the relative weights or importance of the goals. With such a scale, a **3** means highly important relative to the other goals. A **2** means middling

important, and a **1** means having relatively low but positive importance.

In the minimum wage context, liberals tend to assign 'decent wages' a
relatively high weight and assign 'avoiding overpayment' a relatively
low weight. Liberals would thus implicitly or explicitly multiply the
scores in the decent-wages column by a 3, and multiply the scores in the
avoid-overpayment column by a 1. Doing so results in a liberal total
score for the conservative alternative of 10, which is $(3 \times 2) + (1 \times 4)$.
The liberal total for the liberal alternative is 14, which is
$(3 \times 4) + (1 \times 2)$, and so on for determining the other numbers in the
liberal total column.

The Total Scores and the SOS

The conservative total scores are calculated in a similar way. Conservatives tend to give 'decent wages' a weight of 1 and 'avoiding overpayment' a weight of 3. The conservative alternative thus receives a
conservative total of 14, which is $(1 \times 2) + (3 \times 4)$. Neutrals tend to give
all goals a middling weight of 2. The conservative alternative thus gets a
neutral total of 12, which is $(2 \times 2) + (2 \times 4)$. An easier way to calculate
the neutral totals is simply to add the raw scores of $2 + 4$ to obtain 6,
and then doubling that unweighted total.

Notice that on the liberal totals, the liberal alternative wins or ranks
first before taking into consideration the SOS alternative, and the
conservative alternative ranks third. Likewise on the conservative
totals, the conservative alternative ranks first, and the liberal alternative scores last, before considering the SOS alternative. That is a check
on **internal consistency**, although such consistency may not always be
completely present.

Under the SOS alternative, each worker receives 101 pesos a day as a
minimum wage. Each employer, however, pays only 89 pesos per day
to the workers. The difference of 12 pesos comes from a governmental
minimum-wage supplement. By each worker receiving more than 100
pesos, the SOS alternative has exceeded the best expectations of the
liberals. By each employer paying less than 90 pesos, the SOS alternative has also exceeded the best expectations of the conservatives.

The SOS alternative receives a 5 on the goal of 'decent wages'
because it involves paying the workers even more than the liberal
alternative which received a 4 – assuming one wants to round off to
whole numbers on the 1–5 scale, although that is not necessary. The

SOS alternative also receives a 5 on the goal of 'avoiding overpayment' because it involves employers paying even less than the conservative alternative which received a 4. The SOS alternative thus receives a total score of 20 on the neutral totals which is 10×2. It receives a score of 20 on the liberal totals which is $(3 \times 5) + (1 \times 5)$, and it receives a score of 20 on the conservative totals which is $(1 \times 5) + (3 \times 5)$. It is a super-optimum solution because it **exceeds the best expectations of both liberals and conservatives simultaneously**.

Potential Criticism

To be truly super-optimum, however, the SOS alternative should not involve liberals and conservatives both coming out ahead at the expense of other major parties or viewpoints. In this context, one might argue that the government or the general public comes out behind as a result of the extra tax-cost to provide for the minimum wage supplement. It is a subsidy to the wages of the workers, and a subsidy to the available payroll money of the employers.

A well-placed subsidy is professionally administered and involves enough money to get the job done; it especially involves 'strings attached' that make the subsidy more than worthwhile to the government and the taxpayer. In the context of a minimum wage supplement, one important 'string' might be to require the employers to hire people who would otherwise be unemployed, and to require the workers to be willing to move to jobs where they are needed. Another important 'string' would be to require the employers to provide on-the-job training to upgrade the skills of the workers so that they will be more productive than 101 pesos per day, and to require the workers to participate in the training so they can pass whatever performance tests are involved.

With those strings attached, the taxpayers would be relieved from various welfare burdens such as providing medical care, food stamps, unemployment compensation, public housing, aid to dependent children, social security, disability aid, and other forms of public aid. Providing jobs to the unemployed and upgrading job skills facilitate better role models, thereby relieving the taxpayers of the possible welfare burdens of the future generation. The new employment and increased income lessens costly anti-social behavior and attitudes, such as crime, drugs, vice, bitterness, and depression. The upgraded employment adds to the gross national product (GNP), helps create jobs for others, and adds to the tax base.

One objection might be that paying the unemployed 101 pesos per day will antagonize those who are already employed at the old minimum wage of about 95 pesos per day. That is not a serious problem in the United States because there are relatively few workers right at the minimum wage, and they tend to be non-union with little political power. In the Philippines and other developing countries, however, there is a relatively high percentage of the work force at the minimum wage, and they tend to be unionized and more aggressive. The string about on-the-job training might thus have to be emphasized in the Philippines more than the hiring of the unemployed, as compared to the United States.

Another objection might be that employers will resist providing the on-the-job training; they are less likely to do so if it is being partly subsidized by the wage supplement of 12 pesos a day. They are also less likely to object if the training is reasonably well planned so that worker productivity increases more than the cost, thereby increasing the profits of the employers.

This is thus a potential super-optimum solution for conservative employers, liberal workers, and the total society of taxpayers. A key reason this and other super-optimum solutions are sometimes not adopted is because the policy-makers until recently have **not been thinking along these lines**. Another reason is that too often liberals are too concerned that conservatives might gain by a super-optimum solution, even though liberals also gain. Likewise, conservatives may be too concerned that liberals might gain, even though conservatives also gain.

One might also argue that there is something about the minimum wage situation which makes things too easy to find a super-optimum solution. The examples which follow deal with a variety of subject matters and approaches to arriving at super-optimum solutions. They include (1) bicycles versus cars in Beijing, (2) trying to commute to and from Manila, (3) food prices in China, (4) land reform in the Philippines, (5) raising faculty salaries without raising taxes in China, (6) trilingualism in Philippine education, (7) the Asian labor shortage, and (8) American military bases. These examples draw upon the author's 1989–90 experiences in China and the Philippines, but they could apply to any developing or developed country by reasoning from analogy.[2]

TRANSPORTATION POLICY

Bicycles Versus Cars in Beijing

The most exciting presentations in China were those that involved systematic policy analysis, decision-aiding software, multi-criteria decision-making, and super-optimum solutions. One example was the problem of how to deal with the substantial and increasing quantity of night-time accidents involving cars crashing into bicycles in Beijing and other Chinese cities. There are over seven million bicycles in Beijing – which is more bicycles in Beijing than there are people in any American city except Los Angeles and New York.

The material which follows briefly describes how one might systematically analyze the basic alternatives available for dealing with the problem, the goals or criteria for choosing among the alternatives, and relations between alternatives and goals in order to choose or explain the best alternative, combination, allocation, or predictive decision-rule.

The material which follows includes both a verbal analysis and a computer output. The computer output involves a matrix or table of columns and rows in which the goals are on the columns, the alternatives are on the rows, the relations between goals and alternatives are in the cells, the overall score for each alternative is at the far right, and the system provides for doing an analysis whereby one can determine what it would take to bring a second-place alternative or other-place alternative up to first place.

The Inputs

The basic alternatives

(1)   **Having reflectors on bicycles** in order to decrease the increase in the number of night-time accidents between cars and bicycles.

(2)   **Having battery-operated lights on bicycles**. The word 'having' for alternatives (1) and (2) means **requiring by law**.

(3)   This is the alternative of **doing nothing**, just leaving things the way they are.

(4)   This involves **prohibiting bicycles at night**.

(5)   This involves **giving away the reflectors free** at government expense instead of having people buy the reflectors.

(6)   This involves **having people buy the reflectors**. Alternatives (5)

and (6) are thus subdivisions of alternative (1), which just talks about requiring reflectors but does not clarify **who is going to pay for them**.

(7) This is requiring manufacturers and sellers of bicycles **to put reflectors on them before they sell them**.

(8) This involves **subsidizing manufacturers to get them to put reflectors on bicycles**.

(9) Requiring manufacturers in the future to use **reflective paint** on bicycles so that the bicycles can be seen better by cars at night than by using either reflectors or lights. Using a reflective paint costs no more than using regular paint; there is no extra cost involved but a lot of extra benefits. (See Table 2.2 for the nine alternatives in the Beijing bicycle problem, and Table 2.3 for how they are grouped.)

The criteria (see Table 2.4)

(1) **Reduce the number of accidents**, especially where there are fatalities or personal injuries or even just property damage.

(2) **Keep the cost down** to the taxpayer, and to society.

(9) The third especially important criterion (which is 9th on the list but is one of 3 that is starred in Table 2.4) is **equity**, meaning avoiding solutions that unduly burden the poor. Stated more positively, we should seek solutions that do not discriminate against any major groups of people in terms of who **benefits** and who **pays the costs**.

(3) Criteria 3, 4 and 5 all relate to benefits that come from **reducing bicycle–car injuries**. 3 has to do with the cost to the injured person and to the economy as a result of that person's productivity being lost.

(4) That is the cost with regard to the **disruption of traffic** that could cause hold-ups where everybody is late for wherever they are going.

(5) That is the cost to the government in **sending out an ambulance or a police car to take a police report**. Items 3, 4 and 5 are **benefit items** in the sense that if injuries are reduced then the benefits of no lost productivity or lost medical costs are saved and there is no lost disruption of traffic or lost governmental involvement.

(6) Criteria 6, 7 and 8 are 3 subdivisions of the cost that are expressed in 2 above. One cost has to do with the cost of

Table 2.2   The alternatives in the Beijing bicycle problem

Alternative	Alternative
1*FANGUANGJ.	1*REFLECTORS
2*CHE DENG	2*LIGHTS
3*BAOCHIYUANZHUANG	3*DO NOTHING
4*YEWANYANJINWAICHU	4*NO NIGHT BIKES
5*MIAN FEI FAN GUANG	5*FREE REFLECTORS
6*BI MAI FAN GUANG J	6*BUY REFLECTORS
7*CHANGJIA, SHANGREN BI MAIOU	7*REQUIRE MANUFACTURING
8*DUI CHANGJIA, SHANG REN DE BU TIE	8*SUBSIDIZE MANUFACTURING
9*XIN XING ZI XING C CHE ZUIJIAXUANZ	9*SOS

Table 2.3   Grouping the alternatives in the Beijing bicycle problem

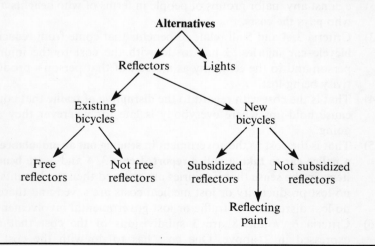

equipment, such as what it would cost people to buy reflectors versus lights with batteries.

(7) This is the cost of **enforcement**, since some solutions require more police enforcement than others.

(8) This is the cost of **interference with the economy and productivity** as a result of such solutions as prohibiting bicycles at night.

(9) **Equity**, as mentioned above.

(10) This is **political feasibility**, since different proposals have different degrees of likelihood of being adopted, and some have no likelihood at all.

(11) This is **administrative feasibility**, since some proposals (like prohibiting bicycles at night) may be almost administratively

Table 2.4   The criteria in the Beijing bicycle problem

Criterion	Meas. unit	Weight	Criterion
1*JIAN SHAO SHI GU	1–5 FEN	1.00	1*+SAFETY
2*JIANG DI CHENG BEN	1–5 FEN	1.00	2*−COST
3 −SHANG HAI	1–5	1.00	3 −INJURIES
4 −JIAO TONG ZU SAI	1–5	1.00	4 −TRAFFIC DISRUPTION
5 −JIU HU ZHI CHU	1–5	1.00	5 −AMBULANCE
6 SHE BEI CHENG BEN	1–5	1.00	6 −EQUIPMENT COST
7 SHENG CHAN LI CHEN	1–5	1.00	7 −ENFORCEMENT COST
8 QIANG ZHI CHENG BE	1–5	1.00	8 −INTERFERENCE COST
9*GONG PING	1–5	1.00	9*EQUITY
10 ZHENG CE KE XING X	1–5	1.00	10 POLITICALLY FEASIBLE
11 GUAN LI KE XING X.	1–5	1.00	11 ADMINISTRATIVELY FEASIBLE

impossible even if the proposal is adopted. See Table 2.5 for how the eleven criteria in the Beijing bicycle problem are grouped.

The data matrix (see Table 2.6)   Looking at the greater detail from the data matrix, first going down the injuries column from the highest to the lowest:

(1) **Reflective paint** does best.
(2) Then comes **battery-operated light**.
(3) Then comes **subsidized reflectors put on by the manufacturer**.
(4) Then **requiring manufacturers and sellers to put on reflectors**.
(5) Then comes **free reflectors** for existing bicycles.
(6) Then comes **requiring people to buy reflectors**.
(7) A distant last is **keeping things as they are**.
(8) Since there are 9 altogether, 2 must have been left out. One is reflectors in general, that does worse on reducing injuries than lights but is less expensive than lights.
(9) Also left out was prohibiting bicycles at night, which would be near the top with regard to reducing injuries if it could be adopted and enforced.

Table 2.6 is a data matrix that relates the nine alternatives to the three main goals.

Table 2.5   Grouping the criteria in the Beijing bicycle problem

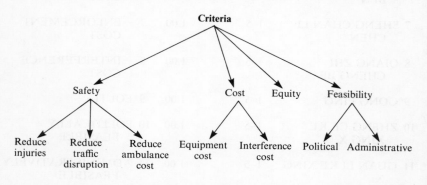

Table 2.6 Relating the nine alternatives to the three main goals in the Beijing bicycle problem

	ALTERNATIVE/CRITERIA SCORING			
	JIAN SHA	JIANG DI	GONG PIN	
1 FANGUANGJ.	4.00	3.00	0.00	1 REFLECTORS
2 CHE DENG	5.00	1.00	0.00	2 LIGHTS
3 BAOCHIYUANZHUAN	2.00	4.00	0.00	3 DO NOTHING
4 YEWANYANJINWAIC	5.10	1.00	0.00	4 NO NIGHT BIKES
5 MIAN FEI FAN GU	4.10	2.50	4.00	5 FREE REFLECTORS
6 BI MAI FAN GUAN	3.90	3.50	2.00	6 BUY REFLECTORS
7 CHANGJIA,SHANGR	4.30	3.70	0.00	7 REQUIRE MANUFACTURING
8 DUI CHANGJIA,SH	4.50	2.30	0.00	8 SUBSIDIZE MANUFACTURING
9 XIN XING ZI XIN	5.10	4.50	4.50	9 SOS

The Outputs

The overall winner   The overall winner is to **give free reflectors for existing bicycles**, but to require manufacturers and sellers to **put reflectors on future bicycles at their own expense without a subsidy**.

That is the combination solution before considering the SOS which outscores every alternative on every criterion, at least for long-run adoption, namely the **reflective paint**. It is a long-run solution but there would be a lot of existing bicycles that would need to be taken care of in the meantime. Therefore, the best solution would be free reflectors for existing bicycles and requiring reflective paint for all future bicycles rather than requiring reflectors for future bicycles which are more expensive and less effective. (See Table 2.7 for the total scores of each of the nine alternatives.)

Analyzing the alternatives in groups   One could go down the cost to the taxpayer and society column in the same way. The best way to deal

Table 2.7   The total scores for the nine alternatives in the Beijing bicycle problem

Alternative	Combined Rawscores	
1 FANGUANGJ.	7.00	1 REFLECTORS
2 CHE DENG	6.00	2 LIGHTS
3 BAOCHIYUANZHUANG	6.00	3 DO NOTHING
4 YEWANYANJINWAICHU	6.10	4 NO NIGHT BIKES
5 MIAN FEI FAN GUANGJ	10.60	5 FREE REFLECTORS
6 BI MAI FAN GUANG J.	9.40	6 BUY REFLECTORS
7 CHANGJIA,SHANGREN	8.00	7 REQUIRE MANUFACTURING
8 DUI CHANGJIA,SHANG-	6.80	8 SUBSIDIZE MANUFACTURING
9 XIN XING ZI XING CH	14.10	9 SOS

with this problem, though, is to go down the complete list of nine alternatives, but to **analyze them in groups**. The sequence is:

(1) First compare **reflectors and lights**. On that, lights do better on reducing injuries, reflectors do better on being cheaper. The important thing is that the analysis enables one to see what the **threshold figures** are, so that one can make a decision as to which alternative to adopt.

(2) Make the assumption that **reflectors would win out** because they are less expensive and China is a poor country and the severity of the injuries are not so great in terms of the present number of fatalities, although they may be increasing. Therefore, after deciding in favor of reflectors, reject other more extreme alternatives like prohibiting bicycles or doing nothing. One can also then analyze **how the reflectors should be paid for**. One can also then separately analyze what to do about existing bicycles versus new bicycles. In that sense, items 1 and 2 are a pair, 3 and 4 are a pair, so are 5 and 6, and so are 7 and 8. We thus have a series of paired comparisons rather than have to face the more difficult question of which combination of nine alternatives is best. There may be a million, or at least many thousand ways, in which nine alternatives can be combined, although we are interested only in the combinations, not the permutations. The answer would be to figure out how many different ways we could take nine things two at a time, nine things one at a time, nine things three at a time, and so on up to nine things nine at a time.

That is unnecessarily complicated since so many of the combinations do not make sense: one needs to **group various alternatives**. If there are three pairs of supposed alternatives, then we eliminate three alternatives by deciding those three paired comparisons. That brings the total of nine down to six. It is more like a tree diagram than a series of paired comparisons, as is shown on p. 3 (Table 2.3). First, we decide between reflectors and lights. Then we subdivide reflectors into existing bicycles and new bicycles. Then we subdivide existing bicycles into free reflectors or not free. Then we subdivide new bicycles into those that have been subsidized to provide reflectors and those that are not subsidized. This requires us to make not 1000 different decisions among 1000 different combinations, but a grand total of three. We first decide reflectors rather than lights, and then we decide reflectors rather than free for existing bicycles, then we decide not subsidized rather than subsidized for new bicycles, and that is it.

The SOS does not apply to existing bicycles. It just adds a third alternative as to how to deal with new bicycles. We still have only three decisions to reach, except now the third decision has three alternatives to it instead of two.

Threshold analysis and multi-dimensionality   The threshold analysis which is done in Table 2.8 not only compares reflectors and lights, but also does so in terms of exact figures showing **how many lives will be saved** and **how many yuan will be the cost**. The threshold figure is 0.40. Working just with the raw scores, reflectors win out over lights. If, however, instead of giving injuries and cost equal weight one considers a half an injury to be worth 1000 yuan, then there would be a tie; that is the same as saying if one were to consider one injury to be worth 2000 yuan, then there would be a tie. Thus if a municipality considers one injury to be worth more than 2000 yuan then it should provide free lights instead of free reflectors. If it considers one injury to be worth less than 2000 yuan then it should go with the cheaper alternative of the reflectors. Some cities that are wealthier than others could thus subsidize lights and others could subsidize reflectors. Maybe no city would consider itself wealthy enough to subsidize lights. Maybe even no city would consider itself wealthy enough to subsidize reflectors. Or maybe all cities might be wealthy enough to subsidize lights, or at least reflectors.

Points this Example Illustrates

(1)   The importance of considering **benefits**, **costs**, and **equity** as the three main criteria of effectiveness, efficiency, and equity.

(2)   The importance of also considering **political and administrative feasibility**.

(3)   The usefulness of **1–5 scales** if one has no better measurement available.

Table 2.8   Comparing reflectors and lights on lives saved and monetary cost

| | THRESHOLD ANALYSIS | | |
	CHEDENG	FANGUANGJI	Weight
JIANSHAOSHIGU	260.00	240.00	− 0.400
JIANGDICHENGBEN	120.00	− 40.00	− 2.500

(4)   The desirability of **measuring in injuries saved** and **incremental monetary units** if that kind of information is available.

(5)   The usefulness of developing a **threshold expression** for dealing with the kind of multi-dimensionality that occurs when the benefits are measured in injuries and the costs are measured in dollars or yuan.

(6)   The desirability of providing **subsidies** in order to increase compliance, but at the same time noting that the incremental subsidy may be more expensive than the benefits from the incremental compliance: in other words, subsidies do increase compliance, but that does not mean that the subsidies are worth it in view of the fact that the increase may be trivial and the cost may be high. That is especially the case with regard to requiring manufacturers to comply with manufacturing standards in consumer products where safety is involved, as contrasted to requiring ordinary people to have to adopt something expensive on their own like seatbelts or air bags. In other words, manufacturers can easily be required to comply with certain standards or be shut down if they fail to do so. Individuals are not so easy to get to comply by ordering them to take an action, as contrasted with simply giving them whatever it is they would otherwise be ordered to buy.

(7)   This illustrates the kind of SOS that dominates all the other alternatives on all the criteria. It could be called a **dominating SOS** or simply a dominating solution. It lacks the key characteristic of a policy-oriented SOS because there is no strong liberal versus conservative split on reflectors versus lights. The liberal position would be that if reflectors are to be required, then they should be provided for free; a liberal position in this context might be to require automobiles to bear the burden of avoiding crashing into bicycles rather than putting the burden on the bicycles to have either reflectors or lights. That, however, would be old-fashioned knee-jerk liberalism that looks to what class of people should bear the burden, rather than to what pragmatically it takes to get the job done. For example, car drivers could be required to get more powerful headlights at substantial expense, but that would probably be less effective incrementally in reducing accidents than requiring bicycles to have cheap battery lights. The problem is that a bicycle with no reflectors and no lights is virtually invisible until it is too late to avoid hitting it.

(8)   The problem also nicely illustrates how one can subdivide general criteria to be more specific if one wants to disaggregate into more **itemized criteria**; and likewise with more specific itemized alternatives.

(9)   The problem illustrates that one can have lots of alternatives and still not overwhelm the decision-maker if the alternatives are grouped and sequenced so that at no time does the decision-maker have to decide among more than three alternatives.

(10)   The main thing about this example is that it is a very real-world example suggested by real policy-makers about a real problem with real data. Table 2.9 provides a summary of the situation with nine alternatives on the rows, five major criteria on the columns, and relations between alternatives and criteria in the cells. It also shows the total scores for each alternative using neutral, liberal, and conservative weights.

The Beijing bicycle problem thus illustrates such broader aspects of public policy evaluation as (1) the role of effectiveness, efficiency, and equity as goals, (2) the importance of considering political and administrative feasibility, (3) the use of 1–5 scales for expressing relations between alternatives and goals, (4) the need for dealing with multiple measurement on multiple goals, (5) the usefulness of threshold analysis, (b) in dealing with both multi-dimensionality and missing information, using subsidies to increase compliance with the law, (7) the nature of a dominating SOS solution which does better than the other alternatives on all the goals, (8) working with groups of criteria, (9) working with groups of alternatives, and (10) the importance of working with realistic problems.[3]

Trying to Commute To and From Manila

The Manila commuting problem is a good example of how people in developed countries may have the false stereotype that policy problems in developing countries are simpler and less urbanized than policy problems in more developed countries. There may be no country in the world that has a worse commuter problem than the Philippines: commuting is relatively simple in New York, London, Paris, Berlin, Moscow, Tokyo and elsewhere, by contrast.

It is more complicated in the Philippines because:

1. The Philippines has only **one really big metropolitan city** to which people are flocking, whereas countries like the United States have many such cities – New York, Chicago, Los Angeles, etc.

2. Metropolitan Manila may be bigger in population and area than most other big cities where there are a lot of complaints about the difficulty of commuting. Metropolitan Manila consists of **five adjacent cities**, including Quezon City which is a big city in itself.

3. Greatly complicating the commuting problem in Manila is that it is on an **island**, and the Pacific Ocean is just waiting to flood any attempt to build a subway system; further complicating matters is the lack of money for an expanded elevated or surface train system.

4. It has been proposed that there should be **more vehicles** to carry **multiple passenger loads** to and from work to ease the commuting problem (Washington, DC, for example, makes a big thing of providing special lanes for cars and buses that have multiple passenger loads, especially as part of a pooling arrangement). The Manila area probably has more small buses per capita than any city in the world; they have developed a mass transit system based on the extended jeep (jeepney) carrying a dozen or more passengers crowded closely together.

5. Having more jeepneys, small buses, and big buses would just **further clog the highways and streets** into and out of Manila. They would thus worsen the problem and make commuting even more time-consuming.

6. Having more bicycles will not handle the Manila commuter problem the way it helps in Beijing; poor people and middle-class people have too far to travel to do it on a bicycle, and they can also ride the jeepney buses for only 1 peso, which is about 1/20 of an American dollar. It thus is **not cost-effective to buy and ride a bicycle to work**; the more influential car drivers would also not tolerate giving up an auto lane on each side of the streets to be used by bicycles only.

7. This commuting phenomenon is not peculiar to the Philippines as a developing country; many developing countries have a capital city or central city to which rural people flock looking for jobs. The people build whatever shanties they can; the city becomes highly over-crowded, not just relative to the jobs available, but in an **absolute sense** given the limited space and the limited technological capabilities of moving people around in that limited space.

Table 2.9 The problem of collisions between bicycles and cars

Criteria / Alternatives	L goal +Safety	C goal −Cost	L goal Equity	N goal Political feasibility	N goal Administrative feasibility	N total (Neutral weights)	L total (Liberal weights)	C total (Conservative weights)
L Alternative Reflectors	4	3				14	15	13
L Alternative Lights	5	1				12	16*	8
C Alternative Do nothing	2	4				12	10	14*
C Alternative No night bikes	5.1	1		1	1	12.2	16.3	8.1
L Alternative Free reflectors	4.1	2.5	4			21.2	26.8*	15.6
C Alternative Buy reflectors	3.9	3.5	2			18.8	21.2	16.4*

L Alternative						
Require manufacturer	4.3	3.7	16	16.6*	15.4*
C Alternative					
Subsidize manufacturer	4.5	2.3	13.6	15.8	11.4
SOS Alternative					
SOS	5.1	4.5	19.2	19.8**	18.6**

Notes:

1. The **benefits of increasing safety** include reducing injuries, reducing traffic disruption, and reducing ambulance costs. The **components of the cost variable** include equipment costs and enforcement costs, and interference costs. Scores are not shown on those goals because they are subgoals of the main goals of safety and cost, although scores could be shown if one wanted further details.

2. Scores on the equity goal are shown and added only for comparing free reflectors with buying free reflectors, since that is where the **equity goal** is mainly involved. Likewise, scores on the feasibility goals are shown only for prohibiting bicycles at night since that alternative is **not politically or administratively feasible**.

Alternatives

Table 2.10 shows the Manila commuter problem in the context of a decision-analysis table or a super-optimizing framework. The conservative alternative (as is often the case) is to **leave things as they are**, or **leave it up to the marketplace to change things**. Some conservatives like to talk about people 'buying' cities the way they buy products; in that sense, people supposedly vote with their feet by going to Manila, and the 'invisible hand' of Adam Smith may eventually cause them to change their votes and go back to the countryside. That runs contrary to the 'invisible hand' of somebody else who said that once you have tasted the big city it is hard to go back to the farm, especially if the landless peasants have no farm to go back to. In the extremely long run, things may get so bad in overcrowded cities that medieval diseases return periodically to decimate the population: that, fortunately (or unfortunately), is not so likely given modern public health care.

The liberal solution tends to be **spending big money**, but often with no strings attached and with an unduly narrow focus on the immediate problem, rather than on the bigger picture. Liberals also tend to project their middle-class New York or Chicago values on to poor people, rural people, and people in developing countries. In this context, this means proposing a New York or Chicago subway or elevated line or Washington, DC car pooling. Those alternatives were mentioned above as being inapplicable to Manila and may be inapplicable to most developing countries for lack of capital: the available capital could probably be better spent in upgrading human skills and machinery for producing goods. It should also be noted that at least some developing countries may be in a good position to act fast in time to prevent potential urban congestion, rather than trying to cure it or alleviate it afterward.

The neutral alternative, as in many situations, tends to involve splitting the difference between conservative expenditures or recommendations and those of the liberals. If the conservatives say 'spend nothing on mass transit' (since it will overburden the taxpayer and may encourage people to move to Manila), and if the liberals say 'spend many millions', then the neutral compromisers try to find a figure in between. Doing so may result in half of a train system and may be an example of where half a loaf is worse than none: a half-way system could be **expensive without adequate incremental benefits**. Neutrals also tend to emphasize trying a lot of things simultaneously: in this context, that would mean a few more jeepneys, small buses, big buses, bicycles,

Table 2.10 The Manila commuter problem

Criteria / Alternatives	L goal −Time commuting	C goal −Taxes	N total (Neutral weights)	L total (Liberal weights)	C total (Conservative weights)
C Alternative Leave as it is	1	4	10	7	13*
L Alternative Mass transit	4	2	12	14*	10
N Alternative Hodgepodge: more jeepneys and buses	2	2.5	9	8.5	9.5
SOS Alternative Suburbs, regional cities, overseas, and other employment centers	4.5	4.5	18	18**	18**

and subsidized taxis. The result would probably be more congestion and more commuting-time wasted, as mentioned above. Building wider highways for the additional vehicles is also not likely to help; many of the commuting roads in Manila are already much wider than Chicago's Outer Drive. The ultimate would be to clear out all the buildings, and have nothing but commuting roads.

Goals

A key goal is to **reduce the tremendous amount of time wasted** getting to and from work. Only the richest of Filipinos can afford to live near the central city, or the poorest (who set up illegal shanties in whatever alley might be available). The people who live in those shanties frequently do not have jobs to commute to, and neither do the people who live in the rich villas. The working people tend to live substantial distances away, and they may spend approximately two exhausting hours getting into central Manila and then getting out again. Those hours are literally exhausting because the exhaust fumes are unbelievable due to the stop-and-go operation of many diesel-fueled vehicles and propane buses. Many of the drivers and street vendors wear handkerchiefs over their faces.

Delays are also caused by numerous trucks going to and from factories that are in the central city, along with office buildings. Delay is also caused by many beggars and street vendors who interfere with traffic at intersections. A further factor is having large military barracks in the central city that could be used for residential housing. Camp Aguinaldo, which is one of the leading army camps in the Philippines, is in downtown Manila; Americans reading about soldiers from Camp Aguinaldo invading the Makati business district think they may have come as paratroopers: the soldiers simply walked down the block into the high-rise buildings. The hot climate further adds to the problem by making the commuting less bearable and causing a lot of overheated cars that stall and block traffic.

The second key goal is to **keep the tax burden down**. On the matter of the tax burden, though, one has to distinguish between the short-run burden and the long-run burden. The long run (if it is not too far away) is more important since it **lasts longer**. In this context, it may be necessary to spend a lot of money to do something about the problem in order to save a lot of time-cost later. More important, by enabling people in the Manila area to be more productive and healthy, GNP may benefit substantially, thereby increasing the tax base. If that happens then the percentage tax rate can be subsequently lowered, and still bring in more money for other projects.

Saving commuting time for workers tends to be a relatively liberal goal, and saving tax money for taxpayers tends to be a relatively conservative goal. As with other SOS analyses, however, both liberals and conservatives endorse time-saving and tax-saving. It is just a matter of the relative emphasis of liberals compared to conservatives.

Scoring and Totals

In scoring the alternatives, leaving things as they are is terrible for saving commuting time, but it does have a positive relation with short-run tax saving. Spending a lot of money on a train system that would run through developed areas of Manila or on a median strip of widened highways could save commuting time, but it does have a negative relation with short-run tax saving. The neutral compromise is not much help on saving time, although it is not as bad as doing nothing. Likewise it does have a short-run incremental tax burden, although not as bad as liberal mass-transit expenditures.

Looking at the totals in Table 2.10, the conservative alternative comes in first using the conservative weights, with the liberal alternative in third place. Likewise the liberal alternative comes in first using the liberal weights, with the conservative alternative in third place. The neutral alternative is everybody's second choice. It is possibly even the second or third choice of the neutrals since the hodgepodge–neutral alternative does poorly on both goals, although it is not the worst on both goals. In arriving at a super-optimum solution, the important thing is finding an alternative that **exceeds both the liberal and conservative initial best expectations**, not necessarily those of the neutrals.

The Super-optimum Solution

The super-optimum solution in this context has at least **three parts**. The first is to **build up employment opportunities in the suburbs or outlying portions of Manila**. The commuting is highly unbalanced: it is nearly all inward in the morning starting about 5.00 a.m., and it is nearly all outward in the evening starting at about 3.00 p.m. This is unlike American cities, where there is an increasing growth in the suburbs as places for employment opportunities, not just bedrooms; farmland northwest of Chicago in places like Schaumberg Township now have skyscraper office buildings and low-pollution factories.

It is amazing that the University of the Philippines which is located in Quezon City outside of Manila does not have a **high-tech area** around it; that would take advantage of the fact that the University is the leading university in the Philippines and possibly the leading university in Southeast Asia. Most American universities that have engineering schools attract high-tech employment in their areas; the Philippine government could provide subsidies to create a high-tech employment area around the university. This would make a dent in the commuting problem, and set a useful precedent for other subsidized suburban employment. It would also help subsidize technological innovation and diffusion: doing that could have broader useful effects on the Philippine economy than just alleviating the Manila commuter problem.

The second part of a possible super-optimum solution is subsidizing the development of **regional cities** throughout the Philippines; certain cities in the southern provinces of Mindanao and the middle provinces between Manila and Mindanao could be made more attractive to rural people from those provinces as places to migrate to, rather than going to Manila. They could even be made attractive enough to attract some people to move from Manila back to those regional cities in their home provinces; this is a kind of subsidization that has been done in the Soviet Union to encourage people to move west. It was also done by the United States to encourage people to move west, although more a matter of providing people with land for farming in the west than for urban employment opportunities. The Rural Rehabilitation Administration during the 1930s, however, did provide low-interest loans to enable rural people from Oklahoma, Arkansas, and elsewhere in the southwest to go to Los Angeles and establish gas stations and other small businesses or become automobile mechanics, rather than going to Chicago, Detroit, Cleveland, and New York, as was the case with poor southern blacks and whites.

The third part of the solution might be for the Philippine government to work more actively with a number of other governments that have labor shortages, and who could **hire some of the excess labor in the Manila area and other parts of the Philippines**. This may be true of Hong Kong, Singapore, Taiwan, Malaysia, Korea, and even Japan; it might also be worthwhile for the Philippine government to do more to **upgrade labor skills** to make that kind of guest-worker program more attractive. Those guest workers also send back lots of money to help the Philippine economy, which may be even more important than relieving the Manila commuter problem. The Philippine government has developed labor-exporting relations with Arab countries on the

Persian Gulf, and Philippines Airlines stops at more Persian Gulf cities as a result than almost any other non-Arab airline. This is another illustration of the need for elevating some of the policy problems of individual countries to a more **international or global level**.

With that kind of three-part super-optimum solution, commuting time could be substantially reduced, more so than doing nothing, having a mildly effective train system, or a hodgepodge of miscellaneous vehicles rivaling the evacuation of Dunkirk every morning and evening in Manila. Likewise, that kind of super-optimum solution could not only save taxes in the long run by increasing GNP and the tax base, but it could also help resolve lots of other policy problems besides the Manila commuter difficulty. An increased GNP through suburban employment, regional cities and overseas employment can do wonders with regard to reducing the problems of crime, poverty, discrimination, and lack of money for education, health care, housing and other public policy expenditures. The SOS shows up in Table 2.10 as being a substantial winner on the liberal, conservative, and neutral totals. That includes winning over the previous liberal and conservative alternatives or expectations even with liberal and conservative weights.

AGRICULTURE POLICY

Food Prices in China

An SOS Spreadsheet Perspective

High farm prices is the conservative alternative in this context and low prices is the liberal alternative. The liberal weights involve a 3 for urban desires, a 1 for rural desires, and a 2 for all the other goals. With the liberal weights, the SOS wins 76 to 48 for all the other alternatives (see Table 2.11). We then go back and put in the conservative weights. The conservative weights give a 2 to all the neutral goals just as liberal weights do, but they show a reversal on urban and rural desires. For the conservative in the context, rural desires get a 3 rather than a 1, and urban desires get a 1 rather than a 3. The SOS is a winner even with the conservative weights, although now the high prices do better than they did before, but still not as well as the SOS.

The neutral perspective is not to give everything a weight of 1, but rather a weight of 2. If the neutrals gave everything a weight of 1, they would be giving neutral goals less weight than either the liberals or the

Table 2.11   Pricing food in China and elsewhere

Criteria / Alternatives	C goal Rural well-being	L goal Urban well-being	N goal Administrative feasibility	N goal +Farming methods	N goal +Export	N goal +Import technology	N goal +GNP	N goal Political feasibility	N total (Neutral weights)	L total (Liberal weights)	C total (Conservative weights)
C Alternative High price	5	1	3	4	4	4	4	1	52 (18)	48* (14)	56* (22)
L Alternative Low price	1	5	3	2	2	2	2	5	44 (18)	48* (22)	40 (14)
N Alternative Compromise	3	3	3	3	3	3	3	3	48 (18)	48 (18)	48 (18)
SOS Alternative Price supplement	5.1	5.1	3	5	5	5	5	5	76.4 (26)	76** (26)	76** (26)

Note:

1. The intermediate totals in parentheses are based on the first three goals. The bottom line totals are based on all the goals, including the indirect effects of the alternatives.

conservatives give them. Thus the neutral picture is that rural desires get a weight of 2, and so do urban desires. To the neutral, everything gets a weight of 2. The SOS wins with the neutral weights too. It is super-optimum, because it is out in front over both the conservative and liberal alternatives using both the conservative and liberal weights. It also wins over the compromise. The SOS involves the farmers **getting better than high prices** and the urbanites **paying lower than low prices**, with the government providing a supplement like the minimum wage supplement, provided that administrative feasibility is satisfied.

Administrative feasibility involves the use of **food stamps**. They are given to urban food buyers and they cannot be easily counterfeited. Food buyers give them to retailers, who in turn give them to wholesalers, who in turn give them to farmers, who turn them in for reimbursement. The eighth criterion in Table 2.11 just talks about political feasibility. There should be a separate criterion for administrative feasibility.

Of special importance is the fact that no farmer gets the supplement unless he agrees to adopt more modern farming methods; otherwise it would be just a handout for subsidizing inefficient farming. By adopting more modern farming methods, productivity goes up; food becomes available for export; foreign exchange then gets acquired for importing new technology. The new technology increases GNP, and everybody is better off, including the taxpayers who pay the supplement. They are better off because with increased GNP, the government can even reduce taxes if it wants to: it can reduce taxes below a 20 per cent level and still have more tax revenue if the GNP base has increased substantially. Table 2.11 summarizes the relations between various ways of pricing food in China and rural versus urban well-being. The super-optimum solution promotes both rural and urban well-being **beyond the original outside bargaining positions of each side**.

An Economics Perspective[4]

The food price has long been a big problem in China. Since the foundation of the People's Republic of China, the government, influenced by the Soviet economic model, had adopted the policy of an extremely low price of agricultural products, and a high price of industrial products; there was thus a big gap between the price of industrial products and that of agricultural products. The farmers paid a high 'tax rate' through the form of a low selling price. For this reason the farmers got little profit from agricultural production, which in return meant the farmers had not enough financial input in farming. This led to the shortage of agricultural products, as shown in Figure 2.1.

At the low price of p_0, farmers were willing to produce and sell agricultural products only at the quantity of q_0. If the price were settled by the market, the equilibrium quantity would be q_1, the price would be p_1, and Δq, which is the gap between q_1 and q_0, is the shortage (Figure 2.1c).

The urban people want from agriculture an abundance of farm food products at reasonably low cost, while the farmers wish to sell their products at the highest price possible. This is the conflict met by the government in the agricultural policy-making process, the solution to which can be used as an example of a super-optimum one.

We give the grains price as an example. The producers wish to sell at the price of 50 fen per kilogram ($1 = 3.78 yuan = 378 fen), while the highest price acceptable to the consumers is 30 fen per kilogram, as Figure 2.1b shows.

The line $C'C$ indicates that along with the decreasing of the grains price, it will cost the consumers less to buy the grains. That is to say, the consumers' benefit will increase. The line OF illustrates that the higher the price of the grains the farmers sell, the more benefit they will get from them, and vice versa. If the price at which the farmers sell their products if 50 fen per kilogram, and the price at which consumers buy is 30 fen per kilogram, both sides can get the benefit of B_0. The compromise price would be 40 fen per kilogram, at which the consumers or the farmers might get the benefit of B_1. It might be a loss for both consumers and farmers (as Figure 2.1b indicates, $B_1 > B_0$). It is a loss to farmers if the 50 fen per kilogram is the minimum price for them to cover the cost of the production. The 40 fen per kilogram is a loss to consumers if the 30 fen per kilogram is the maximum price that they can afford to pay at their present wages.

A super-optimum solution to this problem might involve the price at which the farmers sell their products being raised to **60 fen per kilogram**, but simultaneously requiring consumers to pay only **20 fen per kilogram**. The 40 fen difference would be paid by the government through food price subsidies: government collectively buys the agricultural products from farmers at the price of 60 fen per kilogram, then sells then to urban people at the price of 20 fen per kilogram.

In this situation, as Figure 2.1b shows, the benefit that the consumers or the farmers might get increases from B_1 to B_2, and B_2 is higher than B_0, which indicates that through the government subsidies, both the

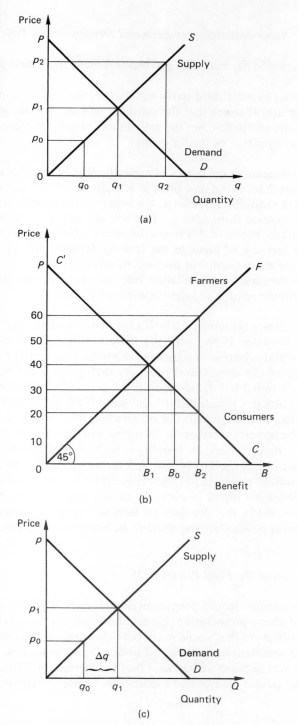

Figure 2.1 An economic perspective in the food pricing SOS

consumers and farmers can get **higher benefit than their best expectation**.

But what can the third party benefactor, the government, get from this program? It seems that the subsidies will increase the government expenditure and deficit, but the government might still come out ahead. This is so by virtue of the following:

1. The **increase of the supply of agricultural products**; this is shown in Figure 2.1c. If the new price p_2 is higher than the original price p_0 and the equilibrium price p_1, the supply of the agricultural products will increase from q_0 to q_2. This will not only resolve the shortage problem, but may also make the country become a food exporter.
2. The **increase of input to the land by farmers**; this in return will reduce the government investment on agriculture.
3. The **decrease of the inflation rate**; this is very important for the economic reform and development of China.

In fact, the beginning of China's economic reform was in the rural area in the later 1970s, with the adoption of the Family-Contract-Responsibility-System in agricultural production and the increase of the price of the agricultural products that government bought from farmers. From 1980–4 the quantity of crops production reached the highest point in Chinese history, but since 1985, agricultural economic growth has been stagnated. The reasons might involve many things, but one of the important factors is the increase of the price of the industrial products that are used in farming – such as farm machinery, seeds, fuels, and pesticides. The benefit that farmers got from the rising price of agricultural products has been covered by the increase in the cost of the agribusiness input; in order to change this situation, the government has made the decision to **increase input on agriculture**: new agricultural policies are expected to be made and implemented in the 1990s.

A Reaction to the Food Pricing SOS

A social scientist from a prominent international organisation came up after the above presentation. He said he could not accept the idea of a food supplement that would make both the rural farmers and the urban workers simultaneously better off in developing countries. The reason he gave was because we had said that the farmers in China wanted 20 cents per pound for rice and the workers wanted to pay only 10 cents per pound. A compromise would have been 15 cents per pound. The food supplement would have paid the farmers 21 cents per pound and the workers would have had to pay only nine cents per pound. He objected on the grounds that he had recently been to China and the price of rice was not what I said it was.

The chair of the panel told him that the exact prices might be an irrelevant consideration – he should just view this as a hypothetical problem helping to clarify the 'bigger picture' (the idea of a third party benefactor making both sides come out better); the chair suggested that instead of 20 cents per pound for rice he just use algebraic symbols and that maybe he would see what was happening better.

That did not seem to help. The problem was that this international organization has spent billions trying to come up with solutions for exactly this kind of problem. His mind apparently was so narrowly focused that he refused to recognize any kind of solution that he or other people at his institution had not thought of; therefore he clutched for whatever straw he could find to argue that this was not a solution. The moral of the story is not to provide any straws. One has to be careful about the details, even if the details are irrelevant. For instance, the correct figure is $200 per week instead of $800 per month for the subscription fulfillment and related costs of the Policy Studies Organization. Which figure one uses makes no difference at all in comparing the alternative proposals; nevertheless, someone like this international executive will say 'we cannot accept this analysis because the correct figure is really $200 per week and not $800 per month'. (The correct figure for a pound of rice in China as of July 20 or so when the presentation was made was actually about 12 cents per pound; I said it was somewhere between 10 and 20 cents, implying that it was 15 cents; if an intelligent international executive could say that that destroyed the whole idea of super-optimum solutions, then less intelligent, less knowledgeable people might be even more likely to find a defense mechanism. Such a mechanism enables them to avoid explicitly or impliedly admitting that they might have been scooped on a solution; it also avoids allowing the opposition side to come out ahead regardless how well one's own side comes out ahead.)

Land Reform in the Philippines

Table 2.12 provides an SOS analysis of land reform in developing countries, although it is especially based on the author's experiences in working with people from the Department of Agrarian Reform in the Republic of the Philippines. Table 2.12 is a classic SOS table in that the rank order of the alternatives on the liberal totals are SOS, liberal, neutral, and conservative. Likewise the rank order of the alternatives on the conservative totals are SOS, conservative, neutral, and liberal.

The Traditional Inputs

More specifically, if we are talking about 100 units of land, the typical conservative approach tends to advocate retaining most of the ownership of the land in the hands of the **traditional landed aristocracy**. The typical liberal approach tends to advocate turning most of the ownership of the land over to **landless peasants** to farm. The typical neutral or compromise approach is something in between, although not necessarily exactly a 50–50 split of the 100 units.

The two key goals in the controversy tend to be **agricultural productivity** and a more equalitarian or equitable **distribution of land ownership**. The conservative alternative (by allowing for economies of scale that are associated with large land holdings) is more productive, but less equitable. The liberal alternative (of widespread land distribution) is less productive, but more equitable. The neutral compromise is somewhere between those relation scores, just as it is somewhere between the conservative and liberal distribution alternatives.

With those relation scores, we logically have the result mentioned above, where the conservative alternative wins with the conservative weights, and the liberal alternative wins with the liberal weights. We are also likely to get the classic compromise, which is everybody's second best alternative or worse. The 'or worse' means that sometimes liberals accept the compromise when the conservative alternative actually does better on the liberal weights, or the conservatives accept the compromise when the liberal alternative actually does better on the conservative weights. Each side may accept the compromise even though it is the third best alternative to them, because they do not want to give in to the other side. That is not the case with Table 2.12, but it does sometimes occur in the psychology of public policy-making.

The Super-optimum Alternative

The super-optimum alternative seems to involve three key elements. The first is that the land needs to be **bought** from the present landowners, rather than confiscated; if the owners are threatened with

Table 2.12 Land reform in developing countries

Criteria / Alternatives	C goal Productivity	L goal Equity	N total (Neutral weights)	L total (Liberal weights)	C total (Conservative weights)
C Alternative Retain land (0 units)	4	1	10	7	13*
L Alternative Divide land (100 units)	1	4	10	13*	7
N Alternative Compromise (50 units)	2.5	2.5	10	10	10
SOS Alternative 1. Buy the land 2. Lots of land 3. Coop action	4.5	4.5	18	18**	18**

confiscation, one possible reaction is to establish death squads, to bring in American military power, or to do other especially nasty things that may easily cost more than the cost of buying the land. The United States probably could have saved a fortune in military and other expenditures on Nicaragua, El Salvador, and Guatemala over the last 10 or 20 years by simply using a fraction of the money spent to buy land from the owners to give to the peasants; the landowners would have probably also saved themselves money by paying a substantial portion of the taxes needed to buy the land.

The second element is that **lots of land** needs to be involved; it cannot be a token program. The landless peasants in developing countries are no longer as passive as they once were. They cannot be easily bought off with relatively worthless bribes or distractions: they have demonstrated a willingness to fight and die for land in pre-communist China, in Central America, and in other developing countries, including the Philippines.

The third element is the need for using **modern technologies** in a **cooperative** way to overcome the divisive effect of distributing the land in relatively small parcels to the landless peasants. Here is where the policy-makers can learn from both capitalistic American farmers and communistic Russian farmers. American farmers are highly individualistic, but they recognize that it makes no sense for each of them to own their own grain elevators, combines, and other big equipment which they can own collectively through producer cooperatives; in the Soviet Union, agricultural efficiency has been promoted through machine tractor stations where farmers can collectively share tractors which they cannot afford to own separately. (This is true regardless of whether the individual farmers are associated with collective farms or private plots.) Cooperative activities also involve the equivalent of county agents who help bring farmers together to learn about the latest seeds, herbicides, pesticides, fertilizers, and other useful knowledge. Cooperative action can also include credit unions and drawing upon collective taxes for well-placed subsidies to encourage the diffusion of useful innovations.

With that combination of SOS elements, one can have **agricultural productivity and equity simultaneously**. Doing so enables that combination of elements to be a strong winner on both the liberal totals and the conservative totals. Appropriate timing may also be required in the sense of moving fast to implement these kinds of ideas – the longer the delay, the more difficult such an SOS solution becomes. (The reason is that the liberal left may acquire such a negative attitude toward the conservative right that the liberal left will consider buying the land to be a surrender to evil people. Likewise, the conservative right may acquire such a negative attitude toward the peasant guerrillas that they can see no respectable solution other than extermination of what they consider to be terrorists.)

Learning Experiences

One of the most interesting aspects of the Philippine land reform experience has been the many mistakes (or one might call them **learning experiences**) that have been made by well-intentioned agricultural experts who may have been overly focussed in their expertise. This can be contrasted with policy analysts who have a more generalist perspective. One should try to see how different policy problems and proposed solutions can interface with each other; some alternatives have a **domino effect**, where the unintended consequences become devastating to what otherwise looks like a meaningful approach to increased agricultural productivity.

Four examples have been provided by people associated with agrarian reform in the Philippines. The first example involves informing farmers as to how they can double their crops through better seeds, pesticides, herbicides, fertilizer, and machinery, **but not providing for any increased storage facilities to put the doubled crop in**. The result was that much of the increased productivity rotted in the fields.

The second example involved informing farmers how they could arrange for as many as four crops per year, instead of one crop per year through special seeds that had a three-month season; the crops thus went from being put into the ground to being ready to harvest every three months. The farmers, however, were not informed as to how a **one-person farm could plow, weed, and harvest four times a year** and still be able to attend fiestas.

The third example involved supplying the farmers with new pesticides that killed all the crop-damaging insects and weeds, but also the frogs and fish that lived on the farms that the farmers liked to eat. After the frogs and fish were killed, the pesticides and herbicides were withdrawn, realizing that the farmers did not want to kill the frogs and fish. The result is the farmers now have no frogs, no fish, and the insects are back. The thing to do might have been to have continued with the pesticides, but give the farmers food stamps to buy frogs and fish from the local markets. The economy would then be better off because the increased farm productivity would more than offset the cost of the frog and fish stamps.

The fourth example involved showing the farmers how they could grow more efficiently with a tractor than with an ox. Such a demonstration, however, failed to recognize that tractors do not make good fertilizer. The demonstration also failed to recognize that if you give one farmer a tractor and not other farmers in the area a tractor, then the other farmers, especially his relatives, come to borrow that farmer's tractor. That farmer then has no tractor, no ox, and no fertilizer. The correct solution might have been to give the tractor to the whole community collectively to share, the way American farmers share grain elevators or Russian farmers share tractors at machine tractor stations.

The idea of one tractor per Philippine farmer is American individualistic capitalism gone berserk, contrary to the realities of farming in the Philippines and other developing countries (or even developed countries). Every farmer in Champaign County, Illinois does not have a combine, and they do not feel deprived; they find it more efficient to hire a combine company, just as every American does not own a U-Haul trailer or a Greyhound bus, although they use them. Farmers want to own their own land, at least in most developing countries. There are many American farmers, however, who own no land, but who farm for land owners; they often make a lot of money getting paid to do it with their equipment. Wanting to own one's own land does not mean one wants to own a combine. The land is used almost all year long if you are a farmer; the combine gets used for one week, and it is recognized as wasteful to have to store it, depreciate it, and make payments on it on a year-round basis. There is a need for **combining individualistic land ownership with collectivistic sharing and renting**.

EDUCATION POLICY

Raising Faculty Salaries Without Raising Taxes in China

This example was developed at the People's University and Beijing University especially by Professor King Chow and a graduate student named Lu Junwei. The example involves the dispute between the government and university professors in China over faculty salaries.

The professors have been seeking a salary of approximately 300 yuan for a certain time period. The government has been willing to give at the most 200 yuan; the object is to come up with a way in which the faculty members could be paid more than 300 yuan, but where the government would be able to pay even less than 200 yuan.

The solution developed by Professor Chow, Mr Lu, and others, is to institute a system of low tuition throughout the Chinese universities while simultaneously increasing the number of eligible students; the money obtained could be used to pay faculty salary increases without having to draw upon the government's limited resources. Provision could be made for low-income students to receive scholarships or loans, especially loans that would be forgiven if the students went into fields of work that were in short supply. The result would be salaries higher than 300 yuan for faculty, with a possible reduction of the government's contribution to less than 200 yuan. The result would also be more people receiving college education, to the benefit of national productivity, which in turn would bring in increased national income and more government revenue. These various relations are summarized in Table 2.13.

This is an example of a super-optimum solution where everyone comes out ahead. The low faculty salaries have also been a point of antagonism between the government and graduate students who anticipate becoming professors, especially when sellers of orange pop and cucumbers can make more in a few days than a university faculty member makes in a month.

The Chinese faculty salaries problem thus illustrates such broader aspects of public policy evaluation as:

1. Having a third party benefactor is a useful way of arriving at super-optimum solutions, but the third party benefactor **does not have to be the government**. That is especially so when the government is one of the two main parties. In this context, the third party benefactor was in effect the students paying tuition.

2. The importance of considering the **side effects** of an SOS solution on GNP. Those side effects include (1) the multiplier effect which occurs as a result of increased income causing increased income for numerous other people via a chain of spending, (2) the compound interest effect which occurs from an increase in the base to which next year's growth rates are applied, similar to getting compound interest on interest, (3) the inter-generational effect as a result of improving parental role models, (4) the taxpaying feedback effect due to increased GNP generating more tax money and subsidy money even if the tax rate is constant or lowered, (5) the export surplus effect which occurs via a productivity surplus that is

Table 2.13 Evaluating policies concerning Chinese faculty salaries

Criteria / Alternatives	L goal Attract faculty	C goal − Cost of government	L goal Equity to students	N goal + Educated population	N goal + GNP	N goal Political feasibility	N total (Neutral weights)	L total (Liberal weights)	C total (Conservative weights)
L Alternative Faculty demand	4	2	3	4	4	2	38 (18)	43 (23)*	33 (13)
C Alternative Government offer	2	4	3	2	2		34 (18)	35 (19)	33 (17)*
N Alternative Compromise	3	3	3	3	3	3	36 (18)	39 (21)	33 (15)
SOS Alternative Tuition and scholarships	5	5	4	5	5	5	58 (28)	62** (32)	54** (24)

61

Notes:

1. For those who prefer numbers to words, the faculty demand can be thought of as 300 monetary units, the government offer as only 200 units, and the compromise as 250 units.
2. The super-optimum solution consists of the government paying the faculty 190 monetary units, but the faculty receiving 310 monetary units. The difference comes from establishing a low-tuition system to replace the current non-existent tuition system. The low-tuition system would provide for scholarships and other forms of student aid for those students who cannot afford the tuition. The SOS would also allow for larger student enrollment without lowering admission standards.
3. The intermediate totals in parentheses are based on the first three goals. The totals not in parentheses are based on all six goals, including the indirect effects of the alternatives.

available for export to obtain new capital goods and technologies which further increase productivity, and (6) the welfare reduction effect whereby the prosperity of an increased GNP means less of a burden on the government to provide for unemployment compensation, public aid, public housing, food stamps, Medicaid, and other forms of welfare. These six points emphasize the upward-spiral benefits of investing in human resources and new technologies for increasing the gross national product.

3. The importance of considering **equity** and not just **effectiveness and efficiency** in evaluating alternative public policies. It is ironic that equity may be more considered in an affluent capitalistic society than in a hard-pressed Marxist society, even though Marxism in theory is supposed to be more sensitive to the spread of benefits and costs across economic classes and ethnic groups.

Tri-lingualism in Philippine Education

The **alternatives** are:

1. **Only English** in the schools.
2. **Only Filipino** in the schools.
3. **Both English and Filipino.**

4. The SOS emphasis is not what language is used, but what the **substance** is that is covered; the emphasis is placed on substance that is relevant to **national productivity**.

All of these alternatives involve the **local dialect** as well. There is no way of avoiding that, which is where the third language comes in. As far as ideological orientation is concerned, speaking only English is associated with conservative elites, and speaking only Filipino has a left-wing nationalism association. Retaining both is the neutral compromise. The SOS can be referred to as the language of productivity, although with English in order to enable Filipinos to have access to the literature of the world that relates to productivity. It does not make any sense to talk about the language of productivity: that is the **subject matter**, it is not a separate language.

The **goals** were:

1. **Access to the world's literature.** That is not an especially good way

to put it – it sounds like access to Mark Twain, Edgar Allen Poe, etc. We are talking about textbook literature, so just say 'access to the world's books'.
2. **National unity**. The first goal is basically conservative; the second goal is basically liberal, although not necessarily so. That is where we developed three groups, **A**, **B**, and **C**, at least with regard to the alternatives.

The A, B, C alternatives are:

1. The **A** alternative is **only English**. That is endorsed by conservative business people who would like to have more access to international trade. It is also endorsed by liberal intellectuals who would like to receive more Fulbright grants and contribute to the literature in their fields.
2. The **B** position of **only Filipino** appeals to cultural conservatives, but also to left-wing nationalists.
3. The **bilingual position** comes out neutral, regardless of whether the first and second positions are considered liberal or conservative.

As for **scoring the relations**, it looks as if in order to replicate what occurred in the course we need a third position which says **only the local dialect**. If we call that position **C**, then it comes out to be a totally dominated position since it provides the worst with regard to access to the world's books and the worst with regard to national unity.

In this context, combining English and Filipino should give the benefits of both. It does not, though, because it detracts from learning English in comparison with teaching only in English; it also detracts from national unity, since both English and Filipino are resented by those people, which is a very substantial percentage, who speak only a local dialect.

The big problem was deciding how to **assign weights** if the alternatives were not clearly conservative or liberal.

1. The people who take the **A** position would give a high weight to access to the world's books, and maybe only a weight of 2 to national unity.
2. The people who advocate speaking only Filipino (**B**) give a low weight to access and a high weight to unity.
3. The people who advocate teaching in the local dialect (**C**) give a low weight to access and a low weight to unity. They give a high

weight to localism. (That alternative may not have been used; it is
one thing to say that there is no way of stamping out local dialects,
it is another thing to say that the national education system should
encourage local dialects by arranging for books and teachers in
every local dialect. We may eliminate that alternative as not being
reasonable.) What we may wind up with, though, is a fairly
traditional analysis in terms of the liberal and conservative nature
of the alternatives and goals.

4. We could say that the bilingual group is group **C**, and that it places
    a high weight on both access and unity. It could be referred to as
    the **D** group, rather than the neutral group.

With these weights, we can calculate four different **total columns**. The
way things are now set up, we are operating independently of liberal
and conservative concepts. The example thus serves the useful methodological purpose of how that can be done. Table 2.14 helps clarify and
summarize the alternatives, goals, relations, and weights.

OTHER PUBLIC POLICIES

The Asian Labor Shortage

The Problem

Speaking before the Hong Kong government, they in effect said that
they did not especially want to hear about solar energy versus nuclear
energy, or trials versus pleas, or getting married, or any of those other
examples. They wanted to know about a SOS to a problem involving
Hong Kong that they considered to be a crucial problem that they were
not able to work out.

The labor shortage was such a problem, which they were approaching from a very traditional perspective. On the one hand was the need
to import additional labor. It in fact required no importing at all: all it
required doing was to just stop arresting people who were seeking to
cross the borders from every direction. These included the Vietnamese
boat people, the people from the Chinese mainland, the Filipinos, and
even some people from English speaking places (although not many)
like Australia, Britain, or India. (Most English speaking people are a
little cautious about settling or staying in Hong Kong given that it will
become a Chinese province in 1997.)

65

Table 2.14 Trilingualism in Philippine education

Goals / Alternatives	Access to world's books	Unity	Totals			
			A Access weight = 3 Unity weight = 2	B Access weight = 1 Unity weight = 3	C Access weight = 1 Unity weight = 1	D Access weight = 3 Unity weight = 3
A Only English	5	4	23	17	9	27
B Only Filipino	2	4	14	14	6	18
C Only local dialect	1	1	5	4	2	6
D Both English and Filipino	4	4	20	16	8	24
SOS Both on productivity	5	5	25	20	10	30

It creates a dilemma that paralyzes decision-making if the choice is one of retaining the labor shortage and thereby missing out on opportunities to make Hong Kong even more prosperous than it is, versus allowing labor in and thereby diluting the population of Hong Kong. This is partly a racist problem, but is also a legitimate concern for the amount of expense involved in education and welfare, although the immigrants may be especially ambitious people who in the long run will pay more than their share of taxes. (This may be especially true of the Vietnamese boat people, although coming by boat from Vietnam to Hong Kong is not much more difficult than crossing the border from Mexico to Texas; they are, however, giving up whatever they had in Vietnam.)

The SOS (that seemed to solve a kind of blind spot by virtue of how the terms were defined) was simply to **redefine the labor force**, and then they suddenly had a labor surplus. 'Redefining the labor force' means recognizing all the potential labor they had – elderly people who are capable of working who are not doing so, disabled people, mothers of pre-school children, people with part-time or seasonal jobs, people who are looking for second jobs, and especially people whose jobs and productivity could be upgraded.

The SOS Table for Conservatives and Liberals

The **alternatives** are:

(C_1) **Import cheap labor.**
(C_2) **Preserve national purity.**
(L_1) **Preserve union wages.**
(L_2) Provide **immigrant opportunities.**
(N) **Import some labor**, but less than either (C_1) or (L_2) would like but more than (C_2) or (L_1) would like.
(SOS) **Add to the labor force and increase labor productivity.** That sounds a bit ambiguous since one can add to the labor force by importing labor; in this context it means adding by drawing upon people who are **already part of the society**.

One key **goal** would be to **increase GNP**, especially by filling orders that otherwise would not be filled. A second key goal is to **minimize disruption to the existing society**. It looks as if a general pattern tends to be emerging in developing these tables of having one relatively liberal goal and one relatively conservative goal with other goals being relatively less important or unimportant.

The **scoring** tends to involve the conservative alternative showing mildly negative on the liberal goal and mildly positive on the conservative goal, and the opposite with the liberal alternative. The neutral alternative shows in the middle on both goals, and the SOS alternative shows especially well on both goals. Table 2.15 gives six alternatives, two goals, and twelve scores, as well as totals reflecting weights for nativism, unionism, and an open door policy.

In this example there are two conservative alternatives and two liberal alternatives. It is not appropriate to say that one conservative alternative is more conservative than another, and that one liberal alternative is more liberal than another – they are just two different kinds of conservatism, and two different kinds of liberalism. One kind of conservatism is basically pro-business and is interested in maximizing business profits. The other kind of conservatism is basically nationalist bordering on racist and is more concerned with ethnic purity than it is with profits. One type of liberalism is pro-union. It is concerned with union wages; it is pocket-book liberalism and it is not concerned with civil liberties. The other liberalism focuses more on civil liberties. For labels, we could say that we are talking about business conservatives versus cultural conservatives, and hard-hat liberals versus civil libertarian liberals. Those are reasonably neutral terms as contrasted to more derogatory or laudatory terms like mercenary conservatives versus racist conservatives, and pocket-book liberals versus intellectual liberals. 'Intellectual liberals' sounds laudatory; Spiro Agnew called them effete, egghead, or pinhead liberals, which does not sound so laudatory.

There are other kinds of conservatives and liberals, but they are not all involved on the immigration issue. There are also religious conservatives who are very strong on issues that have to do with abortion, pornography, or prayer in the schools who are not necessarily pro-business or racist, although there may be overlap. Likewise, one can talk about a set of liberals who are particularly concerned with doing things for poor people. The hard-hat unionists are not very sympathetic to people on welfare. The civil libertarians may be concerned with the free speech rights and due process rights of people, on welfare, but are not necessarily advocates of bigger handouts. They may even be advocates of placing all kinds of strings on handouts, which would go contrary to the welfare liberals, just as the idea of strings goes contrary

Table 2.15 The Asian labor shortage

Alternatives / Criteria	$C_1 L_2$ goal +GNP	$C_2 L_1$ goal – Disruption to society	N total (Neutral weights)	Total L_1 & C_2 weights (Nativism and unionism)	Total L_2 & C_1 weights (Open door policy)
C_1 Alternative Import cheap labor	4	2	12	10	14*
C_2 Alternative Preserve national purity	2	4	12	14*	10
L_1 Alternative Preserve union wages	2	2	12	14*	10
L_2 Alternative Provide immigrant opportunities	4	2	12	10	14*
N Alternative Import some labor	3	3	12	12	12
S Alternative +Labor force +Productivity	5	5	20	20**	20**

to the laissez-faire conservatives. At the present time, one can talk about two kinds of pro-business conservatives – those who want to do things for business but with strings attached, and those who want to do things for business but with no strings attached. Likewise, the liberals can be classified into those who want to do things for poor people with no strings attached, versus those who recognize that strings may be good for poor people and society.

In terms of the **initial totals**, some recognizable patterns are also emerging. All the alternatives tend to wind up with total scores of 12 except the SOS alternative, because they all tend to do mildly well for a 4 on one goal and mildly poorly for a 2 on the second goal, or a 3 on both.

The liberal totals in this context favor alternatives C_1 and L_2. That depends on what kind of liberal we are talking about, though: maybe we have to say that both goals are ambivalent goals. An increased GNP is normally a liberal goal, but would be opposed by unionists in this context if it means importing cheap competitive labor in order to achieve it. Therefore it would only be a liberal goal in the eyes of the L_2 liberals. It is also a conservative goal in the eyes of the C_1 conservatives. This could be a good example of where it is not meaningful to refer to the goals as being 'conservative' or 'liberal'.

Each goal is supported by both liberals and conservatives intensely, but by different kinds of liberals and conservatives. In the usual situation all goals are supported by liberals and by conservatives, but the liberals like some goals relatively better than the conservatives do, and vice versa; here it is not that the liberals like some goals relatively better than the conservatives do, it is that some liberals like some of the goals better than other liberals do. Likewise, some conservatives like some of the goals better than other conservatives do. In other words, there is a kind of **conflict within conservatives** on the **goals** as well as on the **alternatives**, and it might thus be meaningless to talk about a 'liberal total' and a 'conservative total'. One could talk about an L_1 liberal total and an L_2 liberal total and a C_1 conservative total and a C_2 conservative total. In that regard, increasing GNP is a C_1 goal and an L_2 goal. Decreasing societal disruption is a C_2 and an L_1 goal.

That complicates the assigning of **weights**, but not that much. Table 2.15 shows how each group would weight the goals. Knowing that, we can calculate in our heads what the totals should look like. The subtotals could be put on the table. There are only two multipliers, namely 3 and 1; it is easy enough to show what each relation score becomes when multiplied by 3 and when multiplied by 1. We do not have to write anything down to show what each raw score becomes when multiplied by 1.

Calculating the four sets of new totals:

1. For the L_1 or unionist set, the winner is either **preserve national purity** or **preserve union wages**. They both amount to the same thing in terms of whether external labor should be excluded or imported. One could say that the racist conservatives and exclusionary unionists are strange bedfellows: nothing very strange about that at all; it has occurred at many times in American history where otherwise economic-liberal union members have taken sexist or racist positions.

2. The L_2 or civil libertarian column has intellectuals and business people joining together because they share a **willingness to allow for more open immigration**, even though their **reasons may be different**.

3. On the C_1 or business column the results turn out to be the same as the L_2 column because in the context of this subject matter and these goals, the business people who want to **import cheap labor** come out with the same totals as the intellectuals who want to **provide more immigrant opportunities**. We can get differences in those columns if we were to add a goal like 'increase individual firm profits' which would please the business types, but not necessarily the intellectual types. If we added a goal called 'reward ambitious immigrants', that would please the intellectual types, but not necessarily the business types. We would have to add two goals like that in order to get a difference between the L_2 and the C_1 column. We would then have to add 2 more goals to get a difference between the L_1 and the C_2 column.

4. The C_2 or nativist column, which reflects the goals of those who **want to preserve national purity**, comes out the same as the L_1 column, which reflects the goals of those who want to **preserve union wages**.

We could force C_2 and L_1 to be separate in the United States by adding a goal like 'encourage white Anglo-Saxon Protestantism'. That might please those who want to preserve national purity, but it would not please the average unionist who tends to be Polish, Italian, Irish, Hispanic, or otherwise Catholic. Likewise, we could add a goal that would please the unionists, but not please the ethnic purity people. All we have to do is just add a goal that is the opposite of encouraging white Anglo-Saxon Protestantism, such as encouraging **diversity of**

religion and language in the United States. That is the opposite of preserving national purity, but it would be likely to please most unionists since they tend to be minority group people, at least in terms of religion if not race.

All that can be said verbally without cluttering up the table by adding four more goals. As of now the table has seven columns; that would give it 11 columns which is not so horrendous, although the standard table only allows for nine. A main reason for not adding those goals is not because they would make the table too complicated, but because they are **not as relevant to the immigration issue as the goals that we currently have**. We could add just two more columns, since there is no reason why we have to add one column that talks in terms of promoting a single ethnic group (versus pluralism), and then another column that talks in terms of doing the opposite.

The best way to handle the problem is to just note that although the L_1 and C_2 groups come out with the same bottom line and also the L_2 and C_1 groups, they do so for different reasons. This table is not designed explicitly to indicate what those different reasons are; it is just designed to bring out **which alternative is the best in light of the alternatives available and the goals to be achieved**. The verbalization can discuss the motives behind why different groups may place the same high value or low value on a goal for different reasons; it can also say why two groups have the same reasons but yet they are different groups because they differ with regard to other matters.

The SOS Alternative

Instead of concentrating on the diversity within conservatives and liberals, we could put more emphasis on the idea of solving the problem by **raising goals above what is considered the best**. That means raising the unemployment goal to be higher than just achieving zero per cent unemployment in the traditional sense. That sense does not count large segments of the population as being unemployed; it simply defines them out of the labor force. It also does not count large segments of the labor force as being underemployed; instead, it defines being employed as simply having a job, regardless how part-time or how beneath one's capabilities.

Doing better than what was formerly considered the best is now only one kind of SOS. It may be less interesting in at least some ways, because it may be simply a matter of definition, not a matter of actively pursuing well-placed subsidies, tax breaks, or new policies. One does not solve the labor shortage problem simply by defining elderly people as being unemployed, however. One has to go further and talk about how to provide them with **employment opportunities**. We may make a big difference if we start calling so-called retired people unemployed; just calling them unemployed may stimulate them to become more interested in finding jobs, and it could stimulate potential employers into doing more to seek them out. The concept of being 'retired' creates an image of somebody who is practically dead, senile, or decrepit in some sense; the concept of unemployed (especially temporarily unemployed) creates an image of an able-bodied person who is willing and able to work if provided with appropriate opportunities.

In all the examples of **doing better than the best by redefining 'best'**, we are talking about more than just definitions; how things are labeled does influence the behavior of the people who are so labeled, or the doers of the activities: it also influences the behavior and attitudes of **other people toward those activities**. In the Hong Kong labor context, the super-optimum alternative involves the means for achieving the super-optimum goal of doing better than zero per cent unemployment. All the other alternatives focus on the **trade-off between importing labor and disrupting society, or not importing labor and losing additional prosperity**.

Broader Implications

The Hong Kong labor problem illustrates labor problems throughout the world; every country either has a labor shortage or a labor surplus: virtually no country considers its labor situation to be exactly in balance regarding supply and demand. The countries with a shortage are more dramatic like Japan, Korea, Taiwan, Singapore, Hong Kong, Malaysia, West Germany, and to some extent the United States. The countries with a labor surplus consist of most of the under-developed countries that are willing to export labor. That includes all of Central America that exports labor to the US and northern South America that does some exporting to Argentina and Chile (but not much except in the sense of unskilled labor, although that is primarily the kind of labor that is exported). The big export to the US is, however, at both ends – unskilled labor from Mexico but a skilled brain drain from throughout the world, including China, India, eastern Europe, and western Europe. South Africa to a considerable extent operates as a labor importer from the front-line states, but strictly unskilled labor. It loses skilled labor to the rest of the world, including the US and Canada. Israel is another example. They import lots of unskilled labor from the West Bank but lose their skilled labor at the top to the US. The Hong Kong problem is primarily one of the need for **more labor at the bottom**; it is not the kind of unskilled labor that works in the mines of South Africa, but instead the semi-skilled labor that works in the assembly plants throughout Asia (or at least throughout the Asian countries that have that kind of labor shortage).

The problem illustrates the need for having **international economic communities** like the EC (European Community), or the more recent ASEAN (which stands for Association of South East Asian Nations). If such an international community functions properly, then the countries that have **labor surpluses export to the countries that have labor shortages**, and everybody is better off. There could also be interchange between economic communities; there is: not in the sense that the Philippines is exporting labor to western Europe, but in the sense that the Philippines is the largest source of labor in the Arab Middle East, and they send a lot of people to Hong Kong, China, and the US.

On a more methodological level, the Hong Kong labor problem illustrates better than any other problem the idea of **multiple liberal groups** and **multiple conservative groups** that do not get along with each other. Another general principle which this example illustrates is the importance of how a policy problem is labeled. If the problem is referred to as the 'labor shortage' problem of Hong Kong or Asia, then this tends to lead to a solution of **importing more labor**. If the problem is referred to as an 'immigration' problem or an 'ethnic relations' problem, then this tends to lead to a solution of **avoiding the importing of more labor**. The best way to refer to the problem is in such a way that one is pushed toward neither solution, but instead toward thinking in terms of a super-optimum solution in which all sides can come out ahead of their best expectations. That might mean referring to the problem as the 'under-employment' problem of Hong Kong or Asia. Calling it that leads one to thinking about how to make **more effective use of willing and able people who are outside of the labor force**, and of people **inside the labor force who are not working up to their full potential abilities**.

American Military Bases

The problem of the American military bases in the Philippines may be a fitting problem on which to conclude since it is an especially challenging problem, although so are all the others. All the problems in order to qualify as SOS problems need to have the following characteristics:

1. There should be **at least one conservative alternative and at least one liberal alternative**. If there is only one alternative for dealing with the problem, then there is **no problem**, since **there is no choice** – although one could say that there is still a **go/no-go** choice as to whether that one alternative should be adopted.

2. There should be **at least one conservative and at least one liberal goal**. If all the goals are conservative, then the conservative alternative should easily win. Likewise if all the goals are liberal, then the liberal alternative should easily win.

3. The **conservative alternative should do better on the conservative goal**, with the **liberal alternative doing better on the liberal goal**. That is the trade-off requirement; if either alternative does better on both kinds of goals, then that alternative should easily win.

4. It should be possible to say that conservatives give relatively more weight to the conservative goals and relatively less weight to the liberal goals, and vice versa for the assigning of weights by liberals. If that is not so, then it is **not so meaningful to talk about a conservative total with conservative weights and a liberal total with liberal weights**.

5. There should be a super-optimum solution that **does better than the previous conservative alternative on the conservative totals with conservative weights**, and also **does better than the previous liberal alternative on the liberal totals with liberal weights**. That is the most difficult to achieve of these five characteristics, but still manageable.

The problem of what to do about the American military bases in the Philippines is especially difficult because it goes beyond the usual dilemma of choosing between (1) a liberal alternative that clearly wins with liberal weights, and (2) a conservative alternative that clearly wins with conservative weights. An analysis of Table 2.16 tends to show that the liberal alternative barely squeaks by the conservative and neutral alternatives on the liberal totals, and the conservative alternative barely squeaks by the other two alternatives on the conservative totals. We thus have an even tighter than usual dilemma between the liberal and conservative alternatives.

The Alternatives

Working backward from those totals to the alternatives, the conservative alternative is basically to **allow the American bases to remain, but to ask for more money**. The liberal alternative is to **throw the bases out**. The neutral alternative is something in between, generally a **gradual phasing out of the bases**. Other in-between positions might involve throwing out the Clark Air Base but keeping the Subic Naval Base, or vice versa. Another possibility is allow the bases, but with more flying of Philippine flags and the use of other symbols of Philippine sovereignty. A recent middling position is allow the bases, but give the Philippine government **more say in how the planes should be used**, especially with regard to putting down an attempted coup.

The phasing out idea is probably the most common middling alternative. However, it blends into both the conservative and the liberal alternatives. The conservatives are willing to tolerate the bases, but they are going to be eventually phased out to some extent anyhow as the cold war decreases even further; they are also going to be phased out to some extent because they have become rather obsolete in the light of modern defense technology: few if any of the planes or ships could get anywhere without being destroyed by modern missiles (the Russian equivalent of nuclear-armed Trident submarines in the Pacific Ocean could probably wipe out both the naval base and the air base almost before the alarm could ring). There are also bases that are possibly more welcome in nearby Okinawa and Korea.

Likewise, the liberal alternative of throwing out the bases would have to be phased in; they cannot be thrown out within a matter of hours – for one thing, the liberal and conservative members of the Philippine House of Representatives would not tolerate a rushed departure without allowing for substitute employment opportunities and some substitution for the large amounts of money that are spent by Americans with the bases (the Philippine Senate is elected at large and is not so sensitive to Luzon constituency pressures where the bases are located).

One might therefore think there is really only one alternative here, namely to phase out the bases. This problem, however, illustrates the importance of **symbolism and language** in political controversy. Whether the liberals really mean it or not, they talk about throwing out the bases now, not phasing them out; whether the conservatives really mean it or not, they talk about retaining the bases indefinitely. The controversy needs to be resolved in terms of **what each side argues**, not

Table 2.16 The Philippine–US military bases

Criteria / Alternatives	L goal Liberal concerns	C goal Conservative concerns	L goal Sovereignty	N total (Neutral weights)	L total (Liberal weights)	C total (Conservative weights)
C Alternative Bases and more money	3	4	2	18	19	17*
L Alternative No bases	3	2	4	18	23*	13
N Alternative Phase out	3	3	2	16	18	14
SOS Alternative Bases and massive credits to upgrade economy	5	5	3	26	29**	23**

necessarily in terms of the realities beneath the surface: perceptions, value judgements and symbolism are often more important in resolving political controversies than empirical reality, especially in the short run.

The Goals

As for goals, Table 2.16 lists the first goal as 'Liberal concerns'. That means a whole set of interests that liberals are especially sensitive to, including workers rather than employers, consumers rather than merchants, tenants rather than landlords, small farmers-businesses rather than big farmers-businesses, debtors rather than creditors, minority ethnic groups rather than dominant ethnic groups, and in general the **relatively less well-off segments within society**. The second goal is in Table 2.16 listed as 'Conservative concerns'. That means a set of interests to which conservatives are especially sensitive, including employers, merchants, landlords, big farmers, big businesses, creditors, and dominant ethnic groups. One useful aspect of this problem is that it **goes to the heart of liberal versus conservative interests and constituencies**, as contrasted to lower impact problems.

The third goal is in Table 2.16 **(national) Sovereignty**. In some contexts, that can be a conservative goal (such as where Russia nationalists talk about restraining the Lithuanians, expelling the Jews, or otherwise discriminating against citizens of the Soviet Union who are not ethnic Russians). In other contexts, sovereignty can be a liberal left-wing goal (such as where Vietnamese advocate becoming sovereign from China, France, Japan, France again, the United States, and China again during various points in Vietnamese history). Likewise it is a liberal concept in the Philippines when Filipinos talk about getting rid of the Spanish colonialists or the American imperialists, including what they consider to be military-base imperialism. That makes sovereignty in this analysis a relatively liberal goal. Obviously the goal of conservative concerns is a conservative goal, and the goal of liberal concerns is a liberal one.

Scoring the Relations

As for scoring the relations of the alternatives on the goals, both the liberal and conservative concerns are to some extent favorably benefited by present and additional American dollars; these dollars benefit both workers and employers, consumers and merchants, tenants and landlords, small and large farmers, small and large businesses, debtors and creditors, and both minority and dominant ethnic groups. The amount of money is quite substantial: the Philippines is one of the top three recipients of American foreign aid in the world along with Israel and Egypt, whose aid is lessening. The liberal and conservative concerns, however, do not benefit equally. The American presence has a conservative influence; the United States tends to be supportive of conservative pro-American politicians, especially in a country that has American military bases like Korea, Greece, Turkey, West Germany, Spain and the Philippines.

To be more specific, the conservative alternative of retaining the bases with even more money is a bit of a wash-out or a 3 on a 1–5 scale with regard to liberal concerns. The money is at least a 4 on liberal concerns, but the conservative influence of the United States is a 2 or lower; these two subscores average a 3. On the conservative concerns, the conservative alternative of the bases and more money gets at least a 4. On sovereignty, the conservative alternative is at least a 2 on a 1–5 scale, which is the equivalent of a −1 on a −1 to +2 scale.

The liberal alternative also produces a washed-out 3 on liberal concerns. It gets a 4 with regard to getting rid of some of the American conservative influence, but it gets a 2 on losing the American money. The liberal alternative of no bases gets a 2 or lower on conservative concerns. It does relatively well on sovereignty, as both liberals and conservatives can recognize, although they may disagree on the relative weight of sovereignty in this context.

The neutral phase-out approach does about middling on liberal concerns. It provides some money for a while, which is good, but not as good as a lot of money for a long time. It provides a diminishing of American conservative influence, but not as fast as the liberals would like, and not as slow as the conservatives would like. By allowing the Americans to retain the bases even under a phase-out arrangement, the neutral alternative does have a negative effect on Philippine sovereignty, although not as negative as the conservative alternative. We could show that difference by giving the neutral alternative a 2.5 on sovereignty or the conservative alternative a 1.5. Either way, the overall results are not affected.

A Super-optimum Solution

These overall results are that the liberal alternative wins on the liberal totals and the conservative alternative wins on the conservative totals – although not by much, as previously mentioned. Finding a super-optimum solution may be especially difficult where the alternatives are so nearly tied and where the problem is so filled with emotional symbolism. A possible super-optimum solution would involve two key elements. The first is a recognition (as much as possible on all sides) that the bases are probably going to be phased out in the future; this will not be due to the United States surrendering or to the Philippines overcoming the US opposition, it will be due more to defense technology changes (as mentioned above) that makes these bases about as meaningful as the Maginot Line in France in 1940, Pearl Harbor in the United States in 1941, or the Singapore guns pointing to the sea in 1942. The phasing out will also be due to recent world changes that seem greatly to decrease the likelihood of a world war between the Soviet Union, Eastern Europe, and China on the one hand, and the United States and its allies on the other.

More important than a natural rather than a forced phase-out is a second key element of a possible super-optimum solution. This element emphasizes massive credits to upgrade the Philippine economy; it could involve no payment of cash whatsoever on the part of the United States and yet provide tremendous economic benefits to the Republic of the Philippines. It involves a number of characteristics. First of all, the United States makes available an **amount of credits** that when expressed in dollars would be about twice as many dollars as the United States would be willing to pay in the form of **rent or a cash payment**. The United States would be willing to pay more in the form of credits because:

1. It is normally a lot easier to **give credit than to pay cash**. An example might be returning merchandise to a store and asking for cash: one may receive various negative reactions as to why the merchandise should be kept; if, however, one asks for a credit slip, the decision-maker is likely to be much more accommodating.
2. The American economy would substantially benefit if the credits could only be used in the United States to **buy American products and services**. That would benefit the United States more than paying out cash that then gets spent in Japan or elsewhere. At the same time, it does not substantially hamper the Philippines in buying products and services needed for upgrading its economy.
3. The US economy would also substantially benefit indirectly from an upgrading of the Philippine economy, since that would enable the Philippines to buy **even more American products and services in the future**.

As for what the credits would be for, that is where the Philippines could especially benefit. The shopping list might include such things as:

1. Credits to pay for personnel and facilities for on-the-job training and adult education to **upgrade worker productivity**.
2. Relevant credits for upgrading Philippine **higher education**, especially in fields that relate to engineering and public policy which could have high marginal rates of return.
3. Relevant credits for upgrading **elementary and secondary education** as part of a large-scale investment in human resource development.
4. Relevant credits for seeds, pesticides, herbicides, and farm equipment to make the previously mentioned **land reform programs** more successful, including the hiring of experts for training programs.
5. Relevant credits for subsidizing **suburban job opportunities**, regional cities, and overseas employment opportunities.
6. Relevant credits to improve **energy and electricity production** in the Philippines which is such an important aspect of improving GNP.
7. Relevant credits for buying **technologies** that can improve productivity along with upgraded skills, including modern assembly line technologies.
8. Relevant credits for **health care and housing** that can be shown to be related to increased worker productivity.
9. Other credits for buying American products and services that relate to **upgrading the Philippine economy**, as contrasted to buying consumer goods or other products and services that have little increased productivity payoff.

There are additional benefits for both sides that should be mentioned. By 'both sides' in this context is meant the Republic of the Philippines and the United States; 'both sides' also refers to the liberals and conservatives **within the Philippines**. Some additional features are:

1. By providing credits rather than cash, there is a **minimum of loss due to corruption**; it is a lot easier to pocket money than it is to pocket a new schoolhouse or an expert consultant in on-the-job training.
2. By providing credits that are earmarked for upgrading the economy, there is a minimum of loss due to **wasteful expenditures, including bureaucratic administration**.
3. Waste is not going to be completely eliminated; we would not want a straitjacket system that **discouraged experimentation with innova-**

tive ideas for increasing productivity. If innovation is going to be encouraged, some waste must be expected since not all innovative ideas work out well.

4. This could set a precedent for future American aid to other countries and future aid by other developed countries to developing countries. The key aspect of the precedent is emphasizing credits for **upgrading the economy**, as contrasted to an emphasis on food, shelter, clothing, and other traditional charitable 'do-gooderism'.

5. In that regard, we are talking about teaching people **how to fish**, rather than giving them a fish. The fishing analogy is endorsed by liberals who founded the Peace Corps and conservatives who believe in workfare rather than charitable handouts. Actually we are talking about teaching people how to develop and apply new technologies for doing such things as fishing, growing crops, manufacturing products, transporting commuters, and making public policy decisions.

6. The kind of program that most wins friends and influences people in favor of the United States might be programs that involve bringing left-wing anti-Americans to the United States to receive training or having American trainers go to work with Philippine union leaders or Mindanao farmers. People acquire a much more favorable attitude toward Americans in that context than by **receiving a sack of flour labeled 'Made in the USA'**.

It might be noted that if the Filipinos emphasized how obsolete the bases were becoming, they might succeed in getting rid of them faster. On the other hand, it might be wise to emphasize how valuable the bases are in order to get even more credits as payment for retaining them. On the third hand, the United States is not so unaware of the empirical realities, and it is not so unaware of bargaining techniques; this idea of retaining the bases along with an inevitable at least partial phase-out and massive credits for upgrading the Philippine economy should not be approached as a matter of traditional negotiation and game playing: rather it should be approached as a matter that can be resolved to the **mutual benefits of all sides** in the sense of a superoptimum solution with all major viewpoints coming out ahead of their initial best expectations.

SOME CONCLUSIONS

A concluding section to a conference paper or a chapter frequently summarizes what has gone before. That might seem a bit redundant in view of the summarizing nature of the last two policy problems on the Asian labor shortage and the American military bases. They both cover basic ideas regarding alternatives, goals, relations, and the drawing of tentative conclusions as part of a super-optimizing analysis. The problem dealing with the Asian labor shortage comes to grips with the basic concepts of liberal, conservative, and neutral alternatives, goals, and totals. The problem dealing with the American military bases comes to grips with what constitutes an SOS problem, and the relevance of well-placed subsidies and tax breaks toward increasing national productivity.

One point that was made by the participants in the seminars where materials like these were presented was that developing countries like China and the Philippines cannot afford the luxury of super-optimum solutions; instead, they should perhaps be satisfied with something substantially less than the super-optimum (that point sometimes implied that super-optimizing was too complicated except for people trained in computer science, mathematics, statistical analysis, operations research, and other sophisticated methodologies).

After making the presentations though, the consensus generally was that those methodologies are largely irrelevant. They can sometimes be even harmful if they cause paralysis or an over-emphasis on unnecessary measurement and data. The prerequisites for super-optimizing analysis are basically to have (1) some knowledge of the **key facts** relevant to the problem, (2) an awareness of such **political concepts** as 'conservative' and 'liberal', (3) an understanding of such **decisional concepts** as 'goals', 'alternatives', 'relations', 'tentative conclusions', and 'what-if analysis', and (4) some **creativity** in developing appropriate super-optimum solutions. That kind of creativity is made easier by having the first three of the four prerequisites above. It is also made easier by having access to case studies like the ones previously discussed so that one can learn from the experiences of other groups or individuals in trying to develop related super-optimum solutions.

The point about not being able to afford the luxury of super-optimum solutions may, however, in fact be the opposite of empirical and normative reality. The United States and other developed countries have less need for super-optimum solutions than developing countries do; the United States can probably go for a whole generation without developing any innovative ideas or coming close to solving any of its policy problems. If that happened, the US would still have a high quality of life because it has such a well-developed cushion to fall back on. Developing countries, on the other hand, cannot afford to be satisfied with merely getting by; doing so will put them **further behind** relative to other countries that are advancing rapidly – including countries that were formerly developing countries like Japan, Korea, Hong Kong, and Singapore.

In that context, super-optimum solutions are like free speech. Sometimes people in developing countries say they cannot afford free speech because it is too divisive; after they become more developed, then they can allow opposition parties and not have one-party systems with presidents for life. The reality is that they especially need to have free speech in order to stimulate creative ideas for solving their policy problems; those problems are much more in need of solutions than the policy problems of well-developed countries.

A concrete example is the polio problem in Malawi. It is not a problem that is solved by Malawi needing a Jonas Salk to invent a polio vaccine; it has already been invented: they just need to use it. They do not use the vaccine adequately, not because they lack the technology of having bottles of vaccine to pour into paper cups to give to the children to drink; they do not use it because Malawi happens to have a one-party state with a president for life who thinks that only doctors can give out vaccines, partly because he happens to be a doctor himself. Anybody who speaks out against that nonsense may find themselves in jail or worse. The problem is thus a free speech problem, not a technology problem.

On a higher level, the problem is an SOS problem. Polio could be greatly reduced or eliminated in Malawi by explaining to the headman in each village how to pour the vaccine from the bottles into the paper cups, and how to have the children drink the vaccine; doing so would probably mean the end of polio in Malawi as it has meant the end of polio in the United States. President Hastings Banda could get the credit for having been responsible for ending what has been a horrible disease since the dawn of history in Central Africa. That should please the liberals, who are interested in better public health care; it should please the conservative president, who wants to be admired. More important, if this situation can be used for establishing a precedent about the importance of free speech in stimulating better public health care and better resolution of other public policy problems, then the impact might extend to numerous ways in which the quality of life could be improved in the developing country of Malawi.

This is not an isolated example. Numerous examples have already been given in the previous case studies, and more past examples could be given. What is needed are more applications of the basic ideas mentioned above, including what constitute the prerequisites for super-optimizing analysis. It is hoped that this chapter, and the book of which it is a part, will help stimulate those applications toward achieving super-optimum solutions to the public policy problems of developing and developed countries.

Notes

1. For further material on super-optimum solutions where both liberals and conservatives come out ahead of their initial best expectations, see Lawrence Susskind and Jeffrey Cruikshank, *Breaking the Impasse: Consensual Approaches to Resolving Disputes* (Basic Books, 1987); S. Nagel, *Decision-Aiding Software: Skills, Obstacles, and Applications* (Macmillan, 1990); and S. Nagel, 'Super-Optimum Solutions in Public Controversies', *World Futures Quarterly*, 53–70 (Spring 1989).

2. For further material on Philippine public policy problems, see Raul De Guzman and Mila Reforma, *Government and Politics of the Philippines* (Oxford University Press, 1988); David Wurfel, *Filipino Politics: Development and Decay* (Cornell University Press, 1988); Gabriel Iglesias (ed.), *Implementation: The Problem of Achieving Results: A Casebook on Asian Experiences* (Eastern Regional Organization for Public Administration, 1976); and Richard Kessler, *Rebellion and Repression in the Philippines* (Yale University Press, 1989).

3. On policy problems in post-1945 China, see Harry Harding, *China's Second Revolution: Reform After Mao* (Washington, DC: Brookings Institution, 1987); John Burns and Stanley Rosen (eds), *Policy Conflicts in Post-Mao China* (M. E. Sharpe, 1986); and John Major and Anthony Kane (eds), *China Briefing* (Westview Press, 1987).

4. This portion of the China food-pricing problem is authored by Tong Daochi of the People's University of China; he also inspired the basic idea of applying super-optimizing to the food-pricing problem.

3 Global Policy Studies and the Nation-state

Louise G. White

INTRODUCTION

The title of this volume uses the terms 'global' as opposed to 'international' policy studies. The distinction is significant. Internationalism assumes a cluster of nation-states, each with its own interests, and examines how they relate to each other. A global perspective begins with the globe as a socio-technological system. It focuses on the variety of linkages throughout the system, many of them policy issues that spill across national boundaries. It studies how these linkages create problems for the global system and explores what mechanisms can be created to deal more adequately with the problems, and what further linkages can be crafted.[1] Global policy studies as a body of theory and research cannot avoid dealing with the role of the nation-state, however. Policy problems are often created by the actions of national governments and nation-states can potentially help deal with the problems. The field of global policy studies, therefore, needs to consider whether the nation-state is an obstacle to be overcome, a potentially valuable resource, or increasingly irrelevant.

This chapter identifies and compares four ways of thinking about the role of the nation-state in a global policy arena. Three of the perspectives dominate current discussions; they focus on the international economic activities of nation-states. Proponents generally assume that nations pursue their economic interest which is defined as growth in economic productivity. The fourth perspective is more complex. It considers how nations deal with a variety of global policy issues, including but not focusing exclusively on economic development. Not only do nations have a stake in a number of issues, but their interests are not always immediately apparent and they are not simply determined by the dominant economic interests in a nation. This view predicts that state interests often emerge out of an interactive learning process. Therefore, the procedures and institutions that allow states to interact become critically important in enabling them to formulate their interests and develop global strategies. It also assumes that states can play an autonomous role in determining their interests, in persuading others, and in deciding on a framework of obligations and responsibilities.

THE NATION-STATE – HINDRANCE TO A GLOBAL ECONOMY

According to this first perspective, states represent the apparent interests of the major social and economic groups in the society. Since economic interests are the most salient forces, economic groups pressure the state to erect protectionist barriers which in turn impede global interdependence. The sources of this perspective are numerous, ranging from Marxism to pluralism to public choice theory. All of these view the state as a product or reflection of social and economic forces in a society. For pluralists the state referees or brokers among competing interests; for Marxists the state registers the dominant interests in the society; for public choice theory the state is coopted by narrow producer interests that form spending coalitions devoted to expanding public power. A particularly interesting version of this latter position is found in Mancur Olson's study of nation states in which he argues that those countries where interest groups have a major role are most apt to pursue short-sighted policies that impede their economic growth in the long run.[2]

This first perspective contrasts the actions of nation-states with the logic of a global economy in which national borders are less important. The nation-state, in fact, is a hindrance to dealing with global problems. According to the eminent economist Robert Heilbroner (1989), nation-states inevitably build protective barriers and thereby impede free flows of technology and goods across national boundaries. In fact, he makes the interesting prediction that as economic forces move more and more toward a global economy, nation-states will become increasingly important, precisely because groups within those countries will urge the nation-state to afford them protection.

This dynamic is particularly true for states in capitalist systems. They have an advantage because those in power can claim that their system is based on the moral value of economic growth. Instead of critiquing their economic arrangements, members of capitalist systems develop a general sense that business works to benefit the whole society, that 'the class of businessmen is the only group that naturally thinks of itself, and is generally thought of, as speaking for the social order as a whole'.[3] It is not that economic forces dominate the government as claimed by Marxists. Instead the state and businesses have the same interests. 'This business-oriented cast of mind is partly a consequence of the fact that the political realm, having surrendered authority over the workings of the economy, is now dependent on its smooth running to provide the wherewithal to carry out government programs.'[4] The coexistence remains an uneasy one, however, since businesses are oriented to pursue their own profit while the political system is concerned with the whole unit.

Heilbroner concludes that the political realm will continue to be enlarged at the expense of economic interests for a number of reasons. First, technologies have major impacts on the environment which in turn will need government protection. Second, urbanization is increasing, with the enormous complexity that represents. Third, economic actions are so interdependent that business will increasingly call on governments to 'cushion, restrain, or offset disruptions'.[5] Finally, the basic dynamic of capitalism stems from political institutions rather than economic ones. 'The economy inspires people to work; the polity inspires them to work together ... The ultimate mobilizing power of capitalism lies in its political, not its economic, half, even though its dynamism and drive derive from the latter.'[6] The end result is that capitalism reinforces both the demands for protectionism and the capacity of the state to pursue this course.

THE NATION-STATE – IRRELEVANT ACTOR

The second perspective predicts that trends will be exactly the reverse of those predicted by Heilbroner. Economic institutions, not political ones, will become increasingly determinative as groups increasingly benefit from global economic integration and perceive that protectionist barriers hurt them. Representatives of global economic interests, for example, view the global economy as a single unit dominated by large economic units. These global economic forces make nation-states increasingly irrelevant. Some who hold this view acknowledge that states will not give up their prerogatives easily. For example, a collection of essays on the international economy notes that 'the main question is no longer whether the United States will become more fully involved in an emerging global economy. (It will.) What has now become evident is that the many dimensions of the links that have emerged since the late 1970s have created a number of problems of adjustment'.[7] Even as states erect barriers in the short run, however, in the long run they will succumb to the logic of economic markets, as the benefits are more widely dispersed and as appropriate adjustments are made.

According to a speech by a Japanese management consultant, Kenichi Ohmae, national security, national pride, and national concerns for the environment or social welfare, are all outdated issues. In this view the major economic actor of the future is the corporation, whose role is to serve the customer and the stockholder rather than the state. Ohmae predicts a 'new world without borders in which nations no longer contend with military might. Instead the battles will be fought between NEC and IBM, between Mitsubishi and General Motors; and the prize will be the fluctuating loyalty of the world-class consumer whose search for the new and best will drive tomorrow's world economy'.[8] Nation-states are irrelevant at best, and at worst a hindrance. To quote Ohmae, 'Years ago, territories meant something. Resources meant something. Today, those are very old notions. Economies, such as Singapore, Taiwan, Switzerland and Japan, are people-driven. We have to redefine the role of government, which is no longer so important.'[9]

The primary basis for this reasoning is that economic interdependence penetrates all relationships. Businesses are not only increasingly dependent on markets in other countries. Businesses and financial interests are also investing in other countries, with the result that capital flows have become even more important than international trade in goods and services. Presumably states will have less need to protect themselves, since outsiders with extensive financial interests in a country have a vested interest in maintaining the strength and vitality of that economy. Those who take this perspective are generally optimistic that as activities are increasingly dominated by economic rather than political logic, businesses and publics will be better off.

A number of writers, reflecting on economic problems within the poorer nations, come to similar conclusions about the irrelevancy of the state in the face of economic forces. Because the governments in these countries are weak with little moral legitimacy among the populace, they increasingly rely on corruption to remain in power. As a result they are unable to perform effectively for the public at large, they do nothing to stimulate and facilitate private enterprise, and their legitimacy further declines.[10] In this setting the populace increasingly relies on the informal economic sector to earn a living and according to

some at least, are much better off in the long run if the state remains
weak.[11]

THE NATION-STATE – RESOURCE FOR ECONOMIC
DEVELOPMENT

The literature associated with the third perspective emphasizes that
states can take autonomous initiatives to stimulate their economies.
Unlike the first view states do more than reflect the social and economic
interests in a society, and unlike the second view, they are not
necessarily irrelevant in the face of economic forces. This view fits with
a broader development in the political sciences. Quite apart from any
concern for internationalism and globalism, a growing number of
scholars are taking another look at the role of the state and finding that
it is more important than often thought.

The central argument is that the state is not just a creature of its
socio-economic setting. It can act autonomously to pursue goals of its
own and it also influences the values and preferences in the society.[12] As
a partially independent body, it struggles for power with internal social
forces, articulating and presenting a position of national interest. For
example, a study of United States policy towards raw materials
demonstrates that the 'objectives sought by the state cannot be reduced
to some summation of private desires' and that states 'can be treated as
unified actors pursuing aims understood in terms of the national
interest'. State autonomy, the author finds, explains investments in raw
materials better than any theory about the role of political interests.[13]
Studies show that states are particularly apt to be independent in the
European context where administrators play a more decisive role, but it
is also true in the United States, a country where there is less structural
basis for autonomy than elsewhere.[14] The theory is particularly relevant
to the concerns of global policy studies since state autonomy is said to
increase as international issues become more salient. The reasoning is
that officials generally gain greater autonomy from internal groups as
they get involved in the international arena.[15]

An important version of this perspective urges the state to use its
position and resources to stimulate economic productivity. Whereas
the first view assumes that states will accede to economic interests and
follow protectionist policies, this view assumes that states have an
interest in being members of a relatively free international economic
system. By promoting more productive economies they will undercut

the need for protectionism and thereby help to bring about a more prosperous international economy. In this sense the nation state is a potential resource to promote a more interdependent world economy and can use its autonomy to make protectionist barriers unnecessary. Proponents fear that the dominant economic interests will fail to see that the nation has a long-run interest in a healthy economy, and they urge that pursuing this national interest requires a much stronger role for government.

For example, Robert Reich stresses that the nation-states are increasingly interdependent as their economies become more intertwined. United States businesses, however, are ill-prepared to cope in this international arena, and the government needs to be much more assertive in helping them compete internationally. Reich looks to the public sector to develop a broad package of incentives and programs to retrain the work force and increase its skills to produce sophisticated technology and hence make businesses more competitive.[16]

Proponents of a larger role for the state in promoting competitiveness tend to assume that the result will be a more vital and productive international economy, that national interests, intelligently pursued, are consistent with an increasingly interdependent world. If the United States eschews a protectionist policy and becomes more competitive, the benefits will redound on the international economy. Reich, for example, critiques the United States for its 'mob at the gates' mythology, through which it tries to protect itself by keeping others out. Instead he argues that the international economy will be better off with a number of strong, independent states maintaining open relations with each other. And the states are major actors in these relationships, rather than simply acceding to corporate interests or economic forces.[17]

THE NATION-STATE – CUSTODIAN OF MULTIPLE POLICY VALUES

These three perspectives dominate current thinking within the United States, primarily due to the problems the country is facing in remaining competitive in the international economic arena. None of them, however, takes into account the full range of activities associated with global policy issues. According to a fourth perspective the nation-state is not a monolithic player with a clear economic national self-interest to protect or promote. Nation-states exist in an uneasy relationship with other nations and share a number of policy problems, from a depleting ozone shield to a burgeoning drug traffic. For some issues it is clearly in a nation's interest to share information and look for common solutions. For other issues there is a clear national interest in being more competitive or protective. And for yet other issues, a nation's interest is not that clear-cut. It may gradually emerge as interested parties interact with each other and learn more about what is at stake. Or other parties may take over the debate and work out accommodations among themselves that never become part of a national policy.

In this view, the nation-state is not defined solely by its relationship to economic forces. Like those who hold the third view, the state is often an autonomous force. States do more than represent dominant economic interests; they do more than erect trade barriers or go to war with each other. They may also choose to act as 'custodians of public goods – things like clean water and air, secure neighborhoods and protection for families from the vagaries of illness, disability, old age and natural catastrophe'.[18] Nation-states in this view can stifle global interactions or facilitate them depending on two types of activities – first, how the state defines its interests and second how it defines what is appropriate in the situation. Neither of these definitions are self-evident and predetermined. The state can exercise discretion in determining where its interests lie and in deciding on rights and duties in the international arena.

Like proponents of the third view, those who think of the state as the custodian of multiple values agree that the state has some autonomy, but they view the arena as a global one rather than an international one. The difference is evident in two books on foreign policy published in 1989. One, a study of foreign policy under President Kennedy, describes United States policy towards every region of the globe, and underscores a 'politics among nations approach' with the US striving to achieve supremacy. A second study, by a group of scholars at the Brookings Institution, pays little attention to bilateral interactions among states. Instead it focuses on global policy issues such as trade and technology and underscores the limits on national power and the increasing interdependence among nations.[19] According to this second study, 'American officials must move from habits of conflict and domination to those of consensus if they hope to put their economy in order . . . However circumspectly, they must see in Soviet and Chinese economic reform the instruments of international stability. Facing a relative decline in American power, American policymakers must be genuinely internationalist (globalist), must understand economics at least as much as politics, must free themselves of Cold War cliches, and must let go of the myths of supremacy and empire'.[20]

According to this fourth perspective a nation's interest is not well defined and fixed, as is usually assumed in policy analysis models that rely on economic methods of analysis. Rather the content of national interest evolves and shifts as new information is brought to bear. From this perspective, the procedures for interacting with other nations and for bringing interested parties together assume greater importance. What processes for debate and dialogue are set up? Policy analysis consistent with this perspective explores the assumptions and values implicit in different positions, and acknowledges the validity of multiple political interests. It is a much more open and indeterminate political and communication process than is assumed in the first three perspectives.

Moreover, the role of the state varies according to the nature of the policy. According to Katzenstein nations manage interdependence in the world economy through policy networks within their own borders. This emphasis on the relations between the nation and other social and economic units, means that policies reflect the positions and alliances among the state and key social and economic groups.[21] The state does not simply reflect nor negotiate among the different interests but has its own positions and develops alliances with supporting interests. Based on a study of the role of the state in Peru, Stepan notes that the extent of a state's commitment to clear goals, its technical capacity, its monitoring ability, its investment resources, and its international position will vary by policy area.[22]

According to this perspective there is no guarantee that different interests will arrive at cooperative solutions. In an important essay, March and Olsen note that most contemporary models presume that actors behave rationally and seek to optimize their respective positions. The eventual results are 'historically efficient' in the sense that an objective and efficient solution results.[23] This fourth perspective, however, assumes that actors do not necessarily define their interests rationally nor take a long time frame into account. Whether or not that happens depends partly on the effectiveness of the institutions that promote learning and debate and that enable participants to learn what is appropriate in the situation.[24]

Consider the example of foreign debt as a global policy problem. This fourth perspective assumes that there is no clear, well-defined national interest, and that at least in the lending nations, indebtedness affects various groups differently. Investors in banks are clearly hurt in the short run when debtor nations do not repay loans. The same individuals may also be exporters, and are thereby hurt when countries are forced to direct their available resources to repaying debts rather than buying goods. The perspective of the lending states therefore shifts as different groups become involved. In the meantime, the state has an interest in maintaining stable political systems in the debtor countries and argues its case among the affected interests.

The critical issue then becomes the processes and institutions that exist for dealing with this issue, for mediating conflict among the different interests and for learning about and reformulating a nation's own interest. The World Bank and International Monetary Fund (IMF), for example, have only recently begun to facilitate a dialogue among the nations about indebtedness. In the process of the dialogue debtor nations and groups within them are beginning to rethink their original perspectives. Whereas debt forgiveness was not a serious option in the mid-1980s, most parties began to accept it as a reality as the decade drew to a close. This fourth view also assumes that the debt issue cannot be isolated from other policy issues such as military assistance and environmental issues (e.g., the burning of forests in the Amazon basin and the release of CFCs into the environment). It predicts that the outcome cannot be determined ahead of time, but will be influenced by the adequacy of the procedures that are developed for coping with these issues.

This perspective emphasizes the institutions and processes whereby states articulate and formulate their interests and interact with other parties. A number of recent developments in management and administrative theory suggest the kinds of institutions and practices that should prove most appropriate. Most of these have emerged within the domestic policy arena but they are directly relevant to global policies, with the multiple players and their shifting and evolving interests. Some of the relevant developments may be briefly noted.

There is a growing interest in devising **new institutional arrangements**, particularly ones that decentralize and diffuse program responsibilities among a number of organizations. Increasingly responsibilities are contracted out or delegated to a variety of institutions, including private and voluntary arrangements. Traditional governments and market institutions are no longer the only options.[25] Recent theory urges that these new institutions make it possible for states to be more flexible and responsive and that they do not necessarily dilute state authority. Moreover there is a blurring of the lines among the various sectors. Post-industrial society is experimenting with a greater diversity of institutions than was true during the industrial period. In spite of predictions of a convergent, rational view, people continue to be influenced by non-rational and particularist sentiments. Moreover technology has made it possible to tailor goods and services to smaller groups. The result is increasing diversity both materially and intellectually.[26]

The question for the global arena is what institutional arrangements can be developed to handle the kinds of issues that occur across national boundaries. As both the IMF and the World Bank have tried to exert an influence on macro-economic policies within developing nations, they have inevitably invaded each other's domain and are currently reviewing their respective roles. In the meantime the Organization for Economic Cooperation and Development (OECD) provides an important forum for high-level dialogue among 24 industrial nations, but as long as it keeps out some of the fast-growing Asian states, its role will be limited. A number of other arrangements are being developed, many of them described throughout the chapters in the present volume. These include well-publicized conferences to bring together experts and to educate decision-makers about problems. They also include more informal, less visible, procedures in specific policy arenas, such as telecommunications policy.

Second, there is more emphasis on **new roles for the public sector**. There is more interest in the role of the state in determining appropriate norms for coping with policy issues and in educating and persuading interests and individuals. For example regulators are placing more emphasis on imparting state-of-the-art information to different parties and less to holding them strictly accountable to predetermined criteria. Research shows that organizations often perform poorly simply because they are uncertain about the effects of new technologies. In areas such as the international telecommunications arena, governments bring together the different parties to share and review research and information in a particular policy arena.[27] Similarly the state is not just a source of coercion, but it is also a potential source of policy solutions. According to Heclo, 'Governments not only "power" (or whatever the verb form of that approach might be); they also puzzle. Policy-making is a form of collective puzzlement on society's behalf; it entails both deciding and knowing'.[28]

Third, there is more emphasis on **management**, and a recognition that in dealing with complex and rapidly shifting policy issues the answer may lie less in structures of authority and more in the capacity to manage a situation creatively. In contrast to the concept of administration, management usually implies a more proactive and flexible stance. Studies within the general public administration literature refer to the value of communication and negotiation, the importance of gathering relevant information and developing needed resources.[29] There is also a growing appreciation of the **political** dimensions of a manager's job, that managers are operating in a highly politicized arena, that they need to learn to work effectively by motivating and persuading various parties. Management becomes 'an effort to transact with other interests, to take their point of view into account, to rethink and recast programs, and to persuade and convince where possible'.[30]

Fourth, there is a greater appreciation of the **limits of rationality**. According to those who write about organizations as anarchies of meaning, goals often emerge retrospectively to rationalize actions already taken. Interested parties often enter and leave policy arenas depending on what else is currently capturing their attention, rather than on how important the issue is.[31] This theory, with its realistic view of leadership and policy analysis, is highly relevant to the shifting, anarchic characteristics of the international and global policy arenas.[32]

CONCLUSIONS

Those analyzing global policy issues need to examine their assumptions about nation-states in an increasingly interdependent, global system. This study has identified four perspectives on the role of the nation-state. The first three are most fully developed and are well represented in current literature and thinking. They each focus on economic concerns and have arisen to deal with the changing economic fortunes of individual nations. They do not take into account the full range of policy issues that nation-states deal with, nor the ambiguity that is often associated with national policy positions. A fourth perspective views the nation-state as the custodian of multiple policy values and focuses on the processes for dealing with global policy issues. It appreciates that nation-states play a changing and uneven role. On the one hand, their interests emerge gradually as they interact with other parties to learn and discover their goals and as they deal with social and economic interests in their own domestic setting. On the other hand, states have some discretion in defining what is appropriate in a specific policy arena, in specifying obligations, and in using their considerable resources to persuade and educate. This last perspective therefore points to the importance of procedures and forums for carrying out policy discussions and improving the quality of policy debates and decision-making.

Notes

1. Marvin Soroos, *Beyond Sovereignty: The Challenge of Global Sovereignty* (Columbia, SC: University of South Carolina Press, 1986); Robert Clark, *The Future Taking Shape* (Fairfax, VA: George Mason University, 1985); Alvin Toffler, *The Third Wave* (New York: Bantam, 1980).
2. Mancur Olson, *The Rise and Decline of Nations: Economic Growth, Stagflation, and Social Rigidities* (New Haven, CT: Yale University Press, 1982). See also Robert Bates, *Markets and States in Tropical Africa* (Berkeley: University of California Press, 1981); and Douglass C. North, 'A Framework for Analyzing the State in Economic History', *Explorations in Economic History*, 16 (1979): 249–59.
3. Robert Heilbroner, 'The Triumph of Capitalism', *New Yorker* (January 23, 1989): p. 102.
4. Heilbroner, 'The Triumph of Capitalism': 103.
5. Heilbroner, 'The Triumph of Capitalism': 106.
6. Heilbroner, 'The Triumph of Capitalism': 107.
7. John Adams (ed.), *The Contemporary International Economy: A Reader*, second edition (New York: St Martin's Press, 1985): vi.
8. Hobart Rowen and Jodie Allen, 'Brave New World, Inc.', *The Washington Post* (March 19, 1989).
9. Rowen and Allen, 'Brave New World'.
10. Richard Sandbrook, 'The State and Economic Stagnation in Tropical Africa', *World Development*, 14 (3): 319–32.
11. Hernando de Soto, *The Other Path* (New York: Harper & Row, 1989).
12. Theda Skocpol, 'Bringing the State Back In: Strategies of Analysis in Current Research', in Peter Evans, Dietrich Rueschemeyer, Theda Skocpol, *Bringing the State Back In* (Cambridge: Cambridge University Press, 1985): 20. See also Peter Katzenstein (ed.), *Between Power and Plenty: The Foreign Economic Policies of Advanced Industrial States* (Madison: University of Wisconsin, 1978); Stephen Krasner, 'Approaches to the State', *Comparative Politics*, 16 (January 1984): 223–46.
13. Stephen Krasner, *Defending the National Interest* (Princeton: Princeton University Press, 1978): 6, 12, 13. See also the two following sources and their extensive bibliographies: Skocpol, 'Bringing the State Back In', and James March and Johan Olsen, 'The New Institutionalism: Organizational Factors in Political Life', *American Political Science Review*, 78 (3) (September 1984): 734–49.
14. This argument has also been made by those reviewing the growing economic power of 'newly industrializing countries' in East Asia. See Colin Bradford, Jr, 'East Asian "Models": Myths and Lessons', in John P. Lewis and Valeriana Kallab (eds), *Development Strategies Reconsidered* (Washington: Overseas Development Council, 1986): 115–28.
15. Skocpol, 'Bringing the State Back In': 9. For a related study, see Baldwin's study of **how** the state uses its economic powers to promote its

national interests, *Economic Statecraft* (Princeton: Princeton University Press, 1985).

16. Robert Reich, *The Next American Frontier* (Penguin, New York, 1983); *Tales of a New America* (Random House, New York, 1987); Lester Thurow, *The Zero-Sum Society: Distribution and the Possibilities for Economic Change* (Penguin, New York, 1981); James Carroll, 'Public Administration in the Third Century of the Constitution: Supply-side Management, Privatization, or Public Investment?', *Public Administration Review*, 47 (January–February 1987): 106–14; Leonard Lederman, 'Science and Technology Policies and Priorities: A Comparative Analysis', *Science*, 237 (September 4, 1987): 1125–33; and Peter Peterson, 'The Morning After', *The Atlantic Monthly* (October 1987): 43–69.

17. Reich, *Tales of a New America*.

18. Rowen and Allen, 'Brave New World'.

19. Thomas Paterson, *Kennedy's Quest for Victory: American Foreign Policy, 1961–1963* (New York: Oxford University Press, 1988). John D. Steinbruner (ed.), *Restructuring American Foreign Policy* (Washington DC: Brookings, 1989).

20. Robert Beisner, 'Foreign Policy at Century's End', *Book World, The Washington Post* (February 12, 1989): 6.

21. Katzenstein (ed.), *Between Power and Plenty*: 19.

22. Alfred Stepan, *The State and Society: Peru in Comparative Perspective* (Princeton: Princeton University Press, 1978).

23. March and Olsen, 'The New Institutionalism'.

24. March and Olsen, 'The New Institutionalism': 741.

25. Louise White, 'Public Management in a Pluralistic Arena', *Public Administration Review*, 49 (Fall 1989).

26. Clark, *The Future Taking Shape*, Part III.

27. Remarks by Priscilla Regan, Office of Technology Assessment (January 1989). For discussions of regulation in general see John Scholz, 'Reliability, Responsiveness, and Regulatory Policy', *Public Administration Review*, 44 (March–April 1984): 145–53; and Daniel Fiorino, 'Regulatory Negotiation as a Policy Process', *Public Administration Review*, 12 (July 1989): 513–31.

28. Hugh Heclo, *Modern Social Politics in Britain and Sweden* (New Haven: Yale University Press, 1974): 305; cited in Skocpol, *Bringing the State Back In*: 11.

29. Charles Wise, 'Whither Federal Organizations: The Air Safety Challenge and Federal Management's Response', *Public Administration Review*, 49 (1) (January–February 1989): 17–28; Elmer Staats, 'Public Service and the Public Interest', *Public Administration Review*, 49 (1) (January–February 1989): 602–4; Martin Landau and Russell Stout, 'To Manage is Not to Control', *Public Administration Review*, 39 (2) (March–April 1979): 148–56.

30. Louise White, *Creating Opportunities for Change* (Boulder: Rienner, 1987): 196.

31. Michael Cohen and James March, *Leadership and Ambiguity* (Boston: Harvard Business School Press, 1974).

32. Tom Peters, *Thriving on Chaos* (New York: Knopf, 1987).

4 International Cooperation and Political Engineering

Arild Underdal

The main question to be addressed in this chapter may be phrased as follows: to what extent and how can research on collective decision-making processes in general, and the study of negotiations in particular, contribute to the design and 'engineering' of cooperative solutions to global policy problems? My ambitions are strictly exploratory and quite modest; no attempt will be made to provide a comprehensive inventory of findings and hypotheses developed in this field of research, let alone transform such propositions into some kind of integrated 'how-to-do-it' manual.

In political engineering, as in medicine, the prescription of an effective 'cure' depends heavily on accurate 'diagnostics'. Accordingly, the first step towards exploring the potential contribution of decision-making analysis to the engineering of cooperative solutions should be to examine what guidance it can offer in terms of 'diagnosing' collective problems.

'DIAGNOSING' COLLECTIVE PROBLEMS

Inputs from several disciplines and sub-fields will often be required to determine the character and causes of a policy problem. The multidisciplinary complexity of the task can be illustrated by considering one important sub-category of policy problems, that of environmental stress. If we want to know, for example, why fish populations decline in Scandinavian lakes, the 'first order' diagnosis will have to come from natural sciences. Their answer will be given in terms of changes in water quality, the supply of nutrients, the occurrence of epidemic diseases, etc. Such changes may be 'endogenous' to nature itself. If so, the problem would fall entirely within the domain of natural sciences. Most likely, however, at least some of the causes identified by natural sciences can be traced back to some 'exogenous' human activities. This link to human activities is what makes environmental stress a **policy** problem (Soroos, 1987: 265–6). Human activities are, in turn, affected by the economic, political, social, and cultural conditions under which they occur. Insight into systems of human activities will have to come largely from social sciences. Moreover, in cultivating or exploiting nature man uses **tools**, and these tools are products of technology. We may say, therefore, that whenever the problem pertains to the interface between man or society on the one hand and nature on the other, 'first order' knowledge about nature and technology **and** 'second order' understanding of human activities themselves each contributes necessary but not sufficient elements of a comprehensive problem diagnosis.

In this chapter I shall focus on only one aspect of the latter element – the problem of coordination 'failure'. Although intuitively obvious that intergovernmental cooperation may be critical to the solution of global policy problems, it seems worthwhile to explore briefly what characterizes the category (categories) of problems where 'coordination failure' may be part of a valid diagnosis.

Where Can Policy Coordination Make a Difference?

Many of the most severe challenges facing governments today are 'collective' or even 'global' problems in at least one of two senses: some problems are **common** to two or more nations (or generations). Problem similarity provides at least an **opportunity** for learning: when two or more societies face a similar problem, one of them may choose to adopt a solution developed or tested by another, or in some other way base its response on the experiences of the latter. Some problems are (also) characterized by **(inter)dependence**, meaning that actions undertaken by one party can or will affect the welfare of some other(s). A problem may be similar to two or more actors without involving links of (inter)dependence: thus, preventing traffic accidents is a problem facing all cities in the world, but no safety regulation undertaken by (e.g.) the city of Amsterdam will by itself affect the safety of pedestrians and drivers in Oslo, or vice versa.[1] Conversely, a problem may be characterized by interdependence and yet pose quite different challenges to different actors. The petroleum market links producers and consumers in a relationship of interdependence, but the global 'energy problem' as seen from Kuwait or Brunei certainly looks quite different from the one facing Mali or Chad. Most global problems will be characterized by partial similarity as well as by (asymmetrical) interdependence. As indicated by the formation of negotiating coalitions, the agendas of multilateral conferences like UNCLOS, UNCTAD, etc. typically link **all** actors in a network of interdependence, and confront **some** of them with problems that are similar to members of that sub-set (see Table 4.1).

For coordination to be a useful and available device, potential partners must somehow be linked in a relationship of **interdependence**. The existence of similar problems may provide incentives for contact and **learning**; in fact, a substantial part of the everyday interaction occurring among governments seems to be efforts at learning from what other nations are doing. Moreover, there may be a cost-efficiency potential in coordinating efforts at developing solutions. But similarity in itself provides no reason for policy **coordination**; only if actors are linked in such a way that each of them has some amount of **control** over **outcomes** affecting the interests or values of others, can coordination of behavior make a difference. Unless an actor has a reason to **care** about what others are doing, he may as well leave them alone. And unless his behavior can make some difference to others, **they** may as well leave him alone.

In the absence of supranational institutions or the universal, spontaneous compliance with the Kantian ethical imperative,[2] some collective problems can be solved **only** through voluntary cooperation between or among governments. Others **may** be solved through uncoordinated action, but explicit coordination can still be useful in reducing the risk

Table 4.1   A crude typology of collective problems, with illustrations

		(Inter)dependence	
		Low	↓ *High*
Similarity →	*High*	Similar problems, e.g. care for elderly and disabled persons (in industrialized countries)	'Common fate' problems, e.g. conservation and use of common property reserves
	Low	'Individual' problems, e.g. household heating in tropical/arctic areas	(Inter)dependence problems, e.g. producer–consumer relationships

of failure and/or increasing the (cost-)efficiency of the response. Some of the most intriguing collective challenges facing mankind can, however, be met only through **unilateral** action by **one** of the principal parties concerned. Let us briefly explore what characterizes each of these categories of collective problems.

Cooperation is **needed** whenever the 'pursuit of self-interest by each leads to a poor outcome for all' (Axelrod, 1984: 7). The interdependence mechanism leading to this state of collective inefficiency may be labelled **incongruity** (Underdal, 1987). The essence of incongruity problems is that individual actors base their decisions on cost–benefit calculations that include only a 'non-proportional' sub-set of the actual 'universe' of costs and benefits produced by their actions.

To see how incongruity can distort actor incentives, let q_a be the fraction of the universe of benefits from a certain action that enters actor A's own cost–benefit calculations, and k_a be the corresponding fraction of the cost universe. If $q_a > k_a$, meaning that the actual costs are 'underrepresented' in A's own decision calculus, A will himself tend to pursue that line of action 'too far'. Conversely, if $q_a < k_a$, meaning that actual benefits are 'underrepresented', an option will appear as less attractive to the actor than it is to the reference group. Other things being equal, the larger the discrepancy between q_a and k_a, the more A's individual behavior will tend to deviate from the group optimum. This is the rationale behind Mancur Olson's (1968: 29) proposition that a 'large' actor can be expected to behave more in line with the 'collective interest' than 'small' actors.[3] In what Olson calls a 'privileged group' the individual cost–benefit calculations of the 'largest' actor (and possibly others as well) is sufficiently close to that of the group to induce behavior that leads to the group optimum (Olson, 1968: 49–50). By implication, incongruity need not lead to collective inefficiency, but if it becomes sufficiently large, aggregate benefits to the group will fall short of the potential available. When this happens, some form of correction device will be needed to solve or alleviate the problem. And in the absence of supranational institutions (or very strong hegemony) such a device can be established only through 'an exchange of conditional promises' (Iklé, 1964: 7), committing each government to a 'responsible' or 'benevolent' line of action – as long as its partners also comply.

Elsewhere (Underdal, 1987) I have suggested that incongruity can be caused by at least two different mechanisms: **externalities** and **competition**. The term 'externalities' is used here to denote 'leaks', i.e. those consequences of an actor's behavior that 'leak out' to others and hence

are not included in the decision calculus of an actor concerned exclusively with his own welfare. The words in bold type serve to distinguish problems of externalities from those of competition. In a relationship characterized by competition one actor's behavior will obviously affect its competitors, but no rational actor will dismiss these consequences as irrelevant to his own welfare; in fact, they will enter his calculations in a more or less 'inverted' form. The difference between externalities and competition may be described as one between effects that just 'leak' and those that 'boomerang'. Competition can distort actor incentives even more than externalities, and it does so by amplifying the costs of unilateral cooperative behavior and by rewarding defection. Other things being equal, therefore, competition is inherently the more '**malign**' problem.

Explicit cooperation can be **useful** whenever (a) the cost-efficiency of a project depends on the extent to which the inputs of two or more actors are successfully coordinated, and (b) more than one route can lead to the collective optimum. Such a **cost-efficiency potential** may be due to **synergy** or **contingency** relationships. Synergy exists wherever coordination of inputs can reduce the costs of producing or acquiring a certain good, or increase the total amount of that good that can be made available at a fixed cost. Thus, the international pooling of meteorological observations enables more accurate and reliable weather forecasts and/or reduces the costs of weather forecasting. More generally, synergy gains can often be enjoyed by coordinating efforts at developing solutions to problems that are similar to two or more nations. A contingency relationship exists where (a) one actor's choice depends on what some other(s) does (do), and (b) coordination devices can reduce decision or transaction costs, the risk of accidents, or both. Traffic behavior is one of the most familiar everyday contingency situations. The existence of more than one solution implies that we can not **rely** on spontaneous, ad hoc coordination to be effective. The more complex or 'dense' the relationship, the less likely that tacit, ad hoc coordination will succeed (Schelling, 1960; Keohane, 1982: 339ff). Compared to situations of incongruity, cost-efficiency problems are nonetheless '**benign**' (though not trivial); in pure form, they all belong to what Schelling (1960: 89f) calls 'games of coordination' (cf. also Stein, 1982).

Some global problems are characterized by **uni**lateral dependence rather than by interdependence. Externalities **in time** constitute a particularly intriguing kind of political challenge, as one of the parties to this unilateral dependence relationship lacks 'actor capability'

(Sjöstedt, 1974). The problems of resource depletion and environmental stress are collective in the sense that future generations will to some extent share the consequences of human activities undertaken today or even yesterday. Yet cooperation between the principal parties (generations) is an inaccessible device for developing solutions. Problems can be solved only by **actors**, and as only one of the parties to this relationship is (yet) an actor, the **only** kind of solution available is **unilateral** adaptation by present generations. Such adaptation measures will to some extent involve the sacrifice of one's own welfare today for the uncertain benefit of others in what probably appears as a distant and uncharted future. **International** cooperation may, of course, be useful or even necessary to manage **inter**dependence relations among **present** societies regarding measures to be taken today, but the strictly asymmetrical dependence structure of the basic problem implies that unilateral action by one of the principal parties involved is the only strategy available.

We can now see how the potential role of cooperation in solving collective problems depends on the structure of the problem itself. First, the rationale for cooperation is limited to relationships where each party has some amount of control over events affecting the interests or welfare of others.[4] All major policy challenges facing mankind seem to meet this criterion, but some – particularly those involving externalities across generations – are **primarily** problems of unilateral dependence rather than interdependence. Second, only in certain kinds of interdependence situations – notably those characterized by incongruity, a cost-efficiency potential, or both – can cooperation increase aggregate benefits above the level achievable through uncoordinated action. In the absence of universal altruism, optimal solutions to problems characterized by severe and general incongruity **will not be achieved** through uncoordinated action. Cost-efficiency potentials **may** be tapped through tacit, ad hoc adaptation, but explicit coordination will be needed to **ensure** optimal solutions.

From 'Diagnosis' to 'Cure'

The structure of the problem not only determines **whether** cooperation will be needed to achieve optimal solutions, it also determines what **kinds** of cooperative arrangements that will be required. Even the crude typology of problems developed above can be used as a conceptual basis for prescribing (equally crude) categories of 'cures'. As indicated above, incongruity and cost-efficiency problems calls for different kinds of corrective devices. Moreover, they are likely to generate different kinds of negotiation processes, calling for different procedural arrangements and bargaining strategies.

The response to problems of externalities and competition must include some device for 'correcting' actor incentives. Cost-efficiency potentials can be tapped by improving information and communication. Moreover, while cooperative solutions to pure cost-efficiency problems are self-enforcing, meaning that once a solution is generally recognized to have been established, no actor can expect to benefit by defecting unilaterally, cooperative solutions to incongruity problems tend to be unstable in the sense that some temptation to defect or cheat tends to persist. Accordingly, effective mechanisms for monitoring compliance and punishing defection will often be important to the establishment as well as the stability of cooperative solutions to problems of externalities, and even more so to problems of competition (see Table 4.2).

The more malign the 'distortion' of actor behavior, the more difficult it will be to correct. In one important respect we may, therefore, say that the **ability** of actors to achieve cooperative solutions tends to be inversely related to the '**need**' for policy coordination. This paradox is what makes 'political engineering' a potentially important contribution

Table 4.2 The difference between incongruity and cost-efficiency problems

	Incongruity	*Cost-efficiency*
Essence of problem	Incentive distortion	Imperfect information; communication failure
Essence of 'cure'	Incentive correction	Improving information or communication
Game structure	Mixed motive	Pure coordination
Negotiation process	Adversarial bargaining; manipulation or coercion likely	Joint problem-solving and persuasion likely
Stability of agreed solution	Low; incentives to defect unilaterally tend to persist, particularly in competition	High; solution is self-enforcing
Overall character of problem	Malign	Benign

to the solution of global policy problems, particularly those characterized by incongruity.

'ENGINEERING' INTERNATIONAL COOPERATION

'Political engineering' may here be somewhat loosely defined as the development of means enabling actors to solve collective problems as effectively as possible. More specifically, at least three major categories of contributions can be distinguished: one is the design of substantive **solutions** that can be adopted through a given decision-making procedure. Another is the design of **institutions and procedures** whereby 'good' solutions can be developed, adopted and implemented. And a third is the design of **actor strategies** capable of inducing a constructive response from potential partners.

Before exploring how the study of decision-making processes may contribute knowledge and insight relevant to these three 'engineering' functions, it should be pointed out that the focus on 'political engineering' implies a rejection of the 'structural determinism' common to axiomatic–static models of bargaining (e.g., Nash, 1950; Raiffa, 1953; Kalai and Smorodinsky, 1975). Assuming perfect information, definite preferences, and a fixed setting, these models leave no scope for negotiation behavior or interaction dynamics to have an **independent** effect upon the outcome. By contrast, the concern with 'engineering' is based upon the assumption that the structural 'logic' of most negotiation situations is to some extent indeterminate, and perceived to be so by the actors themselves. The relative merits of 'structural' vs 'behavioral' models remain to be determined; what we do assume is that the skill and energy devoted to designing solutions, procedures or strategies **can** make a significant difference (cf. e.g., Rothstein, 1984; Sewell and Zartman, 1984). And if we want to understand the fallacies and opportunities inherent in the process of negotiation, behavior can not simply be appended to 'structural logic' models as a residual and undefined error term; the art of 'engineering' has to be studied in its own right.

Designing Politically 'Feasible' Solutions

To qualify as 'good', a solution to a collective policy problem shall have to meet at least three (sets of) criteria: **efficiency**, **fairness**, and **feasibi-**

lity. Designing solutions is, therefore, a complex task calling for inputs from several disciplines. Using again the problem of environmental stress as an illustration, at least two **efficiency** criteria can be identified: first, a 'good' regime should induce behavior that is ecologically sound. Only natural sciences can tell us what meets this requirement. Second, a regime should induce allocations that are economically efficient, and not all ecologically sound regimes will do so. Here we have to rely on economics to show the way. In turn, the economist will build on inputs from natural sciences, translating ecological impact into social costs and benefits. A 'good' solution is not only efficient; it should also be **'fair'**. In defining concepts like 'fairness' and 'justice', political philosophy offers clarifying advice. Finally, if a solution is not only to be invented but also to be established and implemented, it will have to be **feasible** – politically as well as technically. This is where the study of decision-making processes may contribute.

Clearly, the criterion of (political) feasibility is a secondary concern; its normative merits rests essentially or even entirely on its **auxiliary** function of enabling actors to accomplish as much in terms of one or more of the other criteria as 'circumstances' permit.[5] This auxiliary function is nonetheless an important one; there is a priori no reason to assume that any solution attractive by efficiency or fairness standards will distribute costs and benefits in such a way that it can be adopted through international negotiations.

What can be accomplished through joint decision-making processes can be seen as a function of three basic determinants: the rules of the 'game', among which the **decision-rule(s)** is (are) particularly important; the configuration of actor interests and preferences; and the level and distribution of relevant political resources, including 'skill'.

Cooperation among nations is in principle, and essentially also in fact, a voluntary affair, meaning that the basic decision rule is agreement between or among those who shall contribute to the project. This formulation of the decision rule implies that the question of political feasibility can be approached from at least two different perspectives. We may ask either (1) what characterizes the set of solutions on which a given set of actors can agree, or (2) what characterizes the set of cooperative projects that can somehow be accomplished through voluntary cooperation. In the former perspective the set of participants is considered exogenously **given**; what remains to be determined is which (kinds of) projects can be established by agreement among the actors in this particular set. This is the perspective usually adopted in the study of international cooperation, and particularly in formal theories of negotiation. In the latter perspective, we start out with a given project and ask whether it can be accomplished through voluntary cooperation among **any** set of actors. Sound arguments can be given for shifting more of our attention towards this latter version of the feasibility question (cf. Hovi, 1989).

Clearly, the answer to question (2) will differ from that given to question (1) only in cases where a project can be accomplished by a sub-set or coalition. Fortunately, such a possibility seems to exist for most global policy problems: protection of the ozone layer, eradication of hunger and many other problems can be effectively solved without **universal** agreement on the specific steps to be taken. And, particularly in the field of environmental management, there are several 'promising' indications that many industrialized countries are prepared to accept norms implying that the costs of responding to global policy problems be shared according to 'guilt' in causing the problem or even 'capacity' to prevent or repair damage. For all such projects, however, there will most likely be some critical minimum of 'inclusiveness' below which no sub-set of actors will go ahead alone. And, other things being equal, the more intense the competition among potential partners, the higher will be that threshold.

Thanks largely to developments in game theory, we are able to identify the defining characteristics of politically feasible solutions with a fair amount of precision. Starting with question (1) above, we can conclude that the existence of some **integrative potential** (in n-actor games: the existence of a 'core') is the **minimum** required for (inclusive) cooperation to be possible. The **Pareto frontier** is the **outer limit** of what can be achieved through agreement. From a feasibility perspective, the 'ideal' cooperative project is one where marginal costs are shared in proportion to marginal gains (cf. Olson, 1968: 30), (i.e., one where all incongruities are removed). Formal theories of bargaining provide several 'unique' solutions telling us what perfectly rational actors will converge on under certain more or less plausible assumptions (e.g., Nash, 1950; Kalai and Smorodinsky, 1975). The answer to question (2) is somewhat more complex: for a cooperative project to be politically feasible, it must be sufficiently attractive to all actors in a 'sufficient set'. A project is sufficiently attractive if it is 'Pareto-superior' (or at least not Pareto-inferior) to the best available alternative that can be accomplished unilaterally or by a sub-set of actors (i.e., if it belongs to the 'core').[6] A set of actors is 'sufficient' if it commands the resources needed to accomplish the project by itself without thereby incurring costs impairing the attractiveness requirement as defined above.

The road from conceptual formulas to practical solutions to specific problems is, however, a long and thorny one – and all the more so since it is so rarely travelled in this field of study. It seems a safe prediction that attempts at application, were they to be made, would frequently abort or produce false prescriptions because of insufficient or inaccurate information about the specifics of the problem in question. Obviously, the quality of the output of any model can be no better than the data we feed into it. Nonetheless, I would argue that efforts at systematic application to real world cases should be encouraged. Although we certainly are far from a stage where policy-makers can expect to be furnished with a powerful and operational decision-support system, they may at least find some useful conceptual tools and a checklist of hard questions to address. For the research community, feedback from such efforts may provide important stimuli to further development of (empirical) theory itself.

In view of these and other difficulties, I would suggest conceiving of the design of substantive solutions not primarily as a 'one-shot' application of some construct from formal decision theory, but rather as an incremental process of trial-and-error. The latter approach implies rephrasing the question as follows: how can a project be adjusted and redesigned so as to make it achievable through voluntary cooperation (among a specific set of actors)? This version of the feasibility question directs our attention to the **instruments** of project adjustment, a topic that is less well developed in research on negotiation. The repertoire of project adjustments includes techniques such as, inter alia, increasing or decreasing the scope of issues or the range of participants included; decoupling the 'sum-function' of a regime or regulation from its distribution of costs and/or benefits; providing scope and incentives for cooperation to evolve incrementally; and decreasing the precision and specificity of actor commitments.

It is well known that what Sebenius (1983) calls 'adding or subtracting issues and parties' can affect the size and shape of the settlement range. Issue linkages can increase the integrative potential by creating functional synergy gains, by providing for an 'exchange' of items valued differently by the parties, or by allowing for compensatory side-payments (Sebenius, 1983: 298). Also **de**coupling of 'contaminated' issues can facilitate agreement on solutions to remaining problems. Adding and subtracting parties may have similar effects.

If the problem-solving function ('sum-function') of a cooperative solution is inextricably linked to a certain distribution of costs and/or benefits, the fate of that project will be determined by the least enthusiastic party among those needed to establish it. In my own research on international fisheries management I was struck by the fact that thinking in terms of legal **standards** prescribing the same (change of) behavior for all parties frequently produced non-negotiable (and inefficient) solutions to problems where an integrative potential seemed to exist (Underdal, 1980). Standards may be critical in solving cost-efficiency problems, but for problems of incongruity they are a mixed blessing: in certain circumstances, notably where some objective critical threshold can be identified (e.g., relating to health hazards), a standard may be morally compelling as **the** solution to a certain problem. Even when no such critical threshold can be identified, a standard may serve as a 'focal point' (Schelling, 1960: 57ff), giving at least the appearance of 'equality *vis-à-vis* the law'. In many situations, however, there is no functional need for each party to respond exactly as its partners; thus, there is certainly more than one way of reducing the pollution of the North Sea, and there may even be some 'comparative advantage' potential in allowing states to adopt **different** measures.

Moreover, the question of who should **do** what can most often be separated from the question of who shall **pay** how much of the costs. Measures to protect tropical ecosystems obviously have to be **taken** by nations in the tropical zone, but unless other nations are ready to share the (opportunity) costs, the level of protection actually achieved will almost certainly be 'globally suboptimal'.[7] Also the application of 'scientific' standards of optimization – e.g., the maximization of sustainable biological yield or the maximization of net economic gain – frequently produces solutions distributing costs and benefits in a way that stands no chance of being unanimously approved by a 'sufficient set' of actors.[8] The general lesson seems to be that when faced with a severe incongruity problem for which no 'objectively unique' solution can be identified, look for ways of decoupling the 'sum-function' of a regime from its 'distributive' function.

Preferably, a regime should deter actors from defecting, and at the same time provide incentives or at least opportunities for **sub**-sets of actors to develop their relationship further through an exchange of reciprocal favors or concessions (Gwin, 1984; Keohane, 1988). Regulations placing a general ban on 'discrimination', such as the GATT most-favored-nation clause, seem to achieve the former at the cost of deterring also the latter. Admittedly, the optimal combination of deterring deterioration and encouraging incremental evolution and growth of cooperative arrangements can be hard to achieve (Keohane, 1988). But available research at least suggests that we direct our search towards ways of designing arrangements so that they can at least to some extent meet this dual requirement (cf. Hovi, 1989).

Despecifying actor commitments is clearly a more 'defaitist' strategy than the three outlined above. In certain circumstances, however, what Kissinger has coined 'creative ambiguity' might not only be tolerated, but perhaps even encouraged: particularly in the early stages of a negotiation process it may be a useful device enabling parties to circumvent a knotty issue that is blocking further progress on other elements of the project.

Before leaving the topic of solution design, I should like to point out that the feasibility problem has its domestic ramifications as well. Even though the decision rules applied domestically provide national political systems with far greater capacity for aggregating preferences than the rules authorized in intergovernmental organizations or conferences, the unitary rational actor model, applied particularly in formal theories of bargaining, is at best a fair approximation. Referring to a simple typology suggested by Wilson (1973) (see Table 4.3, below), we may expect also political decision-making processes at the national level to introduce a bias in favor of policies belonging to cell *B* (corresponding to problems of negative externalities), while producing 'too little' of policies belonging to category *C* (corresponding to problems of positive externalities).[9] If so, this pattern has important implications for what might be called the 'domestication' of cooperative responses to global policy problems.

Table 4.3   The Wilson typology of policies, applied to foreign aid

		Costs (domestic)	
		Concentrated	*Distributed*
		A	*B*
	Concentrated		
		(Trade)	(Tied aid)
Benefits			
(domestic)			
		C	*D*
	Distributed		
		(Aid as domestic adaptation)	(Transfer of state funds)

Source: Wilson (1973).

Quite often, the general goals and principles of global policies belong to category *D*, while specific implementary measures are likely to fall in cell *C* or (probably less often) in *B* (cf. Jacobson and Kay, 1983: 324). When such a pattern obtains, there seems to be a serious risk of what might be called 'vertical disintegration of policy' (Underdal, 1979: 7), i.e. a state of affairs where 'micro-decisions' on specific measures tend to deviate more or less significantly from what the overall 'macro-policy' seems to require. The basic principle of designing solutions for international negotiations applies to the national level as well: aim at designing policies so that marginal costs will be distributed in a way that is not radically different from the distribution of marginal gains. Or – if your goal is only to maximize the probability of having a certain program adopted – design it so that net gain is distributed in proportion to political influence or power.

Process 'Engineering'

Even a strongly integrative and Pareto-optimal solution may, however, get stuck in the negotiation process. In fact, wherever more than one Pareto-optimal solution can be identified, and actor preferences over the set of optimal solutions diverge so that both or all actors cannot have their most preferred solution adopted, there is some risk that the actors will fail to tap the integrative potential of the policy problem. Negotiation is an extremely vulnerable decision-making process, and one leading economist has even suggested what might be called an 'iron law of negotiation': inherent in the process of (adversarial) bargaining is a serious risk of blocking, perhaps even 'destroying' the integrative potential that it is undertaken in order to tap (Johansen, 1979: 520). The recognition that such a risk exists leads decision-makers as well as students of negotiation to search for institutional or procedural devices that can facilitate effective negotiations. The development and application of such devices is in this chapter referred to as 'process engineering'.

The basic question addressed by process engineering may be formulated as follows: which decision rule(s) and procedural arrangements are required or instrumental in order to enable actors to develop and establish a 'good' solution to a collective problem – given a certain configuration of actor preferences and a certain distribution of political resources? The basic decision rule(s) is (are) rarely open to modification, at least not in the short run, so the would-be 'political engineer' will most likely have to work with less potent instruments.

Regrettably, the impact of institutional arrangements has so far been a somewhat neglected topic in the study of negotiation. Although (yet) in the form of less elegant theory, we nevertheless have some reasonably well established pieces of knowledge suggesting ways of organizing the negotiation process so as to minimize the risk of suboptimal outcomes (cf., e.g., Walton and McKersie, 1965; Fisher and Ury, 1983; Sewell and Zartman, 1984). Before identifying some of these devices, let us take a brief look at the major obstacles to effective negotiation – the twin problems of imperfect information and communication failure, and the problem of 'process-generated stakes'.

In order to make joint decisions, actors need **information** about, inter alia, the actual effects of alternative solutions and the preferences and strategies of potential partners. In adversarial bargaining, however, adequate information and effective communication is hard to establish since it is a generally recognized fact that information itself **may** be distorted and used as a tactical device to mislead one's opponent(s). At least two information problems can be distinguished; one is **uncertainty**, the other is **inaccurate** information or misperception.

The most obvious response to one's own **uncertainty** is to engage in search for additional information. In adversarial bargaining, however, an actor may have sound reasons for trying to conceal his uncertainty; if perceived by his opponent, the latter may be tempted to engage in manipulation of information. If uncertainty cannot be removed or substantially reduced, it is likely to lead an actor to adopt cautious behavior, characterized by low specificity and low commitment. Moreover, uncertainty regarding the consequences of new solutions may introduce a bias in favor of the status quo. A 'veil of uncertainty' may, however, also facilitate cooperation (Buchanan and Tullock, 1962; cf. also Rawls, 1971). Some institutions, notably those of voluntary insurance, are in fact based on the inability of the customers to predict who will benefit and who will lose.

Inaccurate information may have more detrimental effects; thus, it could lead an actor to reject a solution from which he would benefit substantially, or lead him to insist on a proposal that lies outside the acceptance zone(s) of his opponent(s). Also misperception may in particular circumstances actually facilitate agreement, but 'agreement by mistake' is not likely to produce efficient, 'fair' or stable solutions.

The possibility of using inaccurate information to mislead, and the fear that one's opponent(s) might try to do so, can be serious obstacles to effective **communication**. But communication may be impaired by other mechanisms as well (see, e.g., Jervis, 1976), including cognitive predispositions and constraints, attributional biases, and differences in the cultural or ideological background of negotiators.

The concept of **process-generated stakes** refers to potential gains and losses **pertaining to** or **generated by** negotiating behavior or process rather than the explicit issues on the negotiation agenda (Underdal, 1983: 190–1). The verbs in bold type point to two sub-categories of stakes. First, as observed by Walton and McKersie (1965: 304) and others, negotiators are likely to have their performance evaluated not only on the basis of the final outcome, but also to some extent by the way they play the game. By implication, the utility ascribed to the act of **making** a certain move may be different from the utility of the impact (if any) of the same move upon the official, substantive outcome of the negotiations. Second, process-generated stakes may emerge also as a consequence of **previous** moves. Negotiating behavior aimed at influencing other participants may leave some impact on the incentives of the actor himself. Thus, arguing strongly against a certain proposal tends to make it even harder to accept later in the process. This impact may be desired by the actor, as in the case of a deliberate commitment. But it can also be an unintended side-effect; some kinds of bargaining moves undertaken in order to influence opponents tend to be interpreted as staking an actor's reputation and credibility, whether he intends to do so or not. Moreover, some moves designed to put one's opponent under pressure may in fact bolster his incentives to resist (Deutsch, 1973: chs 9, 10; Rubin and Brown, 1975: 285ff). Yielding to blunt threats is likely to be seen as more humiliating than conceding in response to new information or to appeals to widely accepted norms of fairness or to one's generosity.

Process-generated stakes may work both ways, but it seems a safe prediction that in adversarial bargaining they will most often serve to impede rather than facilitate progress towards agreement.

At least two major strategies are available for improving the **information base** of international negotiations. One relies on the services of presumably competent and impartial third parties, such as teams of independent experts, or the staff of an intergovernmental organization. Scott argues that the most important contribution that can be rendered by an intergovernmental organization is 'the production and utilization of accurate information' (Scott, 1976: 185). Such a body of competent and impartial third parties will not always be available, however. Where it is not, establishing one will take time, and its functions and staffing may become topics of rather delicate meta-bargaining. Moreover, it can be used mainly for producing what Haas (1980) calls 'consensual knowledge' about the nature of the problem and the likely effects of possible solutions. It is likely to be less effective in removing uncertainty and misperception regarding the preferences and strategies of potential partners.

The other major strategy provides for open, mutual control of information. The practical arrangements for facilitating such mutual control may vary considerably, but some kind of **joint** commission of experts seem to be a favorite option. This approach has the advantages of (a) being generally available and (b) to some extent committing the actors themselves to any joint conclusions emerging from the commission. The major disadvantage is that the work of such joint commissions themselves may be severely constrained or 'contaminated' by the political conflict which they are supposed to help resolve. Moreover, some governments and political systems are likely to keep their members of such commissions under more strict control than others. If so, the work of a joint commission will suffer from a basic asymmetry of 'politicization'. From what has already been said it follows that the mutual control approach should be seen primarily as a procedure for developing **consensual** rather than accurate knowledge.

The two approaches might be combined, but only to some degree, and mainly for coping with low-intensity conflict. Their basic rationales are different, to some extent even incompatible; thus, in a low-trust relationship providing direct and full participation for the parties' own agents may severely impair the work of the 'independent' members.

Process-generated stakes pose two major challenges to the 'political engineer': preventing or coping with 'adversarial' commitments, and developing and exploiting 'positive' commitments to the official purpose of the process. Among the many instruments that can be used in order to prevent 'adversarial' stakes from developing are informal and confidential meetings; structuring proceedings so that initial sessions can be geared to exploratory work on specific problems rather than exchanges of public declarations of ideological beliefs and principles; providing a chairman, secretariat or mediator with important initiating functions, pertaining e.g. to the drafting of a 'single negotiating text' (Raiffa, 1982), and – in severely contaminated relationships – even minimizing the amount of direct confrontation.

The development of 'positive' stakes can be facilitated or promoted in several ways. Suffice it here to point to two of the most important techniques. One is the functionalist strategy of building momentum through solving the more 'benign' problems first. The basic assumption behind this incrementalist approach is that once some collective problems have been successfully solved, actors will have acquired additional stakes in solving at least functionally related problems. Moreover, progress on the first items on the agenda may help to convince an actor that there is in fact an integrative potential to be tapped, and that his potential partners are serious and even reasonable actors. Another set of techniques builds on the assumption that, other things – including the substance of the outcome – being equal, an actor tends to be more satisfied with a solution that he has himself invented or proposed than one which is 'imposed' upon him (cf. Fisher and Ury, 1983: 27–8). Clearly, the possibilities of manipulating credit for 'good' achievements will most often be quite limited. So will the possibilities of having other actors accept taking the blame for what is seen as severe burdens. Nonetheless, a third party, or even an opponent, may find subtle ways to increase an actor's 'subjective share' in the solutions developed. And to the extent they succeed in doing so, they have probably also succeeded in (marginally) enhancing that actor's commitment to the solution in question.

Designing Actor Strategies

A multitude of 'how-to-succeed' manuals offer advice to individual actors as to how they can design their own negotiation strategies in order to accomplish what can be accomplished. Most of these manuals are based on impressionistic evidence and personal experience rather than on rigorous research. Such 'practitioner wisdom' can be a very important source of insight, but it is less relevant to my concern here (which remains the potential contribution of research). Its relevance for this chapter can be questioned also on the grounds that most of this literature is concerned primarily with **individual** rather than collective success. Interestingly, however, one important key to solving one's own problems is seen to be the ability to induce the constructive cooperation of one's prospective partner(s). Thus, even the pure egoist is generally advised to adopt what is marketed as a 'win-win' approach (Weiss-Wik, 1983). Negotiators are urged to consider the opponent's problems as being part of their own as well.

A common point of departure is the assumption that each actor faces a basic 'negotiator's dilemma', described by Lax and Sebenius (1986: 6) as 'the inescapable tension between cooperative moves to create value for all and competitive moves to claim value for each' (cf. Walton and McKersie, 1965). More specifically, each actor is seen as facing the twin dilemmas of inducing the constructive cooperation of his prospective partner(s) without inviting attempts at exploitation, and at the same time deterring exploitation without provoking fear or anger and thereby increasing the risk of running into a conflict spiral.

In the abstract, we know fairly well what characterizes the optimal strategy for coping with these dilemmas. Four basic requirements are aptly summarized by Axelrod (1984: 54), suggesting that a strategy be designed so as to be **nice** (inviting cooperation and reducing fear by starting out with a cooperative approach oneself), **retaliatory** (responding quickly to attempts at exploitation), **forgiving** (assuring one's partners that mutual cooperation can be (re-)established at any time), and **clear** (minimizing uncertainty regarding one's own strategy). Supplementary advice is provided by Fisher and Ury (1983). One of their principal concerns is how to encourage and facilitate constructive **search** for integrative solutions. Among their general rules of thumb are the suggestion to focus on basic interests rather than on official positions (cf. Nierenberg, 1981), the underlying assumption being that one's interests can often be satisfied through more than one specific solution – some of which may yet remain to be discovered or invented. Negotiators are therefore urged to combine firmness on interests and principles with flexibility on means. To help actors avoid premature commitments, the authors also suggest ways of separating 'inventing from deciding' (Fisher and Ury, 1983: 62).

Such general propositions can, of course, not serve as a precise formula for deciding on specific moves in specific situations. Nor should the advice provided be interpreted as universally valid. Most of the manuals available are developed with reference to Western societies in general and American culture in particular. Moreover, in marketing his particular manual an author may succumb to the temptation to make exaggerated claims regarding the validity of his prescriptions. Research on negotiation strongly suggests that most strategies work better in some circumstances than in others. This suggests that we should be aiming at offering conditional ('if-then') prescriptions; claims that one approach generally **dominates** others (see, e.g., Fisher and Ury, 1983: 95) probably overstate the case. Nonetheless, I think it is fair to conclude that the study of negotiation and problem-solving behavior is capable of providing a conceptual framework for the design of actor strategies, and a number of non-trivial and partly substantiated propositions that can serve as general guidelines for coping with 'the negotiator's dilemma'.

CONCLUDING REMARKS

The argument of this chapter may now be summarized as follows: (1) 'Political engineering' is important to the development and implementation of cooperative solutions to global policy problems. It seems that in most instances of successful international collaboration one or more 'entrepreneurs' can be identified. And such entrepreneurs need not be 'hegemons' providing collective goods out of self-interest; their main contribution often seems to be that of providing 'engineering' skills and energy (Young, 1989). (2) Research on negotiation and to some extent also other decision-making processes **can** contribute knowledge and insight relevant to the 'engineering' of international cooperation, and has in fact already done so. Furthermore, I have argued that it seems worthwhile, at least from the perspective of theory development, to make systematic efforts at applying some of the concepts and propositions available to 'real-life' cases. A case can also be made for making efforts at conceptualizing more of our research questions and conclusions in explicitly instrumental terms. If the study of decision-making is ever to contribute to the development of praxis itself, it will have to do so primarily by providing insight into the functioning of accessible means or instruments (and into strategies for obtaining access to effective instruments).

It should be recognized, however, that we are yet far from having a firm theoretical basis for the practical 'engineering' of international cooperation, particularly when it comes to process organization and management. We should also recognize that efforts at applying available concepts and propositions would frequently abort because of missing or inaccurate data. And even when we are able to come up with some specific prescription, there is likely to be just a small chance of ever seeing it implemented, particularly if that prescription is geared to promote 'systematic' or 'global interests'. 'Engineering' requires an actor or 'engineer'. In the international political system 'global concerns' generally have a weak institutional basis; to a large extent collective benefits are achieved as a **side-effect** of the pursuit of individual gain. Moreover, each government is likely to see substantive proposals as well as procedural arrangements primarily as means to promoting its own interest. And when actor interests diverge, as they normally do in international negotiations, political 'engineering' may itself become a topic of tacit or even explicit meta-bargaining. The 'patient' of political engineering is, in other words, likely to be an unruly one – prone to defying any 'cure' prescribed by a 'political engineer'.

However formidable, none of these problems should be completely demoralizing to research on strategies and techniques for 'engineering' cooperative solutions to global problems. At the very least one might argue that the greater the challenge, the more important it is to develop effective 'tools'.

Notes

1.   There may be an aspect of 'opportunity interdependence', however: to the extent that a solution developed by one society to a common problem is freely accessible to others, that recipe itself may be considered a **collective good**.

2.   'Handle so dass die Maxime deines Willens jederzeit zugleich als Prinzip einer allgemeinen Gesetzgebung dienen können' (Kant, *Kritik der praktischen Vernunft*, quoted from Næss, 1962: 465).

3.   Olson defines the 'size' of an actor as 'the extent to which he will be benefited by a given level of provision of the collective good' (Olson, 1968: 28).

4.   Note that I did not say **each** of the others. A distinction can be made between 'saturated' networks of interdependence, in which each party is directly sensitive or even vulnerable to each of the other 'members', and 'non-saturated' networks, in which some are linked to each other only indirectly, i.e. through their relationships to some third party. Obviously, cooperation may be a device for managing also non-saturated interdependence relations.

5.   A political activist may, of course, complain that the concern with political feasibility is not only secondary, but just another piece of evidence that political scientists easily succumb to weird or even subversive aberrations. Even if we accept the argument that the important task at hand is expanding rather than merely identifying the range of feasible outcomes, we may point out that the chances of succeeding in such an effort to some extent depends on the accuracy of our diagnosis of current constraints.

6.   We might add a requirement of **stability**, demanding that post-agreement incentives to defect be absent or effectively curbed for all partners.

7.   It should be recognized, though, that sharing the costs of measures undertaken by other nations will most often itself be a highly sensitive issue. Industrialized countries may agree to pay some of costs of measures undertaken by Third World countries to protect the global environment, but it does not take an area specialist to predict that the governments as well as the publics of Scandinavian countries will be most reluctant to pay the UK to reduce emissions causing 'acid precipitation'. Moreover, there is a real strategic dilemma between insisting on basic normative principles (e.g., relating costs of reparation to 'guilt' in causing the damage) for the long run, or engaging in 'horse-trading' for short-term results – one possible side-effect being that of encouraging extortion.

8.   For an interesting illustration, see Mäler (1989).

9. This is not obvious, however. Issue categories *B* and *C* may lead to the mobilization of 'the many' or of their representatives. If such a mobilization occurs, and if it is based on self-interest, we would expect the political process to produce a bias in favor of category *C* rather than *B*.

References

Axelrod, Robert (1984) *The Evolution of Cooperation* (New York: Basic Books).

Buchanan, James M. and Tullock, Gordon (1962) *The Calculus of Consent* (Ann Arbor: University of Michigan Press).

Cohen, Herb (1980) *You Can Negotiate Anything* (Secaucus, NJ: Lyle Stuart).

Deutsch, Morton (1973) *The Resolution of Conflict* (New Haven: Yale University Press).

Fisher, Roger and Ury, William (1983) *Getting to Yes* (Harmondsworth: Penguin Books) (first published by Houghton Mifflin, 1981).

Gwin, Catherine (1984) 'Strengthening the Framework of the Global Economic Organizations', in Bhagwati, J. N. and Ruggie, J. G. (eds), *Power, Passions and Purpose* (Cambridge, MA: MIT Press): 125–77.

Haas, Ernst B. (1980) 'Why Collaborate? Issue-Linkage and International Regimes', *World Politics*, 32 (3): 357–405.

Hovi, Jon (1988) 'Hvilke typer av prosjekter kan realiseres gjennom internasjonalt samarbeid?', *Internasjonal Politikk*, 6/1988: 109–20.

Hovi, Jon (1989) 'The Evolution of Cooperation: Some Notes on the Importance of Discrimination', *Cooperation and Conflict*, 24 (2): 55–68.

Iklé, Fred C. (1964) *How Nations Negotiate* (New York: Harper & Row).

Jacobson, Harold K. and Kay, David A. (1983) 'Conclusions and Policy', in Kay, D. A. and Jacobson, H. K. (eds), *Environmental Protection: The International Dimension* (Totowa, NJ: Allanheld, Osmun & Co.): 310–32.

Jervis, Robert (1976) *Perception and Misperception in International Politics* (Princeton: Princeton University Press).

Johansen, Leif (1979) 'The Bargaining Society and the Inefficiency of Bargaining', *Kyklos*, 32 (3): 497–522.

Kalai, Ehud and Smorodinsky, Meir (1975) 'Other Solutions to Nash's Bargaining Problem', *Econometrica*, 43 (3): 513–18.

Keohane, Robert O. (1982) 'The demand for international regimes', *International Organization*, 36 (2): 325–55.

Keohane, Robert O. (1988) 'Bargaining Perversities, Institutions, and International Economic Relations', in Guerrieri, P. and Padoan, P. C. (eds), *The Political Economy of International Co-operation* (Beckenham: Croom Helm): 28–50.

Lax, David A. and Sebenius, James K. (1986) *The Manager as Negotiator* (New York: The Free Press).

Mäler, Karl-Göran (1989) 'The Acid Rain Game', paper prepared for the ESF Workshop on Economic Analysis for Environmental Toxicology (Amsterdam, May).

Næss, Arne (1962) *Filosofiens historie, II* (Oslo: Universitetsforlaget).

Nash, John F. (1950) 'The Bargaining Problem', *Econometrica*, 18: 155–62.
Nierenberg, Gerard I. (1981) *The Art of Negotiating* (New York: Simon & Schuster).
Olson, Mancur Jr (1968) *The Logic of Collective Action* (New York: Schocken Books) (first published by Harvard University Press, 1965).
Raiffa, Howard (1953) 'Arbitration Schemes for Generalized Two-Person Games', *Annals of Mathematical Studies* (Princeton: Princeton University Press).
Raiffa, Howard (1982) *The Art and Science of Negotiation* (Cambridge, MA: Harvard University Press (Belknap)).
Rawls, John (1971) *A Theory of Justice* (Cambridge, MA: Harvard University Press).
Rothstein, Robert L. (1984) 'Regime Creation by a Coalition of the Weak: Lessons from the NIEO and the Integrated Program for Commodities', *International Studies Quarterly*, 28 (3): 307–28.
Rubin, Jeffrey Z. and Brown, Bert R. (1975) *The Social Psychology of Bargaining and Negotiation* (New York: Academic Press).
Schelling, Thomas C. (1960) *The Strategy of Conflict* (Cambridge, MA: Harvard University Press).
Scott, Anthony (1976) 'Transfrontier pollution: are new institutions necessary?', in *Economics of Transfrontier Pollution* (Paris: OECD): 178–218.
Sebenius, James K. (1983) 'Negotiation arithmetic: adding and subtracting issues and parties', *International Organization*, 37 (2): 281–316.
Sewell, John W. and Zartman, I. William (1984) 'Global Negotiations: parth to the future or dead-end street?', *Third World Quarterly*, 6 (2): 374–410.
Sjöstedt, Gunnar (1974) *Integration and 'Actor Capability'. A survey of the theories of regional, political integration* (Stockholm: Utrikespolitiska Institutet).
Soroos, Marvin (1987) 'The Imperative of Global Problem Solving', *Gandhi Marg* (August): 264–80.
Stein, Arthur A. (1982) 'Coordination and collaboration: regimes in an anarchic world', *International Organization*, 36 (2): 299–324.
Underdal, Arild (1979) 'Issues Determine Politics Determine Policies', *Cooperation and Conflict*, 14 (1): 1–9.
Underdal, Arild (1980) *The Politics of International Fisheries Management: The Case of the Northeast Atlantic* (Oslo: Norwegian University Press).
Underdal, Arild (1983) 'Causes of Negotiation "Failure"', *European Journal of Political Research*, 11 (2): 183–95.
Underdal, Arild (1987) 'International Cooperation: Transforming "Needs" into "Deeds"', *Journal of Peace Research*, 24 (2): 167–83.
Walton, Richard E. and McKersie, Robert B. (1965) *A Behavioral Theory of Labor Negotiations* (New York: McGraw-Hill).
Weiss-Wik, Stephen (1983) 'Enhancing Negotiators' Successfulness', *Journal of Conflict Resolution*, 27 (4): 706–39.
Wilson, James Q. (1973) *Political Organizations* (New York: Basic Books).
Young, Oran R. (1989) 'Bargaining, Entrepreneurship, and International Politics', paper presented at the 30th annual convention of ISA (London, 28 March–1 April).

5 The Comparative Study of Global Policy Problems

Andrew M. Scott

INTRODUCTION

This chapter makes three, linked points. The first section emphasizes the importance of the **comparative** study of very large-scale problems. The second section stresses the potential usefulness in this connection of remote sensing from satellites. The third section argues that the remote sensing capabilities that have been developed with such great success by the military and the intelligence community, at great cost to the taxpayer, should now be made available for the pursuit of national security objectives broader than purely military ones.

COMPARATIVE ANALYSIS OF VERY LARGE-SCALE PROBLEMS

The nations of the world face a growing number of serious large-scale problems such as global warming, deforestation, and ozone layer deterioration. These difficulties represent a somewhat different **class** of problem that those to which international relations analysts are accustomed and therefore a different mode of discourse is called for. The terms of analysis will not be military strength, alliances, sending signals to an aggressor, and so on. Nation-states may not even be the focus of attention.

As recently as 1970 many of the problems troubling the world today were either totally unknown or perceived by only a handful of specialists:

- AIDS
- destruction of tropical rainforests
- desertification
- ozone layer problems
- toxic wastes

121

- ground water contamination
- acid rain
- Third World indebtedness
- solid waste disposal
- the drug onslaught ... and so on.

Taking social, economic and environmental problems together, it appears that, on the average, we are creating, or discovering, somewhat more than one very large-scale problem per year. The socio-biosphere has clearly become an efficient producer of very large-scale problems.

Why are problems emerging at such an impressive rate? The answer turns on the nature of the global system and changes taking place in it. Each year there are more actors in that system than the year before, and perhaps new kinds as well. Together they are taking more actions than ever before, including new kinds of actions. Therefore there is a continuing increase in the amount of interaction and complexity in the global system. Aggregate economic activity continues to mount, technological development accelerates, and population increases. Each of these factors impinges on the socio-biosphere and contributes to problem production.

Very large-scale (VLS) problems are not altogether new, but until the 1950s they were uncommon. Now they are numerous. Furthermore, since the impact of humankind on the biosphere continues to mount, not only should new VLS problems be expected to appear, the **rate** at which they will appear must be expected to increase. What forms will these new problems take? What new surprises await us in the capacious reservoir of the as-yet-unperceived-problems?

Information in large quantities will be needed if these VLS global problems are to be recognized and assessed. That means that VLS problems require special study as a **class**. While attention has been devoted to **individual** socio-biospheric problems, they have not been perceived as constituting a class meriting study as such. We have tended to assume that each problem is unique and capable of being understood and dealt with only on its own terms. This way of thinking has deterred researchers from fashioning a broad data base and seeking insights that move beyond the individual problem in the direction of generalization.

Rather than assume, tacitly, that each problem is unique, newly-minted, and unlike any other, it is time to look at these problems systematically in a comparative framework. The comparative perspective is a familiar one in the social sciences and once analysts see the need for such a shift in approach it should not be difficult to make it. How might the enterprise be set in motion?

Unique in some ways, each of these VLS problems also has characteristics that will allow it to be compared with others. What, then, are some of the features that allow for comparability? Or, to put it another way, what are some of the questions that might be addressed to VLS problems if we were to seek to compare them? Here are a few.

1. **What is a 'problem'**, in the sense that the term is being used here? The question seems simple but the answer is not self-evident.

    A starting point would be to see the socio-biospheric system as consisting of a large number of interacting variables and processes. One of those variables (or a process incorporating one of them) might increase or decrease so that its relationship to a second variable, or to some constant, changes. For example, if the amount of solar radiation penetrating the ozone layer (variable 1) begins to approach the upper limits that humans can tolerate (variable 2), a 'problem' will be conceived to exist. Since the consequences will be planet-wide, this would qualify as a VLS global policy problem.

    This way of defining a 'problem' recognizes the importance of **information**, of **measurement**, and of the **interpretation** placed on information. Change in the variables is one thing and the determination that those changes constitute a 'problem' is another. Problem definition is a **social** process and must always incorporate a **subjective** element.

2. **What caused the problem?** More precisely, what factors contributed to changes in the variables of interest to us?

3. **When did significant change** in those variables begin?

4. What is the **extent and severity** at present of the problem under consideration?

    Determining severity requires **measurement**. For any one problem, an appropriate unit of measure will probably not be difficult to find. The difficulty arises when we try to weigh different units of measurement in an effort to compare the impact of one problem with that of another. Yet the task must be addressed, and on an urgent basis. It will not be easy to construct a composite metric but, if it is understood that it is better to have an imperfect measuring device than none at all, it should be possible to devise a workable tool.

    In the absence of a metric, all 'problems' are born equal and there is no way to assess relative threat with any precision. In the absence of a metric there can be no agreed basis upon which to establish priorities among perils, or to allocate resources among them wisely.

5. What does the **trajectory** of a given problem look like?

    For each problem of concern, an effort should be made to fashion an **impact schedule** – that is, to indicate how great the expected impact will be at different points in time. These values could then be plotted to depict the anticipated trajectory of a problem.

    Once an agreed metric exists, the trajectories of various global problems can then be plotted simultaneously and informed judgements might then be made about priorities.

6. Does a given problem seem to be **linking up** with other processes and problems? And, if so, what are the dynamics of the linkage process?

    Because VLS problems emerge in a highly interactive socio-biospheric system they tend to diffuse easily and rapidly. For example, the drug problem was first viewed in the United States as a matter to be dealt with by local authorities. Then it was perceived as a national problem and, fairly soon thereafter, was perceived as an international problem. Furthermore, again because of the interactive nature of the system, problems not only diffuse on their own, they link up with other VLS problems. For example AIDS quickly moved from being a local to a national to an international problem and, at the same time, it ceased to be just a medical problem and became a serious social, political, religious and economic problem as well. In the same way, it is possible to see the issue of global warming being perceived, from month to month, as broadening out and becoming tied-in with an ever wider range of other issues.

    Complexity mounts rapidly as problems link up with one another and this makes it extremely difficult to disaggregate elements of an overall problem for purposes of analysis or action. For example, on October 19, 1987 the Dow Jones average plunged 508 points. In one day the securities traded on that market lost 22.6 per cent of their value. Shock waves were felt in markets all around the world: Tokyo, Hong Kong, Singapore, Australia, London, and Switzerland. The panic reverberated around the world but the process was fortunately brought to a halt before it spiralled down into total collapse.

    Many explanations were offered for the collapse of the US

markets but the Presidential Task Force looking into the matter noted that the system of markets has grown geometrically with the technological and financial revolutions of the 1980s. On a normal day the two main electronic clearing services in the United States, CHIPS and Fedwire, clear the astounding amount of close to $700 billion in payments. Markets in the United States that had previously been separate had become linked in ways that had been little noted and less understood and they, in turn, had become linked to markets abroad. The emergence of vast, unregulated, global markets, electronically linked, meant that panic and destabilizing actions could be quickly transmitted throughout the system.

As the system became more intricate and globalized, its complexity outran the understanding of those who were part of it. It may seem strange that humans can create something more complex than they fully understand, but they do it all the time with social systems. The secret is that complexity is added incrementally, by the actions of countless individual actors who are seldom aware of the changes they are inducing. For example, tens of millions of investment decisions are made globally each business day, and many of those decisions involve transnational flows of funds. The individuals involved in a given decision are thinking of their own gains and losses rather than system change, yet, as a consequence of countless numbers of such micro-decisions, the nature of international finance is changed. The value of world financial movements is now fifty times the value of world trade flows!

One of the distinctive features of VLS socio-biospheric problems is the way in which micro-actions often aggregate into macro-problems. A problem may be created by a multitude of small actions and yet grow into something so large and complex as to challenge human efforts to comprehend and manage it. Thus, the casual release of chlorofluorocarbons (CFCs) has grown to something beyond human scale – degradation of the ozone layer. Or, again, millions of micro-actions over decades resulted in changes in the chemistry of the atmosphere which are now producing the phenomenon of global warming.

7. Should there be an attempt at **intervention** in a given problem? What will the consequences be if there is **no intervention**? How confident can one be of estimated **trajectories**? What will the **costs and consequences** be if there is only a moderate intervention? What new problems might emerge out of the planned solution to the present problem?

If there is to be an attempt at intervention, **when** should it come?

What happens to both cost and consequences if intervention is delayed for three years? Five years? By whom would the **decision to intervene** have to be taken? Are there **moral dimensions** to this matter? Are some forms of intervention unacceptable? Are some forms of intervention more **equitable** than others?

8.   What about the **aggregate impact** of a number of VLS socio-biospheric problems?

Those familiar with a particular problem will sometimes parade the impressive probable consequences if no action, or inadequate action, is taken. However, since human society must deal with a number of **concurrent** problems and their consequences, a way is needed to estimate the **aggregate burdens** that will be imposed at a given time in the future. Awareness of likely aggregate future burdens might help provide motivation for a determined effort to head off some problems before their consequences join with others and the situation becomes unmanageable.

REMOTE SENSING AND SYSTEMATIC MONITORING

As noted earlier, vast quantities of information will be needed if emergent VLS problems are to be recognized and if management capabilities are to be developed. Because of the character of VLS problems the data needed will often be **global or regional** in nature and will be needed in a **continuing flow**.

Such data will also be needed promptly. The early identification of changing circumstances is important because a problem that might be relatively easy to deal with if recognized early in its career might well become much more difficult to cope with at a later date.

Too often large-scale problems are perceived tardily. This tardiness is sometimes related to 'attention bias'. Investigators do not at present scan the socio-biosphere using systematic search procedures but, instead, focus on what they believe to be 'important', and the definition of 'important' reflects habit, assumptions, and the conventional wisdom of the moment. A definition of what is 'important' implies a perception of what is **not** important, and this is where the difficulty often lies. In addition, however, systematic global scanning requires information technologies that have not, until very recently, begun to become available.

The tools available for systematic scanning of global conditions are improving all the time and one of the most important of the new tools is remote sensing from satellites. The Global Environmental Monitoring System (GEMS), which grew out of the 1972 Stockholm Conference on the Human Environment, did much to illustrate the potential of systematic global monitoring. The seven GEMS categories adopted by UNEP (United Nations Environmental Programme) were:

- expanded warning system for threats to **human health**
- assessment of **global atmospheric pollution** and its impact on **climate**
- assessment of the extent and distribution of **contaminants** in **biological systems**, particularly food chains
- improved system of **international disaster warning**
- assessment of the state of **ocean pollution** and its impact on **marine ecosystems**
- assessment of the response of **terrestrial ecosystems** to **environmental stress**
- assessment of critical problems arising from **agricultural** and **land use practices**.

The idea of systematic monitoring of features of the global environment is now firmly established, but the scope of that monitoring could be extended in response to improved technological capabilities and a broader range of concerns.

In general, international relations scholars have not been much interested in exploiting the source of data represented by remote sensing. Perhaps this will change as its potential begins to be more fully appreciated. Just as intelligence analysts continue to find new questions they can address by means of remote sensing, so those interested in the identification and analysis of emergent VLS problems would also uncover new possibilities as they became familiar with this tool. If social scientists and environmentalists had at their disposal the capabilities of several of the more advanced intelligence satellites, with their cameras, radars, and multi-spectral scanners, it would certainly allow them to investigate a wider range of important issues than at present.

Might it be feasible to trace the movement of refugees as well as rural migration to the cities? Might it be possible to develop 'quality of life' measures by looking at air quality, water quality, crowding, adequacy of housing, schools, waste disposal facilities, recreation facilities and hospitals? Could not indicators be devised for economic development, rate of technological change, and so on? Scores of variables relating to international affairs could be monitored – such as the size, location and movement of military forces, movement of freight by rail, truck and ship, and the extent of air travel and electronic communications.

While some of this data might be available from traditional sources, the advantages of remotely sensed information are impressive. The data can be made available in a matter of **hours** instead of months or years. It will have a high degree of **reliability** (in many circumstances information from traditional sources – for example, data gathered via Third World governments – have a modest level of reliability). Also, if information is available from other sources, remotely sensed data could provide a useful **reliability check**. Remote sensing also makes it possible to gather data for a region or for the entire globe at the same moment in time and therefore to have **simultaneous**, or **near simultaneous**, readings for a given variable. Finally, now that the development costs of the technology have already been paid for, it is a relatively **economical** way to gather data on a large scale.

There are many things that remote sensing cannot do but there are also many things it can do. It can be used to monitor, simultaneously, a multitude of variables and to detect rates of change, degrees of intensity, and frequency of occurrence. In tandem with computers, it can detect **departures from norms** and discern **patterns** and **pattern change**.

The program being organized by social scientists, the Human Responses to Global Change Project (HRGCP), complements the natural scientists International Geosphere-Biosphere Programme (IGBP) begun in 1986. Remote sensing needs to be made an important part of the HRGCP.

GLOBAL POLICY PROBLEMS AND THE INTELLIGENCE COMMUNITY

As the Soviet military threat continues to decline the preoccupation with East–West conflict, deterrence and weaponry that has governed many minds for decades will weaken. The American people and their government will begin the process of reexamining and redefining the 'national interest'. Socio-biospheric matters that had no chance of gaining serious consideration while the attention of policy-makers was concentrated on military matters will have a chance to get on the action agenda.

The pressure to make cuts in the United States military budget will, in the long run, prove irresistible and, as part of that process, the budget for the intelligence community will come under scrutiny. The development of highly sophisticated satellite intelligence capabilities was justified budgetarily by the nature and magnitude of the Soviet threat. As that threat declines, and as Soviet responsiveness as well as on-site inspection provides alternative sources of intelligence, there will be a reduced need for the military intelligence provided by national technical means. As the US enters an era of more relaxed East–West relations the mission of the intelligence community must be reexamined and its budget scrutinized.

Might it not be in the interest of the intelligence community therefore to try to roll with the punch and to fashion a new justification for national technical means? 'Yes, the national interest now needs to be redefined in much broader terms, economically and environmentally, than it has been. A preoccupation with military capabilities and threats needs to be replaced by a concern with a range of existing and emergent large scale problems. The intelligence community has developed, and is developing, the means for monitoring and analyzing those problems.' That is to say, the purely military justification for satellite funding could be complemented by a second justification, the use of remote sensing to deal with a wide range of social, economic and environmental issues. National technical means could then emerge as an instrument supporting an enlarged conception of the national interest: swords **plus** plowshares.

There are many forms that this kind of civil–military cooperation could take. For one, the chances are that vast quantities of data could be released by the intelligence services for use by natural and social scientists without threat to military security. And, since the information was gathered with the taxpayers' money, why should it not be made available to other agencies, governmental and non-governmental, working for the national interest? In these circumstances might not a dog-in-the-manger attitude on the part of senior intelligence officials be politically risky?

Cooperation might also take the form of consultation between intelligence agencies, on the one hand, and other governmental agencies and groups of natural and social scientists, on the other, while the missions of individual satellites were being devised. Alternatively, a percentage of satellite time might be allocated to systematic socio-biospheric scanning. Perhaps a civilian group could be set up to coordinate the information requests of other agencies (Agriculture, AID, Interior, Commerce, EPA, etc.) as well as non-governmental research requests.

CONCLUSION

The need for a systematic comparative study of existing and emergent VLS problems seems evident, and that need will grow with the passage of time. The national interest requires that such problems be identified, analyzed and, if possible, dealt with. For that, socio-biospheric scanning capabilities are required. If remote sensing technologies did not already exist there would be pressure to create them to meet that need.

But those capabilities already do exist. They were developed by the Defense Department and the intelligence agencies, at great cost to the taxpayer, as part of the response to the Soviet military threat. Thus far those advanced technologies have been utilized almost exclusively for military purposes. Now they should be put to work in support of a concept of the national interest that perceives the importance of other challenges as well.

If a greater effort were made, problem recognition and early warning could certainly be improved. After all, as Kenneth Boulding once remarked, 'We have to be prepared to be surprised by the future, but we don't have to be dumbfounded'.[1]

Note

1.   Repeated in a phone conversation with Stuart Nagel as of May 8, 1990.

6 Eastern Europe and Global Issues

Longin Pastusiak

The future always begins and never ends. A man constantly chases future trying to shape it according to his own interest and sometimes against his own long-term interest.

For centuries a man has lived under the threat of the end of the world. Various religions, including Christianity, contributed to that feeling. The self-proclaimed prophets are constantly issuing warnings that the end of the world is inevitably approaching. The authors of contemporary science fiction books offered many scenarios in which the end of the world might come.

But the problem today, the problem of global threats, is much more serious to be left only to religions, prophets or the authors of the science fiction novels.

A human being since his first existence has been struggling with nature although he is a part of that nature. And it wasn't peaceful coexistence. On the one hand a human being benefited from the generosity of nature. But on the other hand a man was basically distrustful towards nature and was often a victim of nature. Before a man was being killed by another man he was often victimized by various natural cataclysms and disasters.

Gradually a man learned more and more secrets of nature and learned how to coexist with it. It wasn't ideal or totally harmonious coexistence, but gradually it led to the establishment of some kind of a biological and ecological balance between man and nature.

Today we are witnessing a new situation. This long-existing balance between man and nature is threatened. Contemporary man possessed tools which allow him to subjugate, to enslave and even to destroy nature. The balance of power between man and nature does not exist any more. This process of disturbing the balance between man and nature is taking place before our eyes and is taking place often with our own participation. Today it is a problem of local, regional and global dimensions. And it has reached such a magnitude that if not contained it may lead eventually to the total destruction of mankind.

131

Not long ago my generation in the socialist countries was proud of intensive industrialization process, mass motorization, etc. Today we know that besides the obvious economic benefits of those processes, we also paid a high ecological price. Many of those programs made our life and the future generation's life in the socialist countries easier. But socialist enterprise can pollute air as badly as the capitalist one if left out of social control. Theoretically, there is no reason why a socialist enterprise should carry its production plan at the expense of ecological interest of society.

The extent of the devastation of nature has already reached such a level that if the process of deterioration of the environment continues further, the time will come to introduce on an international scale a new kind of a crime, **a crime against nature**. A crime against nature in a contemporary state of the problem is equally a crime against mankind. A human being can exist only in symbiosis with nature. The perspective of symbiosis of a man with technics and the most modern technology, but without natural environment, is frightening.

In the situation where a human being has equipped himself with the most sophisticated tools of ecological crimes and when he is using those tools under the banner of development of civilization, nature is increasingly more and more threatened and more and more vulnerable. Therefore, the world community of people should abandon the program of fighting with nature and should replace it with the program of fighting for the preservation of nature.

I started my chapter raising the problem of protection of the natural environment, but in reality it is only one of many other threats of global dimension in contemporary world.

In Poland as well as in other Eastern European countries there seem to be growing awareness of the following three trends:

1. The contemporary world is shrinking but its problems are more and more **widely spread** and more and more **intensified**. In other words, through the development of communications systems, transportation, through the flow of people and ideas, the world is somewhat smaller, and not only individual people, but whole nations are more interdependent – culturally, economically, and from the point of view of feeling of security. From the point of view of the global threats our planet has become a small island from which one practically cannot escape and from which one has no safe place to escape.

2. But this process of relative shrinking of our planet is just one of

many phenomena. This process is accompanied by another one which could be called **globalization** or **universalization** of problems facing our generation and the generations to come. Up to now most problems faced either one country or one region only. There were always certain zones which were untouched or not threatened. One could call these **safe zones**, or **reserve zones** of mankind. Today such reserve zones practically do not exist anymore. A human being is practically threatened in every corner of our globe. Even during the last two **world wars** most of our earth was not touched by destruction. This cannot be said or assured in the event of total nuclear war in the future.

3. Most of the disasters in the past which a man experienced had some kind of **spontaneous** or **quasi-natural** character. Often those disasters were beyond control of a human being. Contemporary threats, however, and threats in the near future derive mostly from our civilization. Those threats are products of activity of man and man therefore should be obliged to find solutions for those threats.

The attitudes of the socialist countries toward global issues varies, but generally there is growing concern that time is running out and that there is a need for more coordinated or international scale efforts to solve those issues.

This growing concern of the socialist countries toward complex global issues is rather a new phenomenon. The socialist countries since mid-1950s strongly stressed the danger of nuclear war and the necessity to avoid total nuclear annihilation. There were also early concerns with such global issues as world hunger, colonization, regional and global security. But there was also a tendency to treat many global issues as a product of another socio-political system, namely the product of capitalism (or state-monopoly capitalism) and thus of not being of interest to the socialist countries. 'For many years', writes Polish economist, professor Pawel Bozyk, 'the socialist countries held the view that global threats are of external origins. According to this point of view planned economy is able to eliminate hunger and malnutrition, unemployment, illiteracy and many other shortcomings of industrial civilization which are unavoidable in the conditions of capitalist and market economies. Now wider and wider are views that the development of civilization in the countries of planned economy is causing threats of global dimension. For instance: deterioration of the environment, crisis of raw materials and energy resources, inflation, indebtedness, bureaucracy, etc. Those threats are created unintentionally. One can counteract ... them but one cannot avoid them. They are results not only of the mistakes made, ... they have an objective character.'[1]

So the prevailing view in the socialist countries now is that global issues are not any more solely of external origins but are also the result of their own industrial development. So far the socialist countries have successfully solved those global issues which they inherited from the past, from the capitalist system, e.g.: hunger, malnutrition, social inequalities, economic insecurity and economic instability, illiteracy, etc. These issues received high priority in the socialist countries. But at the same time speedy process of industrialization were accompanied by other undesirable effects: socialist enterprise if left out of social control can pollute just as badly as the capitalist one. 'Initial spectacular successes of the socialist countries caused them not to pay attention to new global threats. They did not work out preventive measures protecting themselves against pollution and other threats. ... Intensive industrialization had adverse effects upon the environment which hampers normal development of man and limits further industrial development.'[2]

The socialist countries of Eastern Europe of course benefited from industrial and social development. For years they used extensive methods of development which later hampered the utilization of intensive methods of economic development. The cold war atmosphere in international relations and the political, economic division of Europe lead to some kind of autonomic regional isolation of Eastern Europe from Western Europe. This situation created a feeling of economic security on the part of socialist countries and the feeling that the socialist countries were in fact immune from global threats.

Up to the 1970s there seems to be polarized opinions in Eastern Europe as to the methods of reacting to global challenges. As Pavel Bozyk puts it in the book *Global Challenges and East European Responses*,[3] there are two distinctive approaches toward global challenges in Eastern Europe.

The first approach, which interprets global challenges only in terms of constraints which menace the development of the socialist economy, identifies them with the diffusion of adverse effects of the capitalist relations of production and the resulting economy ruled by the laws of the market. According to this approach, capitalist relations of production and market mechanisms lead to a world-wide cumulation of adverse phenomena, which are reflected in the appearance of crises. The capitalist economy is by its nature incapable of preventing these crises; it is, however, capable of diffusing their negative effects and this, especially at the present levels of internalization of economies, has a destructive impact on the development of the socialist countries (as well as a good number of less developed economies). As a planned economy, the socialist economy is capable, according to this view, of eliminating most of the global constraints, especially those such as hunger and malnutrition, unemployment and illiteracy, as well as several other shortcomings of the capitalist mode of development. If such constraints emerge in the planned economy, they can result only from subjective errors of social and economic policy and could be prevented through institutional methods (choice of proper development strategies, correct measures of socio-economic policy, etc.). According to this approach global constraints are of an objective nature only in the capitalist economy; in the socialist countries they should be viewed as external constraints to their development.

The second type of approach, which regards global challenges as an expression of the changing conditions of economic activity in the contemporary world, identifies them with the effects of civilizational development. According to this point of view, such challenges as environmental pollution, energy and raw materials crises, inflation, disruption in international payments, bureaucracy, etc. also lead to negative effects. Constraints of this type can be counteracted, but not avoided. According to this point of view, global constraints are for the East European countries not only a product of the external environment, but also an effect of their own development. They can slow down this development, damage living conditions, increase mortality rates or result in other disruptions. Their global character consists in the fact that they apply to all countries regardless of their socio-political systems or level of development. These constraints appear simultaneously; they are interrelated and dependent on a great number of factors.

The period of detente and growing interdependence contributed toward the change of attitudes of the socialist countries towards many global problems. This is also reflected by various public opinion polls measuring attitudes and perceptions of Polish society toward the world and toward the world problems.

The outside world is perceived by Poles as a factor which should be taken into consideration in analysis of chances and threats of personal as well as national destiny. According to data of the Center of Public Opinion Research in Warsaw (Centrum Badanic Opinii Publicznaj, hereafter CBOS) only 2.6 per cent of the respondents in Poland said that world events had no meaning for Poland.[4] Every fourth person recognized the existence of political and economic ties between Poland and other states. Every fifth respondent stressed the idea that in contemporary times all states were interdependent. Every fifth Pole recognized also the immediate consequences of world developments upon social, economic and political life in Poland. Every sixth person stressed that Poland belonged to one of the blocks between which there were tensions and rivalries. Stressing interdependence between other nations and Poland, respondents mentioned such factors as: economic restrictions, geographical location of Poland in Central Europe, military obligations to allies, world peace and threat to Poland's own boundaries.

It is interesting to note that the division of the contemporary world into blocks was more often stressed by men than women. High school, vocational school graduates and the inhabitants of villages tended to stress more the geographical location of Poland and Poland's ties to the outside world.

As far as the connection between personal destiny and the outside events were concerned, 19.9 per cent of respondents saw no connection whatsoever. For 61.3 per cent such a connection existed. To 19.9 per cent this connection was based on the conviction that there was no direct link between personal destiny and the destiny of his or her own nation. Every tenth respondent had a clear view about consequences of eventual war for his life and for the life of his family; 7.2 per cent of the respondents underlined the thesis that world peace and peace within the country gave them and their family a stronger feeling of security; 8.1 per cent of the respondents said that shortage of import products in Poland was an example of the direct effect of an international situation upon their personal life.

Some people in Poland saw a psychological link between themselves and the world. The following percentage of respondents approved the following statements: 'This what happens in the world influence my personal feeling and my personal situation' (6.9 per cent); 'Everyone wants to live and work in peace, for family and wants to raise his children and grandchildren' (6.3 per cent); 'Threat of war depresses me, creates bad feeling, instability of the world makes me nervous' (5.9 per cent).

Some respondents even when they denied the existence of a link between their personal destiny and the world events in a way confirmed the existence of such linkage. They said: 'I am an unimportant person, I can do nothing to change the situation' (3.9 per cent); 'I am interested only in personal and family affairs' (2.9 per cent); 'I have to do my own work, regardless what's going on in the world' (2.7 per cent); 'Personally the world situation does not concern me' (2.3 per cent).

Women more often than men in Poland perceived war as a supreme threat to the world. Farmers stressed more often the view that the world events had little or not at all impact upon their personal way of life. Craftsmen in Poland more often stressed the idea that the limitation of imports had direct impact upon their life.

The data quoted above show that autarchic thinking in Poland is rather marginal. The adult Polish population understands that more an open society and more open Polish economy will lead inevitably to closer linkage of personal and national destiny with the destiny of the world. To a substantial part of Polish society, personal fate and the fate of his or her nation is closely tied to the fate of the world. This is also a lesson which Polish society drew out of its own historical experiences, out of the tragic fate of Polish history.

Three-quarters of the respondents agreed with the following statement: 'Politics should not disturb economic relations between states.' They also would like to see the United Nations prohibiting the conduct of economic warfare. This is also a result of the adverse effects of all kinds of restrictions and embargoes, imposed on Poland by NATO countries after the proclamation of martial law in Poland on December 13, 1981. Those sanctions adversely affected Polish society as a whole, and clearly demonstrated how Poland was dependent upon trade with other countries, and demonstrated how the standard of living of every citizen and the well-being of every Pole was dependent upon the links with the outside world. The damage NATO sanctions did to the Polish economy contributed also to the development of a global consciousness in Polish society.

More than half of the respondents (54.6 per cent) expected in 1985 an increase of military spending in the world in the near future. They perceived this trend as undesirable and unfortunate. As far as 'desirable and most advantageous for Poland' trends in the world are concerned, Poles mentioned: progress in development of sciences, technology and medicine (46.3 per cent), international convertibility of the Polish currency, the zloty. Every third Pole saw clear advantages from convertibility of the zloty. Three-quarters of respondents would like to enter the 21st century with a convertible Polish currency. Poles seem to pay much attention to convertibility of their currency; the lack of convertibility was also mentioned as the most undesirable thing by 42.3

per cent of respondents. This exceeded even military spending (32.4 per cent) and the limitation of political sovereignty of Poland (23.1 per cent) as the most undesirable thing.

The opening of the Polish economy and Polish society to the world was connected with expectations that 'developed countries should help the less developed nations'. This conviction was shared by 35 per cent of the respondents, who treated this idea as a part of a moral order in the international system. As many as 95.1 per cent of the respondents shared the view that all people should contribute to the elimination of world hunger. Part of that thinking involved a view that Poles living abroad should contribute to a more favorable climate for Poland (37.8 per cent) and also a view that politics should not create obstacles in international economic and cultural relations (83.8 per cent).

Indebtedness, which is one of the global problems in the contemporary world, was also viewed by Poles as an important national problem linked in some way with the international situation. Women (15 per cent) more than men (13.2 per cent) agreed with the notion that Poland should join the countries which refused to repay 'excessive debts'. Women (47.6 per cent) also more often than men (33.8 per cent) thought that Poland should not take new credits before she had repaid the existing debts. Every second person with higher education and every third person with elementary education did not agree with the idea that Poland should refuse to repay her debts.

World peace was clearly recognized in Poland as one of the most important global issues. Poles have also perceptions as to the countries which constitute threat to the world peace. The Center of Public Opinion Research in 1985 asked the Poles which countries constituted the greatest threat to world peace. In the first place most often mentioned were the following countries: USA 63.7 per cent, FRG 15.1 per cent, USSR 12.1 per cent, Germany 2 per cent, Israel 1.3 per cent. In the second place most often indicated were the following countries: FRG 36.7 per cent, USA 23.3 per cent, USSR 20.9 per cent, Israel 3.3 per cent, Great Britain 2.9 per cent, China 2.9 per cent, Germany 2.4 per cent, South Africa 1.6 per cent. The third place was much more differentiated: FRG 21.2 per cent, USSR 14.3 per cent, Great Britain 13.7 per cent, China 11.3 per cent, Israel 9.2 per cent, France 6.5 per cent, USA 6 per cent, Japan 3.2 per cent, Germany 1.3 per cent, Iran 1.1 per cent.

Another question was asked related to that mentioned above: 'which countries Poland should be afraid of most'. The responses were not much related to the question on which countries constituted the greatest threat to world peace. Poles differentiate between those countries which in their perception threatens world peace and those countries which are potentially threatening to Poland. As enemies of Poland, the following countries were indicated: in the first place FRG 43.3 per cent, USA 19.2 per cent, USSR 9.3 per cent, Germany 9 per cent, NATO countries 4 per cent, all countries 1.7 per cent, socialist countries 1.6 per cent, 'there are no enemy countries' 2.6 per cent. In the second place the following countries were indicated as enemies of Poland: FRG 32.2 per cent, USA 29.8 per cent, USSR 10.9 per cent, GDR 7.5 per cent, Germany 4.1 per cent, Czechoslovakia 3.2 per cent, Great Britain 3.2 per cent. In the third place the following countries were mentioned: Great Britain 17.3 per cent, FRG 14.1 per cent, France 12.5 per cent, USA 12.1 per cent, USSR 12.1 per cent, GDR 9.5 per cent, Czechoslovakia 6.5 per cent, China 3.6 per cent, Germany 2.4 per cent, Israel 2 per cent, NATO countries 1.0 per cent. We should note that this poll was conducted before the late 1989 events in Poland and Eastern Europe.

Poland's historical experiences have had some influence upon contemporary perceptions by Poles of the enemy countries.

Of all the issues and values for most of the Poles, peace is of the highest priority. Peace is more important than civil liberties, religions, beliefs and human rights. As many as 87 per cent of the respondents held such a view. Poles are concerned with world peace. For 16.4 per cent of the respondents outbreak of another world war in 10 years seemed inevitable. A great majority, however, believed that world peace could be preserved on global scale and they expected some kind of action coordinated on an international scale to consolidate world peace.

Polish diplomacy is particularly active in the field of European security and European cooperation. The Rapacki plan of 1957 (denuclearization of Central Europe), Gomulka plan of 1963 (freezing of nuclear arms in Central Europe), a Polish proposal of 1964 to hold all European conferences on security with the participation of USSR and USA, the Jaruzelski plan of 1987 for military disengagement in seven European states (Poland, Czechoslovakia, GDR, Hungary, Belgium, Holland, and Denmark) and many other Polish initiatives has made this field a specialty of Polish diplomacy. Public opinion polls indicate that Polish society gives stronger support for foreign policy of the Polish government than for its domestic policies. In the foreign policy area the Polish government was supported by 56.2 per cent of the respondents; 24.3 per cent denied such support. In domestic policies

51.1 per cent of the respondents supported the Polish government, while 38.2 per cent denied such support.

The political beliefs of the individual shape his or her attitudes not only towards domestic issues in Poland, towards allies and economics, but also towards universal human values. Those respondents who supported the Polish government gave high priority to the issue of world peace (52.8 per cent) while among those who denied such support only 39 per cent indicated that world peace was for them of the highest priority. The same thing applies on the issue of domestic peace in Poland (25 per cent and 14.8 per cent respectively) and on domestic military spending (6.7 per cent and 3.8 per cent respectively). Those who did not support the domestic policies of Polish government gave higher priorities than those who supported the Polish government to such values as: personal freedom (13.9 per cent and 2.7 per cent respectively), civil rights (9 per cent and 2.7 per cent respectively), elimination of world hunger (5.2 per cent and 3.2 per cent), respect for religious beliefs (4.9 per cent and 1.8 per cent), protection of the natural environment (4.5 per cent and 1.9 per cent respectively). The poll indicates clearly that those indifferent towards domestic policies of Polish authorities tended also to be indifferent towards the issue of world peace (32.3 per cent), and also towards civil rights (2 per cent). They gave the highest support to such issues as: elimination of world hunger (8.7 per cent), religious beliefs (7.4 per cent), equality of both sexes (0.7 per cent).

The poll also indicated the existence of correlation between political orientation and social status of the respondents. It is illustrated by Table 6.1.

Another poll was taken by the Center of Public Opinion Research (CBOS on August 4–6, 1985, which also gives some indication how the Poles perceived some important world issues. Respondents were given a list of generally accepted values concerning world, Poland and family. They indicated those which consisted for them of the highest priorities.

On the basis of this poll one can definitely say that the issue of world peace was clearly perceived by Poles as a global and universal threat. Older people (40 years old and older) tended to pay more attention to domestic Polish problems while younger people (up to 39 years of age) were more concerned with world problems. Generally speaking, every third respondent was concerned with global issues (see Table 6.2).

People were asked what favorable trends they expected in the coming 10–15 years.[5] Out of a representative sample of 150 interviews, 72 said they expected further progress in economic growth, 53 expected better

Table 6.1   Correlation between political orientation and social status

Selected social groups (%)	Supporting domestic policies (%)	Denying support for domestic policies (%)	Do not see an ally of Poland (%)	Members of Polish United Workers' Party (%)
Managers with				
higher education	61.6	34.1	17.6	63.7
high school education	59.4	37.9	30.3	40.5
Regular employees with				
higher education	41.0	54.8	30.1	22.3
high school education	44.0	45.8	21.0	16.4

Source: Centrum Badania Opinii Publicznaj, CBOS, (Center of Public Opinion Research) BD/380/23/85. *Opinia o polityce zagranicznej (Views on Foreign Policy)* (Warsaw) (November 1985).

Table 6.2   Perception of world issues

World		Poland		Own family	
Values	Indications (%)	Values	Indications (%)	Values	Indications (%)
World peace	54.1	Domestic stability	29.5	Stability in family	16.4
Well-being	31.2	Wealth of the country	46.8	Well-being	22.0
Freedom	29.3	Independence of the country	46.9	Personal freedom	23.8
Friendship between nations	34.8	National solidarity	16.8	Personal friendship	18.4
World progress in science and technology	21.3	National progress in science and technology	37.9	Modernization of own house	20.7

Source: Centrum Badania Opinii Publicznej, CBOS, (Center of Public Opinion Research), *Jubileusz ONZ – Konsultacja Spoleczna (UN Anniversary – Public Consultation)* BS/278/5/85 (August 1985).

cooperation and more agreements in East–West relations. When asked what would be the most disadvantageous developments in the world for Poland, 91 said that escalation of armaments particularly in its economic and human aspects. Armaments are clearly perceived in Poland as a burden for the economy, although very few question Poland's obligations to the Warsaw Pact.

The threat of world war is often perceived by Poles through their own memories and through the collective memory of a nation. For instance, the question was asked whether looking to the past they could recall events which worried them as events which might lead to a new world war. Every fifth person living in peaceful Europe for the last 40 years did not recall any event which in his perception could lead to the outbreak of world conflict. Two-thirds indicated at least one such international event. The rest of the respondents admitted that they lived in constant fear of the outbreak of world conflict.

What kind of events, in perceptions of Poles, are likely to cause the new world war? Four clusters of factors were most often mentioned.

First, **domestic instability**. Every fifth person mentioned martial law as a threat to world peace, and every fourth person mentioned a Polish crisis, and the chaotic situation of 1980–1 in Poland as a threat to world peace.

Second, the **tensions between the two superpowers** were also mentioned. The following events were recalled by Poles as possibly leading to the world conflict: Cuban missile crisis (30 indications), Vietnam war (11), Afghanistan (9), Berlin crisis of 1953 (8).

The third cluster of events dealt with the **conflicts between the socialist countries**: Czechoslovakia in 1968 (16 indications), Hungary in 1956 (9), and frontier skirmishes between China and the USSR and between China and Vietnam.

The fourth cluster of factors consisted of **single events around the world**. The protracted conflict in the Middle East (12 indications), and the Malvina–Falkland Island conflict were mentioned relatively often. As destabilizing to world peace were also mentioned such events as: meetings of West German Landsmanschaften, claiming Polish territories, introduction of Pershing II and Cruise missiles, in Western Europe, and Iraq–Iran war. Individual respondents mentioned also the following single dramatic events as threatening world peace: mistakes by computers, guiding strategic systems, deaths of great leaders, the American invasion on Grenada, the shooting down of South Korean airplane KAL 007, and the situation in South Africa.

One hundred and fifty interviewees were asked in indicate according to their personal views what is the likelihood of world conflict in the next 10 years. The results are shown in Table 6.3.

The poll indicated also that men felt less threatened by world conflict than women. The higher the level of education the more people were concerned with the possibility of world conflict in the next ten years.

Deeper analysis of relations between subjective views of probability of war and the substantiation of those views lead to the identification of the following four categories of reasoning.

First is the kind of **wishful thinking** reasoning, illustrated by the following statements: 'I am an optimist', 'I would like to live in peace to raise my child', 'World conflict is for me an abstraction'.

The second type of reasoning tends to think that people are **manipulated with the threat of war**. It is illustrated by the following statement: 'They blow up the danger of war to frighten us.'

The third group of people see the primary cause of eventual war in **Soviet–American rivalry**. It is illustrated by the following statements: 'Because Poland is closely allied with the Soviet Union which is in conflict with United States, therefore Poland is implicated in that conflict'. 'We are just pawns in that rivalry'.

The last type of reasoning places the source of world conflict **within Poland** or **within the block of socialist countries**. The most drastically stated one of the respondents: 'Socialism was born as a result of World War I and perhaps the end of socialism requires World War III'.[6]

Every third respondent clearly stressed that Poland should conduct peaceful policies. Every sixth person was in favor of alliance with the Soviet Union and every sixth was in favor of neutrality. A third of the interviewees stressed the lack of possibility of conducting a completely independent foreign policy, stressed the necessity to protect Polish economic interests and underlined the thesis that Poland should keep good relations with all the states regardless of their socio-political system.

Table 6.3   Perception of probability of outbreak of world conflict

Scale of probability	0	10	20	30	40	50	60	70	80	90	100	*Don't know*
% of modifications	26.0	14.0	10.0	1.3	1.3	19.3	4.3	1.3	2.6	4.0	2.6	4.0

Source: Centrum Badania Opinii Publicznej, CBOS, (Center of Public Opinion Research), *Jubileusz ONZ – Konsultacja Spoleczna (UN Anniversary – Public Consultation)* BS/278/5/85 (August 1985).

Poles watched closely the summit meetings between Gorbachev and Reagan in Geneva in November 1985 and in Reykjavik in October 1986. The poll taken in December 1985 made on the basis of a 1479-member representative sample indicated that Gorbachev made a better impression than Reagan. The question was put: who, Gorbachev or Reagan is more concerned with peace? The answers were the following: Gorbachev 42 per cent, Reagan 2.3 per cent. One quarter said that both were equally concerned; 12 per cent of the respondents did not trust either of them.[7]

Poles were disappointed with the results of the Reykjavik summit. For the lack of results 35.6 per cent blamed the United States, 3.9 per cent the Soviet Union, 32.1 per cent both countries, and 28.4 per cent had no opinion.[8]

Many Poles, particularly those who are more educated, see **global problems and global issues**. They tend to think that the world is undergoing a general crisis of our civilization. There is a crisis of creative thinking and a crisis of consciousness. My own impression is that a majority of Polish society still is relatively unaware of other nuclear annihilation global threats.[9] The Chernobyl nuclear power accident made people more aware that global issues do not have national frontiers.

Created in May 1987, the Polish Chapter of the Club of Rome will certainly contribute to the development of global level political thought in Poland and I hope it will contribute to the development of global consciousness.

At the present time we have the following situation. The number of global threats is increasing. The scale and extent of those threats is also growing. Those threats are understood by relatively limited groups of people around the world. Those groups are issuing all kinds of warnings. On the basis of those warnings various social movements are starting, various solutions are offered. Political practice on global scale, however, falls behind conceptual thinking.

There is a clear and urgent need to develop **global consciousness** in societies around the world. More and more people should be aware about the global dimensions of existing threats, about the necessity to develop local, regional and global approaches to the solutions of those universal problems. There is a need to create more effective global social pressure to eliminate existing threats.

To develop a **global-level political thought** and global consciousness is a long process. To overcome deeply rooted nationalism, regionalism, tribalism, and parochialism in the pattern of thinking is not an easy task. As long as a substantial part of the world population today struggles with various basic social and economic problems, as long as for hundreds of millions of human beings hunger and shelter is a basic issue it would be difficult to convert their thinking from everyday worries into global consciousness.

But should we therefore abandon the hope of developing global-level political thought? Of course not. First, some global threats, like the danger of nuclear annihilation, should mobilize people for the survival of mankind and thus for the highest of all possible values – the right to live. Second, global consciousness does not contradict class consciousness or national consciousness. There is no incompatibility between the three. Global consciousness is a reflection of human solidarity in view of new global threats, challenges and concerns. Those dangers are of new, unprecedented dimensions, and as such they require **new thinking** and **new approaches**. A human being needs to develop a self-defense instinct to save himself from self-annihilation. Third, the global consciousness could stimulate the development of various corrective mechanisms eliminating or limiting the negative effects of our model of civilization.

To develop global-level political thought and global consciousness requires some kind of coordinated efforts of all the nations. It requires an effort on **a global scale**.

Our world is gradually shrinking but its problems are becoming more and more widespread. This is a process of **globalization or universalization** of our world. The process basically is characterized by a growing number of problems which most effectively can be solved only on a global scale. Those problems or threats one can ease by seeking solutions on a national or regional scale. But the real and effective solutions can be achieved only through coordinated global effort.

What are those problems? Here are a few good examples:

- The threat of a total nuclear war.
- The arms race and the consequences of it.
- International security.
- Education for peace, building of mutual trust and building of cooperative infrastructure on global scale.
- Access to non-renewable resources.
- A new economic order.
- A new information order.
- Access to food resources. Exploitation of seabeds and oceanbeds.

– Protection of the natural environment.
– International terrorism.

One could enumerate many more problems which are common to all the nations, although different nations have different levels of concerns with various issues. The perception of threats varies among nations but there is no doubt there are problems which are common for all people.

There are two basic ways of reaching solutions of those problems:

(1)   A **regional** approach.
(2)   A **global** approach.

A regional approach can be effective if treated as part of a broader process, as an 'island approach' leading gradually to global arrangements. For instance one could imagine as quite realistic and reasonable that regional security systems are created, regional atom-free zones which in fact are sub-systems of eventual global-level security arrangement.

The global approach could be more effective if the agreed solutions were universally accepted and carried out simultaneously by all the actors in the world. And this is not easy to achieve.

The dispute whether a regional or global approach is more effective in a way is meaningless. Each approach is fine and acceptable as long as it leads to an **effective solution**. Both approaches require global consciousness and require thinking in global terms. And in this respect we are far behind the need. The time factor is very important: each day's delay of our struggle with global problems deepens the scale of the threats, creates new problems and thus weakens the chances to overcome them.

An alarm for mankind has been issued long ago. But the results so far have been rather modest. We cannot afford to tolerate the present state of affairs, and of inertia. If it continues further, the present **problem situation** in the world will become a **crisis situation**. Mankind then might be only several generations from the catastrophic Epoch 'zero'.

Of course a man is not completely idle, and tries to deal with threats and challenges. But he counteracts modestly and mostly locally. Today the scale of many issues has reached such a level that it requires not only imagination but also action within a global framework. Man has a chance to survive; whether he will take advantage of that chance depends solely on him and not on supernatural forces.

Notes

1. Pawel Bozyk, 'Nie Uciekniemy przed swiatem' (We cannot escape from the world), *Polityka*, 8 (February 21, 1987).
2. Pawel Bozyk, 'Nie Uciekniemy przed swiatem'.
3. Pawel Bozyk (ed.), *Global Challenges and Eastern European Responses* (Warsaw: The United Nations University Polish Scientific Publishers, 1988: 10–11.
4. Centrum Badania Opinii Spolecznej (CBOS) (Center of Public Opinion Research) BD/380/23/85; *Opinia o polityce zagranicznej* (Views of Foreign Policy) (Warsaw) (November 1985).
5. Centrum Badania Opinii Spolecznej (CBOS) (Center of Public Opinion Research), *Jubileusz ONZ – Konsultacja Spoleczna* (UN Anniversary – Public Consultation) BS/278/5/85 (August 1985).
6. Centrum Badania Opinii Spolecznej (1985).
7. Centrum Badania Opinii Spolecznej (CBOS) (Center of Public Opinion Research), *Opinie o szczycie genewskim i aktualnej sytuacji miedzynarodowej* (Views on Geneva Summit and International Situation) BD 12/1/86 (January 1986).
8. Centrum Badania Opinii Spolecznej (CBOS) (Center of Public Opinion Research), *Spotkanie w Reykjaviku w opinii spolecznej* (Meeting in Reykjavik in Public Opinion) BD/335/30/86 (November 1986).
9. Longin Pastusiak, 'Swiat na progu trzeciego tysiaclecia: szanse i zagrozemia dla Polski' (The world at the threshold of the third millennium: chances and threats for Poland), Torun 1985, paper presented at the convention of Polish Political Science Association (Torun) (November 1985).

Part II
Specific Policy Problems

7 Labor Rights in a North–South Framework: International Trade Union Solidarity Actions

Inés Vargas

BACKGROUND

Unionization is the most important instrument available to workers in their struggle to achieve their aims, to overcome their difficulties and to create the possibility of their expressing demands and improving social conditions. Workers' organizations are counterparts to management, thus there exists a conflict of interests, values and aims not resolvable by means of legislation alone. As Davies and Freedland point out, 'As a power countervailing management trade unions are much more effective than the law has ever been or can ever be ... Everywhere the effectiveness of the law depends on the unions far more than the unions depend on the effectiveness of the law. The effectiveness of the unions, however, depends to some extent on forces neither they nor the law can control'.[1] Indeed, with their increased strength in the industrial countries, trade unions have established considerable influence, especially in countries with long traditions of cooperation between trade unions and related political parties.

As is stated in the Davies and Freedland version of *Kahn-Freund's Labour and the Law*:

The individual worker is subordinated to the power of management but that power of management is coordinated with that of organised labour. The regulation of labour results from the combination of these processes of subordination and of coordination, of the rules made unilaterally by the employer in conjunction with those agreed between him or his association and the union through collective bargaining, including bargaining at the plant level.[2]

The results of both legislation and the combination referred to are, logically, very different for countries with strong unions than in countries where unions are weak. Here we refer to the Third World, where generally the main task of trade unions is to survive, not only because of problems in legislation, but also because of the consequences of the combination referred to above. And all of these are dependent on the context within the particular country.

In developing countries, regional and national differences clearly exist, because the variety and diversity of the situations and national contexts present differing degrees of economic development, in terms of per capita income and levels of industrialization. This diversity reflects political and cultural factors, including various types of political power, differences between social groups and organizations, and the relations between these bodies and the state. Here the relation between political regimes, the right of workers to organize and trade union rights is crucial. And here arises the twofold relation which trade unions have with respect to human rights. On the one hand, the freedom of workers to organize and trade union rights can develop only where there is a general respect for human rights.[3] And on the other, as groups with recognized rights for promoting and protecting the economic and social interests of their members and themselves as groups, trade unions represent an important means to promote not only trade union rights and collective bargaining, but also other human rights.[4] However, if trade unions are attacked as a result of policies aimed to repress freedom of association and trade unions, then it is very likely that other human rights are thereby violated by the same mechanisms of repression.[5]

INTERNATIONAL SOLIDARITY ACTIONS

In industrialized countries, organized workers have used various methods and forms of solidarity (for example, sympathy strikes, political demonstration actions and boycotts) in struggles to improve their standard of living. Similarly, organized workers and peasants in developing countries have adopted analogous methods in related, but more desperate, struggles. Most of these struggles have remained predominantly within their separate spheres. Nevertheless, in addition to a generalized sense of mutual concern and mutual support, there have been instances when workers in both industrialized and developing countries have acted in solidarity. An example of this form of

international solidarity would be when a labor dispute, the **primary
action**, in the **primary country** is responded to by **solidarity actions of
support** in the **secondary country or countries**. Such solidarity actions
can involve North–North, South–North, North–South and/or South–
South relations. They may entail not only moral and financial support,
but also more direct industrial action such as sympathy strikes and
boycotts.

In some cases, where direct worker actions have taken place within
the supporting country, solidarity actions have proved effective. However, in international boycotts of ships flying 'flags of convenience',
solidarity actions have been far less successful.

Although there have been several interesting cases of solidarity
actions in various industrialized countries, this chapter gives general
examples and concentrates on the situation of Norway as a secondary
country. Norway has had labor relations much more favorable for
workers than in the countries in the Third World, and its trade unions
are strong and powerful. Logically, in this framework Norway will
appear as a supportive country. Furthermore, of the countries where
primary conflicts might take place, this chapter will concentrate on
workers whose human rights are violated, and specifically their freedom to organize and exercise trade union rights. Closely related to the
issue is the situation of crews in ships flying 'flags of convenience'.

CASE STUDIES

The Coca-Cola Case

One successful example of this North–South relation is the labor
conflict (the **primary action**) in Guatemala between Coca-Cola and its
Guatemalan workers and supporting solidarity actions in various
industrialized countries (such as Norway, Belgium, Canada, West
Germany and the USA), as well as some developing countries (such as
Mexico, the Philippines and Venezuela). This case was regarded as a
victory by the International Union of Food and Allied Workers'
Associations (IUF).[6]

The IUF in Geneva became involved with the Coca-Cola case in
Guatemala in 1979, when workers from Embotelladora Guatemalteca
SA (EGSA) made a request for a support action.[7] The owner of EGSA
had hired, as had other factory owners in Guatemala, members of the
PMA, the Mobile Military Police, to act as armed guards in the plant

and deal with workers trying to carry out trade union activities.[8] He also refused to negotiate a new collective agreement in February 1980.

During that period, the rule of the Guatemalean dictator Lucas Garcia was also in the phase of its most severe brutality. On May 1, 1980, 90 people 'disappeared', either picked out of the crowd or taken from their homes later that evening. From the parade in Guatemala City, 30 union members were pulled out, abducted and killed in the most bestial ways. Of these victims, two had been connected with the EGSA Coca-Cola plant. On June 21, 1980, in a massive police raid on the office of Confederación Nacional de Trabajadores CNT (National Workers' Federation), 27 union leaders were abducted (none of them has ever reappeared): two were union leaders of EGSA.[9] The killing of union leader Marlon Mendizabal on May 27, 1980, made the IUF step up their action. Coca-Cola was confronted with a publicity campaign throughout the world, and national branches of IUF prepared supportive actions. These ranged from sympathy strikes, consumer boycotts and publicity campaigns to representations to management. Attempts at tourist boycott also took place. In Guatemala, the EGSA workers initiated a strike which was soon violently broken up by the police.

In Norway the two affiliates of the IUF, the Norwegian Food and Allied Union (NNN) and the Hotel and Restaurant Workers' Union prepared in coordination with the Norwegian Federation of Trade Unions (LO) a three-day sales and production boycott of Coca-Cola in June 1980. The Coca-Cola company internationally and in Norway appealed to the unions in an attempt to prevent the planned action.[10] None of the Norwegian employers brought the case to court, however.

The measurable economic effect of these solidarity actions throughout many countries was very small, but the information and publicity involved had a much larger scope. Under this pressure, Coca-Cola pledged to find new franchise owners for the EGSA plant, who then took control of the plant for Coca-Cola in order to prevent further damage to the company name. The workers became affiliated to the union STEGAC and a new collective agreement was set up in December 1980. The IUF actions were definitely called off one month later.

In February 1984, the Coca-Cola company announced its plans to close down the EGSA plant, complaining of total lack of profit and mismanagement by the former owners. STEGAC and the IUF argued instead that the plant was commercially viable. Moreover, the Coca-Cola Corporation had negotiated with the IUF and signed an agreement in 1980, quite in contradiction to the corporation's traditional refusal to bargain with international federations. But by 1984, Coca-Cola was preparing to abolish all of the gains for labor and union rights achieved since 1980 through the national and international solidarity actions.

In response, the workers occupied the plant on February 18, 1984. This occupation lasted for more than three months, with the initial period of the occupation especially tense. Plain clothes police patrolled outside, and the Army set up roadblocks, stopping passing cars and occasionally firing shots.[11] Once again, the Coca-Cola workers called for international support action. In Norway and several other countries, publicity campaigns and short production stoppages of Coca-Cola plants were staged.[12]

On May 27, 1984, the Coca-Cola Central American subsidiary and STEGAC reached an agreement in San Jose, Costa Rica. The IUF was present at the meeting, but not a formal party to the agreement. This agreement guaranteed continued production, new collective agreements and back pay for the plant workers during the occupation. The international boycott action was cancelled, and the IUF regarded the action as a successful example of international solidarity.

The Coca-Cola example is difficult to compare with other conflicts, for three main reasons. (1) To gain the attention and support of international trade union associations, human rights abuses, especially the right to organize in its relation with other human rights, must be significant and obvious. In Guatemala, the abuses were extreme and blatant. Hence, unlike other cases, Guatemala represented an obvious and legitimate target, for international concern. (2) The Coca-Cola company is in a weak position when confronted with international solidarity actions. The Coca-Cola corporation, as a multinational with branches in practically every country in the world and with a product as world famous as Coca-Cola, could be easily identified for boycott and publicity actions. These sympathy actions were augmented by the ease of carrying out the production boycott actions. In many instances, workers simply had to leave Coca-Cola aside while producing other soft drinks on the same production line. (3) Guatemala's marginal economic and social position in relation to the industrialized countries virtually eliminated any possibility of significant backfire effects from international sympathy actions directed against it.

Thus, from the three preceding points, we can see that if the human rights abuses had been less obvious, if the multinational involved more resilient to attack, and if the primary country a more influential international actor, then the outcome could have been very different.

Ships Flying 'Flags of Convenience'

Very different from the Coca-Cola action are the traditional boycott actions in connection with ships sailing under flags of convenience. And, also unlike the Coca-Cola case, many of these actions have been fought in court.

The 'flags of convenience' ships are usually crewed by men from developing countries. It is frequently claimed that the conditions concerning wages and labor relations (also safety and sanitary standards) are lower in these ships.[13] However, different working conditions for crews are not the only problem: the flags of convenience labor situation also affects the position of unions in traditional shipping nations, representing a threat to shipping in traditional maritime countries as well as to the seamen and maritime traditions in these countries.

There have not been many cases of such boycotts carried out by Norwegian workers. This relative passivity appears to stem mainly from a court judgement rendered concerning the sympathy action taken against the Greek ship *San Dimitris* in October 1954. It flew a Panamanian flag and appeared to be owned by a Panamanian company, but the real proprietor was a Greek shipping company, with administrative officers in London. Its crew were also Greek.

The background for this blockade was the campaign in which the International Transport Workers' Federation (ITF) was engaged together with different unions in many nations. In the aftermath of the Second World War, the traditional shipping nations were selling old ships in order to renew tonnage. Buyers would register them in Panama or other small developing countries who had placed their flags at the disposal of foreign shipowners. Generally these shipowners did not take proper care of these vessels, and the hiring, wages and working conditions for the crew were adjusted solely according to the wishes of the shipowners. This problem had been discussed in many ITF Conferences, where it was concluded that the principal reason for such transferral to Third World countries' open registers was to avoid the social rights that seamen had obtained in the traditional shipping nations, as well as taxes and international provisions concerning security at sea.

Two decisions were reached in the wake of the actions against the *San Dimitris*. The first handling of the case was in terms of sympathy actions, the second in terms of boycott. The Norwegian Labour Court (ARD 1956–7: 16ff)[14] stated that the action was a **sympathy action** carried out in support of an international blockade of ships flying flags of convenience. The Labour Court here referred to the June 11 decision of the Court (ARD 1924/5: 179ff) where it was expressly recognized that a party has the right to employ sympathy actions in support of a foreign primary conflict. The shipowner sued the Norwegian Seamen's Union and the Norwegian Federation of Transport Workers, basing his claim on the assertion that the referred action should be considered illegal under the provisions of the Boycott Act of 1947. The Norwegian Supreme Court declared the boycott illegal under two of these provisions (Rt. 1959: 1080ff). First, the Court found the purpose of the action illegal because those conducting the boycott intended to force the company to sign a collective agreement with ITF and the crew to become members of this organization. The Court also noted that the crew, which was not organized, had not expressed a desire to join the ITF, and that their individual wages were at a level that was not contrary to the applicable Greek National Agreement.[15] The Court held that this meant that the action was unlawful under § 2(c) of the Boycott Act of 1947: a paragraph which forbids, among other things, unconscionable boycotts and actions in situations where there is no reasonable relationship between the interest that will be promoted by the boycott and the injury that it will occasion. Second, the Supreme Court held that the boycott was illegal under § 2(d) of the Act because the workers failed to give an individual concrete notice of their intended action. This Supreme Court decision required the workers to pay compensation to the shipping company.[16]

LEGAL ASPECTS

The legality of sympathy actions, political demonstration actions and boycotts raises complicated legal issues:

(1)   such actions involve the **rule of law in the primary country** – i.e., the country where the primary action is taking place

(2)   in the case of ships 'flying flags of convenience', they may involve the **rule of law of the country of registration**, of the country of the **nationality of the shipowner** and of the country or countries of **nationality of the crew**

(3)   they involve the **rule of law in the supporting country** – i.e., the country where the solidarity action is taking place.

Here, however, our main concern is: what might be the role of human rights in these situations? More specifically, what about international principles concerning the right to freedom of association, the right to organize and the right to collective bargaining?

The Right to Engage in Solidarity Actions

Many legal problems arise from solidarity actions; hence it is important to identify the law applicable to the various legal issues involved. The first point is whether a solidarity action is **lawful in the country concerned**; and if so, what restrictions might exist regarding it, and whether national legislation provides for all or some cases in question. The most widely followed rule here is that the legality of the solidarity action can be judged only by the law of the country **where the action takes place**. A further relevant issue is to determine what should be considered as a 'solidarity action' and the conditions required.

In Norway the peace obligation during the period when the collective agreement is in force means that industrial actions are not allowed during that period. This obligation has both a statutory and contractual basis: it is regulated through the Labour Disputes Act (§ 6, 1 and 3) and the Labour Disputes Act for the Public Sector (§ 20), and by the existence of a concrete collective agreement as a contract, even though it does not include provisions concerning the issue. The Basic Agreement, for example, in its § 2-2, refers to this obligation to refrain from industrial action.[17]

However, labor disputes are permitted in the case of actions outside the purview of questions regulated by the collective agreement. Thus, for example, the obligation to maintain peaceful relations is not a hindrance to **sympathy actions**, because these have the purpose of supporting a party in a labor dispute that does not concern the tariff conditions of the supporting workers.

Jurisprudence has been developed through the practice of the Norwegian Labour Court. Important here is the decision of the Labour Court (published in ARD 1926: 47ff). In this decision, in line with previous decisions of the Labour Court (ARD 1920–1: 1ff and in ARD 1924–5: 179ff), the Court held that for collective agreement parties, an absolute and unconditional obligation to abstain from the use of industrial action during the agreement period could not be assumed without an explicit provision in the agreement. This principle has been maintained ever since. In other words: without a particular basis in a collective agreement, sympathy actions cannot be hindered. That further means that, in Norway, questions concerning sympathy actions might be regulated in collective agreements, and it is possible to include in such agreements rules limiting the admittance of sympathy actions, or even forbidding them. The practice of the Labour Court has laid down the general rules, but concrete provisions about the issue can limit them in collective agreements.

The Basic Agreement deals with sympathy actions in § 3-6. In this provision the acceptance of sympathy actions is recognized, but on the condition that the primary conflict should be lawful and that there exist the consent of the Norwegian Employers' Confederation (NAF) or the Norwegian Federation of Trade Unions (LO).

However, other types of actions – e.g., boycott, political demonstration action – might determine that the action should be treated differently, according to the application of law and court practice.

In Norway, the legality of the use of **boycott**, being an action accomplished by Norwegian workers and union organizations, must be decided within the frame of the Boycott Act (BA) of 1947. Illegal boycotting is subject to punishment (§ 5, BA) and also the liable trade union or unions have the financial responsibility for compensating the boycotted (§ 4, BA). The problem is that the possibility for a boycott to be legal is hardly limited by the provisions of the Act itself. Boycott rules were and are seen as class legislation[18] whose content, structure and organization reveals that boycotting trade unions were to be feared as irresponsible and dangerous for society. From the time of the first Norwegian legislation on boycott in 1933, it was considered that the use of labor boycotts needed to be strictly controlled. Restrictions were approved for calling or implementing a boycott, with all kind of requirements for hampering worker initiatives on such actions. Indeed, it is still extremely difficult to further a legal boycott in Norway today.

Political demonstration strikes are permitted, on the condition that their purposes are real and would not directly or indirectly influence wages or working conditions agreed upon in the collective agreement. The duration of the strike is also used by the courts as a criterion as to its legality. Actions should be short in time. Also, such actions should not be in contradiction with the employer's right to direction.[19]

Cross-national Actions

The second legal question raised by these actions concerns whether traditional industrial actions – such as sympathy actions, political demonstration strikes and boycotts with respect to labor disputes – can be carried out in support of a conflict in another country. It is unusual for national legislation to deal with this issue. As one of the rare examples, S 29 of the British Trade Union and Labour Relations Act 1974 should be mentioned. This explicitly refers to actions in support of a dispute in another country. Here the qualification was that those taking action in Britain must be likely to be affected themselves, in relation to a trade dispute matter, by the outcome of the dispute abroad. This qualification was deleted in 1976, but 1982 Employment Act reintroduced it. The Davies and Freedland edition of *Kahn-Freund's Labour and the Law* states:

> The qualification amounts to a denial of international solidarity: protection is afforded only when those taking action in this country [Great Britain] have an industrial interest of their own for so doing. Both ... restrictions derive from the view of industrial relations as essentially a fragmented activity, as a matter for particular employers and their employees, and not as raising issues of general concern to employees organized in trade unions.[20]

This same argument cited by Davies and Freedland could be used in the cases of boycotts of ships under flags of convenience in Norway. Boycotts are carried out for improving the conditions of work and wages of their crews, as actions within the context of a broader international solidarity and as issues of general concern to workers' organizations. However, they are taken as fragmented problems, and it is not rare that solidarity workers are sentenced to pay compensation.

The legality of sympathy actions in support of disputes abroad is not the only major problem that can arise. In different European countries, courts have recognized in various ways the possibility of such actions occurring, but within certain conditions. In general, the most often used prerequisite would seem that the action supported must itself be **lawful**.

In Norway, the decision of ARD 1924–5: 179ff established the right of the parties to use sympathy actions during the period of validity of the collective agreement in support of a main conflict abroad. There it is stated that according to Norwegian law, employers as well as workers have open access to carry out a work stoppage if nothing else is settled in current legislation or agreements.[21] The Court held in this decision that the issue at stake therefore is not whether there exists a warrant legalizing sympathy actions in support of conflicts abroad, but if the existing collective agreement positively declares that such actions are illegal in the period of validity of the agreement. In other words: since the collective agreement do not explicitly forbid such actions, sympathy actions in support of conflicts abroad are permitted. Norwegian courts have held to this principle ever since.[22]

Political demonstration strikes concerning situations in other countries are permitted to the same extent as they are accepted in the national milieu. Two important decisions of the Norwegian Labour Court relate to this issue and have been resolved in accordance with the principles for the acceptability of political demonstration strikes in the domestic context (ARD 1920–1: 1ff and ARD 1937: 22ff). Further, the basic line of reasoning concerning political demonstration strikes was defined in the former decision, which dealt with actions related to a situation abroad: i.e., that a political demonstration strike obviously not related to the collective agreement, but instead directed against the authorities of the state – not against the employers – was legal. Obviously there will be many cases where it will be a matter of judgement as to whether such an action is legal or not. Therefore the political atmosphere at a given time, the composition of the court and similar factors may influence the decision in each case.

Concerning boycotts, these have taken place mainly in the case of ships flying flags of convenience. Usually, working conditions and social security (if any) applied by shipowners to the crew are those covered by legislation of the country of registration. However, the persons or firms owning these ships will often have only a formal address where the ship is registered.[23] This almost fictive presence makes it very difficult to get reasonable work conditions for seamen or their rights implemented in that country. Working conditions and social security thus become the main element for competition between shipping companies using flags of convenience.

Norwegian trade unions have long been grappling with the question of their possibility of participating in international boycotts. LO has presented several proposals aimed at reforming the Boycott Act. In an answer given at the Question Time in the Norwegian Parliament on January 28, 1981, the Minister of Justice said that the issue had to be seen against the background of actions carried out in recent years by ITF and the Norwegian Unions of Seamen and Transport Workers. The purpose of these actions was to pressure shipowners to enter into ITF agreements with their crews, as well as to pressure companies to pay wages already agreed upon in previously signed ITF agreements.

The Minister of Justice pointed out that these issues raised several questions at both legal and political levels. In the latter area, for example, shipping, navigation and foreign relations policy were all involved.

Legality of Primary Actions

In the Nordic countries, sympathy actions appear to be lawful if the **primary action itself is lawful**. Thus, the problem of legality involves the legal system of two countries. The pivotal question then becomes how the **'lawfulness' of the primary action** will be determined.

Generally speaking, unions need most international solidarity in those places where they are most harassed and repressed. And this situation has close links with the situation of human rights in the country concerned. The Director of ILO has pointed out that restrictions on trade union freedoms are more frequently encountered in cases where civil liberties in the general sense are also curtailed – e.g., the right of association in general, the right of assembly, freedom of thought and expression, freedom from arbitrary arrest, imprisonment or exile, or the right to a fair, public trial before an independent and impartial court, with a presumption of innocence until guilt is proved.[24]

The close relation between workers' freedom of organization and civil and political rights is shown by the fact that a great number of complaints of alleged infringements of trade union rights submitted to ILO arise from alleged violations of the civil and political human rights of trade union leaders and members. The ILO's Director General has indicated that this is the case in roughly the half of the cases brought before the Freedom of Association Committee.[25] It must further be noted that the cases finally examined by the Committee are but a tiny percentage of the realities faced by workers wishing to exercise their right to organize and engage in trade union activities. These cases involve a considerable number of situations, including allegations related to the life, liberty, exile and personal safety of trade union leaders in particular and of members of their organizations.

Here we may cite the example of the situation of labor in Latin America. Violations of human rights occur simultaneously with violations of international standards of freedom of association and the right to organize in trade unions. Latin America provides a sad tale of massive violations of the right to security of the person, with a great number of murders and disappearances, often of trade union leaders and members. In addition, serious injuries, frequent use of torture, ill-treatment, arbitrary arrest and detention, exile, restrictions of move-ment, and summary procedures have been experienced by trade unio-nists in the region.

If the 'legality' to be taken into account is that of the country where the primary conflict takes place, this raises the question of whether a legal system where human rights and international labor standards are respected is to be considered equal to a system where they are violated and workers harassed or repressed. In this last instance, recourse to the rule of law and practices of the primary country could mean that the problem might be resolved in a manner incompatible with the prin-ciples and legislation of the country where the sympathy action takes place, or incompatible with international labor standards.

If then the action carried out in Norway is a boycott, its legality has to be solved through the boycott provisions. In this case the legality of the action would not be based on the legality of the main conflict, but on the rules of the Boycott Act. It could be that there does not appear to exist any main conflict to support, as might happen with conditioned sympathy strike notices, which include calling a boycott concerning a third party if a condition is not covered. They could be declared legal or illegal in relation to this party and such a boycott is covered by Norway's boycott provisions.[26] And as noted above, the possibilities of furthering such actions in Norway are bleak.

This is usually the situation concerning ships flying 'flags of conve-nience', where shipowners literally enjoy full freedom in hiring seamen and deciding their working conditions. Some recruit seamen with no training, unqualified and without certificates as seafarers, which means a safety hazard. All of these create special problems in terms of hiring, contracts, continuity of employment, social security and repatriation: internationally accepted standards are bypassed. The complaints of seafarers 'have ranged from the not being paid the contracted wages to having been abandoned at alien ports without any hopes of repatria-tion. In many cases employers have abandoned their vessels along with men on board, merely to escape fulfillment of contractual obligations. Under such circumstances, crew members find themselves stranded at alien ports without any supply of essential provisions like food, water and fuel for heating and lighting'.[27] To all these has to be added factors clearly jeopardizing the safety of seafarers, as in the continuing armed conflict in the Gulf. Hence, it is of utmost importance to set international minimum standards for these workers, as well as mechanisms to implement such standards and the support of international organizations.

Here, the problem relates to the legislation or standards to be applied in the case of ships. In Norway, there is a tendency to view the **real** connections to a country as decisive. A good example of this is the Norwegian Supreme Court decision in the *San Dimitris* case (Rt. 1959: 1080). Since both the shipowner and the crew were Greek, the Greek national agreement was taken into account. This tendency follows the general choice of law principles. For example, those chosen at the time of the EEC treaty in 1980, where it was stipulated that where circumstances indicated that the employment contract was more closely related to another country than to the flag of convenience country, then the law of that country should be applied. That was also the case with a Norwegian Supreme Court decision (Rt. 1936: 900ff), where it was stated that the legality of a Norwegian seamens' strike on an English fishing vessel should be settled by English and not Norwegian rules.

Still another question involves the relation or connection of the boycotted ship to Norway. The Norwegian courts have held that the closer the connection, the more reasonable would be the demands by the seafarers' union for a collective agreement.[28] However, the courts have also held that the fact that a vessel is owned and/or managed by persons or companies with little connection with the flag state is a point in favour of accepting a boycott action when the ship sails to Norway.[29] Certainly, problems of labor relations exist in ships coming to Norway, no matter what the situation might be in terms of close or loose connections of the ship to the country. The situation has to be evaluated according to the given set of circumstances. In the *San Dimitris* case, the ship came into port in Norway only once. The court, however, did not establish any requirement of more connections as a condition for a legal boycott. Thus, the opinion of Jakhelln on the issue is very appropriate: the question of whether a court is competent should, from a Norwegian viewpoint, depend on whether one of the parties or other circumstances of the case establish sufficient such connections to the country where the court has its seat, so that it would be unreasonable **not** to advance the case.[30]

Undoubtedly, more information and research on international labor issues is needed. This is especially so in light of the explosive growth of multinational corporations, whose technologies and divisions of labor can move capital and build industries or parts of industries wherever labor may be cheap and non-unionized.

This issue is of interest not only in the concrete cases in question, but also throughout the discussion of the enforcement of international labor law and national laws – and, of course, for the situation of the workers concerned.

CONCLUSIONS

A central feature in trade union solidarity actions is that they are directed to support the labor conflicts of others. Power is unevenly distributed in all societies, and even if it is assumed that labor law should serve to equalize the balance in this respect, some legal rules could serve different purposes. When these rules and practices are used to restrict trade union possibilities to engage in industrial actions in support of conflicts in countries where human rights, workers' freedom to organize and trade union rights are violated, then these rules bypass international human rights principles. The same may be said about undue restrictions of boycotts against ships whose crew is not covered by minimum international standards concerning job safety, wages and working conditions.

Generally speaking, when workers' freedom to organize and trade union rights are repressed, other human rights will also be violated. Repression of trade union rights may constitute not only attempts to destroy the development of a genuinely free trade union movement, but also represent an integrated part of a general oppression. Therefore, a country which espouses democratic and human rights principles should ensure that its domestic legislation allows its national trade unions to act in solidarity with workers in more repressive societies.

This principle will apply mainly to industrialized countries, while primary actions to secure trade union rights will generally take place in Third World countries. Trade unions in Third World countries will as a rule be weak, both financially and in the level of unionization, and this will limit their possibilities of performing forceful solidarity actions in their own countries.

In actions of international solidarity, boycotts will be the most efficient weapon. However, as we have seen in the case of Norway, a state may as a matter of principle establish a boycott right and then proceed to qualify it so as to render it almost useless for domestic or international purposes. In order to permit international trade union solidarity actions in the struggle for workers' rights and their freedom of organization, restrictions on boycotts will have to be re-evaluated so as to allow workers to carry out such actions of international solidarity. It goes without saying that such a practice has to be established within the context of the general principles of a society based on the rule of law.

As stated in the beginning of this chapter, my starting point is that trade unions are the most important tools available to workers in their struggle for social justice and improved living conditions. In furthering their demands or in carrying out international solidarity actions, unions are viewed as the organizational or institutional framework for social action by and for workers for their protection and common interests. Unions are **pressure groups**, and in practice their expectations and demands will be expressed in terms of power relations between them and employers, economic groups, public authorities and the state. Trade unions should serve workers and respect and promote their rights, both nationally and internationally. This process raises issues of general concern to workers' organizations. The stronger unions can be very effective in the defence of their common interests and in the promotion and maintenance of workers' freedom of organization and trade union rights. International solidarity actions geared to these aims thus make an important contribution to the realization of human rights.

Finally, concerning the role of trade unions in relation to human rights, I want to point out:

(1)   that through international solidarity actions, trade unions in industrialized countries are an important mechanism for the promotion of workers' freedom of organization and trade union rights, as well as other human rights

(2)   that there are close links between workers' freedom of organization and the human rights practices in a given country

(3)   that the realization of human rights includes the concrete establishment and promotion of these rights, both within individual nations and in the larger international context.

Decisions of Nordic Courts: Abbreviations Used

ARD   Decisions of the Labour Court (Dommer og kjennelser av Arbeidsretten).

DBC   Decisions of the Boycott Court (Dommer m.v. av Boikottdomstolen).

ND   Compilation of Nordic Sentences Concerning Maritime Matters (Nordiske Domme i Sjøfartsanliggender).

Rt.   Decisions of the Supreme Court (Norsk Rettstidende).

Notes

1. Davies and Freedland (1983): 21.
2. Davies and Freedland (1983): 22.
3. For further details, see ILO, 'Trade Union Rights and Their Relation to Civil Liberties' (1970); ILO, 'Freedom of Association. A workers' education manual' (1987): 93–103; ILO, 'Freedom of Association. Digest of decisions and principles of the Freedom of Association Committee of the Governing Body of the ILO' (1985), paras 68–207; and ILO, 'Human rights – a common responsibility' (1988).
4. See I. Vargas, 'Workers' Right to Organize, Trade Union Rights and their Relation with Civil and Political Human Rights' (1988).
5. Vargas (1988).
6. IUF is one of the International Trade Secretariats (ITSs), which are autonomous confederations of unions in the same industry or occupation. It had affiliates in 60 countries, but none in Guatemala. The Coca-Cola conflict was not the first in which IUF had been involved. Previous to the Guatemalan issue, it had undertaken multi-country campaigns on behalf of the workers of other multinationals, such as Nestlé and Unilever.
7. IUF prepared a document (in 1981) concerning the action conducted during 1979 and 1980 in support of the struggle of the Sindicato de Trabajadores de EGSA in Guatemala to secure recognition of their trade union rights: *The Coca-Cola–Guatemala Campaign 1979–1981*. Its Introduction states that 'in several respects [this action has] been the most significant and successful ever conducted by IUF'. In the document there is an exposition of the different actions undertaken in numerous countries (11–14). Some of these are:

   Denmark: 'Hotel- og Restaurationspersonalets Forbund began a consumer/sales boycott of Coca-Cola in February 1980. As this was the first action to take place, the Coca-Cola company was quick to intervene, promising settlement of the issue. The company also threatened layoffs of SID bottling workers which resulted in the bottling workers refusing to support the boycott action. In November 1980 at the SID Congress, the Coca-Cola issue was raised by representatives of the bottling workers. The IUF General Secretary explained the significance of the boycott and the Congress voted in favor of continued support'.

Sweden: 'All five of the IUF's Swedish affiliates, Svenska Livsmedelsarbetareförbundet, Hotell- och Restauranganställdas Förbund, Handelstjänstemannaförbundet, Sveriges Arbetsledareförbund, and Svenska Industritjänstemannaförbundet, conducted consumer, production and sales boycotts during the third week of April 1980 following an extensive publicity campaign. The Socialist Youth staged street theater plays to demonstrate publicly the situation at the EGSA plant and distributed thousand of stickers'.

United States:

(1)   'AFL–CIO president Lane Kirkland stated, during a press conference in Stockholm on May 23, that American workers were being asked not to drink Coca-Cola for as long as violence persisted in the Guatemala franchise operation and that the AFL–CIO supported the labor struggle in Guatemala'.

(2)   'The president of the United Automobile Workers of America, Douglas A. Frazer, wrote to members of the US House of Representatives drawing their attention to conditions in Guatemala and asking them to oppose US military aid to the present government'.

Mexico: 'Sindicato de Trabajadores de la Industria Embotelladora de Aguas Gaseosas, Similares y Conexos de la República Mexicana organized a mass street demonstration on April 20 following a national meeting of all Coca-Cola workers. Preparations were made for a production stoppage to be held at a later date to be specified by IUF, in order to coordinate with other actions'.

Venezuela:

(1)   'Federación Nacional de Trabajadores de la Industria Hotelera y Similares de Venezuela began a national sales boycott of Coca-Cola on July 23, 1980'.

(2)   'FENTRIBEB staged 15-minute demonstration strikes in all five Coca-Cola plants on July 9, 10 and 11. 1,500 workers participated'.

West Germany: Very important were the actions undertaken in West Germany. West German unions contacted major travel agencies to urge cancellation of tours to Guatemala. NGG (Gewerkschaft Nahrung – Genuss – Gaststätten) was in regular contact with the German Coca-Cola management regarding the EGSA situation. Representatives of Coca-Cola in Atlanta, USA, contacted the IUF at this time, urgently requesting a meeting to reach a settlement and expressing fears over planned actions in Germany (and Canada as well).

8.   See Latin America Bureau, 'Soft Drink – Hard Labour' (1987): 8ff; and Jane Slaughter, 'Guatemala's Labor Movement. Coke Victory Spurs Recovery' (1984). The use of gunman from the police at the Coca-Cola

plant in Guatemala was also told to me in an interview with Rodolfo Robles, former general secretary of STEGAC, on 25 November, 1985.

9. Latin America Bureau, 'Soft Drink': 12; IUF, 'The Coca-Cola–Guatemala Campaign': 7–8, and Slaughter, 'Guatemala's Labor Movement': 16.
10. IUF, 'The Coca-Cola–Guatemala Campaign': 13.
11. Slaughter, 'Guatemala's Labor Movement': 15.
12. In 'Soft Drink – Hard Labour': 31 it reads: 'Boycott action began immediately, and spread rapidly. On 7 May production stopped at 13 different Coke bottling and canning plants in Norway. In Italy, several short stoppages occurred at Coca-Cola plants while workers met to hear reports on the situation in Guatemala. Austrian unions wrote to the local Coca-Cola management threatening action. In Mexico, ten different bottling plants held solidarity strikes for three days each on a rotating basis, while in Sweden all five IUF affiliates staged a full production and sales stoppage for three days'. News of further union action plans in different countries reached Atlanta. For the company, probably the most worrying of all was a national boycott campaign by a coalition of IUF's affiliates and church and consumer groups scheduled to start in 16 US cities on 21 May, 1984.
13. See: Schmidt, 'Ships Flying Flags of Convenience' (1972): 77–9; Jakhelln, 'Working conditions and social security on ships under "flags of convenience"' (1985): 571–4; and Jakhelln, 'Boikott av skip under bekvemmelighetsflagg' (1986): 572.
14. For abbreviations used in the decisions of Nordic Courts, see the end of the chapter, p. 167.
15. Where appropriate, for example in instances such as this one, in which the interested parties share a common nationality, Norwegian courts often will consider the terms of such agreements. For more details, see Jakhelln, 'Working Conditions': 578–9.
16. Another important case in Norway concerned the boycott of the *Nawala* ship. In relation to the action against this ship, there were two decisions from the Hålogaland Appellate Court: ND 1980: 282ff (called the first *Nawala* decision), and ND 1981: 177ff (called the second *Nawala* decision). The ship *Nawala* was registered in Hong Kong, and had its place of business in the USA. It appeared, however, to be Swedish-owned. It had a crew of 32 seamen, of mainly Chinese and British nationality. In the first *Nawala* decision, the Appelate Court confirmed the holding of the trial court rejecting the shipowners' request for a temporary prohibition of an intended boycott by Norwegian workers. The Hålogaland Court considered that the intended boycott was not – as it had been in the case of *San Dimitris* – directed towards forcing the crew to become members of the ITF or the shipowner to pay expenses, but instead was part of a policy of Norwegian and international seafarers' organizations: to obtain the ITF minimum standards for crews in ships sailing under flags of convenience. In addition, the Court called attention to the fact that the Norwegian shipowners and shipping

companies had already accepted these minimum standards for foreign crew in Norwegian-owned ships flying flags of convenience. In the second *Nawala* decision, the Court found the boycott by Norwegian Seamen's and Transport Unions, their Federation, and the Longshoremen's Association to be illegal. These bodies were condemned to pay the damages (amounting to US $240,000) incurred through the illegal boycott actions. The Court considered that the demands for a collective wage agreement that included both 'back pay' for the crew from the date they started work on board the ship, and unilateral rights of ITF/ Norwegian Seamen's Union to change the rate of pay upon two months' notice to the shipowner, were an unreasonable burden for the employer and thus were grounds to declare the boycott improper and, therefore, illegal (BA, § 2(c)).

17. The Norwegian Federation of Trade Unions (LO) and the Norwegian Employers' Confederation (NAF) signed a Basic Agreement in 1935 which has been renewed periodically, although there have been several amendments since then. It is considered the first part of every collective agreement signed by the sectors represented by LO and NAF.

18. This feeling of 'class legislation' was referred to in Ot. prp. nr. 73 (1947): 1 concerning the boycott provisions introduced with the reform of 1933 to the Norwegian Labour Dispute Act. This was strongly raised in the statements of the Labour Party faction in the Norwegian Parliament's Standing Committee on Social Affairs in 1933 and in the presentation of LO of April 5, 1933 concerning the proposed legislation. (The letter of LO is included in Ot. prp. nr. 71 (1933): 68–92.)

19. The Labour Court has dealt with more than 20 cases involving political demonstration strikes, even though there have been many of such actions. See, for example, ARD 1920–1: 1ff, ARD 1960: 1ff, ARD 1970: 65ff, ARD 1976: 23ff and 96ff, ARD 1979: 37ff, and ARD 1984: 85ff.

20. Davies and Freedland, *Kahn-Freund's Labour and the Law*: 320.

21. Decision at ARD 1924–5: 179ff; 182.

22. See decision at ARD 1956–7: 16ff.

23. For more details about the problem, see ILO, 'Report of the Director General', for the 74th (Maritime) Session 1987 of the International Labour Conference (1987), and ILO Report III parts 1 and 2 for the same session on 'Social security protection for seafarers including those serving in ships flying flags other than those of their own country' (1987).

24. ILO, 'The ILO and Human Rights' (1968): p. 36.

25. The Committee on Freedom of Association in 1987 had already examined 1,400 cases of allegations of infringements of trade union rights. See ILO, 'Freedom of Association' (1985): 17ff. The statement of the Director of ILO is to be found in ILO, 'Human rights – a common responsibility': 16.

26. DBC 1934: 1ff, especially 16–17.

27. ILO, 'Record of Proceedings' (1988): 7/11.

28. See the decision at ND 1981: 177ff.

29. ND 1981: 177ff.

30. See Jakhelln, 'Working conditions': 577ff.

References

Basic Agreement of 1986 (Hovedavtalen), published by Landsorganisasjonen i Norge (Norwegian Federation of Trade Unions (LO)) and Norsk Arbeidsgiverforening (Norwegian Employers' Federation (NAF)) (Oslo, 1986).

Davies, Paul and Freedland, Mark (1983) *Kahn-Freund's Labour and the Law*, Hamlyn Lectures Series (London: Stevens & Sons) 3rd edn.

Dommer og Kjennelser av Boikottsaker – 1934–1940 (1935–41) (Oslo: Grøndahl & Sønn).

ILO (1968) 'The ILO and Human Rights', Report of the Director General (Part 1) to the 52nd Session of the International Labour Conference (Geneva: ILO).

ILO (1970) 'Trade Union Rights and their Relation to Civil Liberties', ILO Conference, 54th Session, Report VII (Geneva: ILO).

ILO (1985) 'Freedom of Association: Digest of decisions and principles of the Freedom of Association Committee of the Governing Body of ILO' (Geneva: ILO) 3rd edn.

ILO (1987) 'Freedom of Association. A workers' education manual' (Geneva: ILO) 2nd revised edn.

ILO (1987) 'Report of the Director General', International Labour Conference, 74th (Maritime) Session 1987, Report I (Geneva: ILO).

ILO (1987) 'Social security protection for seafarers including those serving in ships flying flags other than those of their own country', International Labour Conference, 74th (Maritime) Session 1987, Reports (III) 1 and 2 (Geneva: ILO).

ILO (1988) 'Record of Proceedings', International Labour Conference, 74th (Maritime) Session 1987 (Geneva: ILO).

ILO (1988) 'Human rights – A common responsibility', International Labour Conference, 75th Session 1988, Report of the Director-General (Geneva: ILO).

IUF–UITA–IUL (1981) *The Coca-Cola–Guatemala Campaign 1979–1981* (Geneva: IUF) (mimeo).

Jakhelln, Henning (1985) 'Working conditions and social security on ships under "flags of convenience"', *Social and Secure* (Sociaas en Zeker) (Leiden Kluver–Deventer): 571–85.

Jakhelln, Henning (1986) 'Boikott av skip under bekvemmelighetsflagg. Noen spørsmål i brytningsfeltet mellom sjørett, erstatningsrett, arbeidsrett og organisasjonrett'. *MARIUS*, 123 (Oslo) (October).

Latin America Bureau (1987) *Soft Drink – Hard Labour. Guatemalan Workers Take on Coca-Cola* (London: Latin America Bureau (Research and Action)).

Ot. prp. nr. 71 (1933) 'Om forandringer i lov om arbeidstvister av 5 mai 1927' (Proposition from the Norwegian Ministry of Social Affairs to the Odelsting on amendments to the Labour Dispute Act of 5 May, 1927).

Ot. prp. nr. 73 (1947) 'Lov om endringer i lov om arbeidstvister av 5 mai 1927' (Proposition from the Norwegian Ministry of Social Affairs to the Odelsting on amendments to the Labour Dispute Act of 5 May, 1927).

Schmidt, Folke (1972) 'Ships Flying Flags of Convenience', *Arkiv for Sjørett (Journal of Maritime Law)*, 12: 77–96 (Oslo).

Slaughter, Jane (1984) 'Guatemala's Labor Movement. Coke Victory Spurs Recovery', *NACLA*, 18 (5) (September–October): 15–17.

Vargas, Inés (1988) 'Workers' Right to Organize, Trade Union Rights and their Relation with Civil and Political Human Rights', paper presented at the International Peace Research Association's General Conference (Rio de Janeiro) (August) (mimeo).

8 Alternative Policies for Dealing with International Communication

Jonathan F. Galloway

Nations of the world have become increasingly interdependent and one measure and cause of this interdependence is the communications revolution of the new information age. Beyond the interdependence of the governments and power structures of distinct nation states, we see the integration of world markets as what used to be national industries become global and what were national stock exchanges become world-wide. For instance, IBM's data management service links 270 cities in America with 60 in Europe and 10 in Japan. Nicholas Brady, head of the US Task Force investigating the October 19, 1987 Stock Market crash, points out, 'We have 300,000 screens around the world connected by electronics and technology ... and we're not talking about individual market places. We're talking about one market that those screens and electronics put together' (as quoted in Dougan, 1988). As Thomas and Brenda McPhail point out, 'Currently, the global telecommunications system links all the countries of the world, includes 600 million telephones, creates U.S. $250 billion in annual revenues, and annually stimulates U.S. $100 billion of investment' (McPhail and McPhail, 1987: 290).

In addition to computers and telephones, communications satellites are necessary to the information revolution in this new, not post-, industrial world society. Without international cooperative ventures such as INTELSAT and INMARSAT and coordination through the International Telecommunications Union (ITU) and the United Nations, the merger of the 'space age' and the 'information age' would be impossible.[1] The story of this cooperation and coordination has often been told (Leive, 1970; Galloway, 1972; Dizard, 1985; Codding and Rutkowski, 1982; and Soroos, 1986), but let us here summarize the background of the specific telecommunications topic which is the subject of this chapter – the use of the geostationary orbit (GSO) and frequency spectrum.

THE GSO ORBIT/SPECTRUM RESOURCE

Policy is made at the global level in allocating frequency bands and slots on the geostationary orbit. This global decision-making process is set up institutionally and legally within the framework of the ITU, a specialized agency of the UN but an agency which dates from 1865 is functional, and is not as politicized as the General Assembly of the United Nations or UNESCO. But politics is inevitable and below we will analyze the characteristics of the environment – e.g., scarcity – which lead to decision-making being politicized, as well as the forces which push towards consensus and cooperation – e.g., the desire to communicate and technological advances.

First, let us describe the physical characteristics of the GSO and the frequency space and the general characteristics of the legal regime which governs mankind's movement into outer space. The legal regime is related to this volume's theme of global policy studies because to a certain extent law is policy but, of course, this does not mean that there are not challenges to the law and different interpretations of agreed texts.

The GSO is 22,300 miles above the equator. Ideally, a satellite in this orbit moves at the same speed as the earth rotates around the polar axis (United Nations, 1980). Consequently, the satellite appears stationary from the earth and ground stations can fix their antennas on a fixed point in the sky rather than having to move across the horizon as is the case with satellites in low-earth orbit. Thus the GSO is the most economic orbit because it cuts antenna costs. In fact, three satellites, one over the Atlantic Ocean, one over the Pacific, and one over the Indian Ocean, can cover most of the globe. The idea for using this orbit in this way for communications was first broached by Arthur C. Clarke in 1945 (Clarke, 1984). He writes, 'All these problems can be solved by the use of a chain of space stations with an orbital period of 24 hours, which would require them to be at a distance of 42,000 km from the centre of the Earth . . . Each station would broadcast programmes over about a third of the planet' (Clarke, 1984: 57).

The elegance of Arthur Clarke's argument was robust and parsimonious. But the real world faces us with some deviations from the ideal. Because of the gravity of the moon and the sun and because the orbit is not perfectly circular (the earth is not perfectly round; but it is more round than flat!), station-keeping devices are required on each satellite in the GSO. Another problem is that GSO satellites experience solar eclipses twice a year around the spring and fall equinoxes. Further, GSO satellites do not have a service arc which enables them to see positions in high latitudes. Thus, communications to areas near the North and South Poles is best obtained by polar-orbiting satellites such as the Soviet Molniya system.

A further deviation from the ideal could not have been foreseen by Arthur Clarke in 1945. This is the crowding of space stations on orbital positions on the GSO. Crowding, or the perception thereof, presents the problem or image of future scarcity of orbital slots and can be graphically illustrated by the satellites using the low-frequency C-band as of July 1, 1985 (see Figure 8.1). As of December 31, 1988, the ITU list of such space stations numbered 534 (ITU, 1989: xii–xxii) (there can be more than one space station on a satellite). With current station-keeping accuracy of 0.1°, 1800 satellites could be spaced uniformly in the 360° of the geostationary arc without risk of collision but not all positions on the arc are equally desirable and, further, one must be aware of the space debris issue – i.e., the problem of satellites or parts of satellites which are no longer performing a useful service in orbit. In the GSO, it takes one million years for such debris to decay (Smith, 1984: 10–12). This is the context we shall return to when discussing global policy-making involving the GSO and the decisions of the World Administrative Radio Conferences held in 1985 and 1988.

THE FREQUENCY SPECTRUM

The frequency spectrum used for radio communications is found between kilohertz and gigahertz. Tables 8.1 and 8.2 below display where this spectrum is located on the total electromagnetic spectrum.

Within the radio spectrum certain space is most suitable for communications satellites and has been used by the early comers. The latecomers may want this space, too, or they may be able to use expansion bands. One important line of inquiry in this connection is the extent to which technological and engineering advances have overcome certain zero-sum game aspects of the allotment problem. If, indeed, they have, as this observer believes and many technical studies indicate, then we see an 'expanding pie', and opportunities for a virtuous rather than a vicious circle of global policy-making.

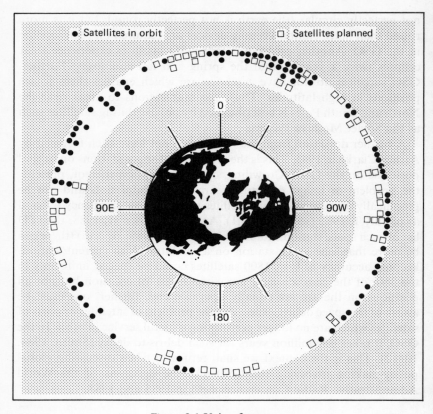

Figure 8.1 Vying for space

THE LEGAL REGIME

One very salient aspect of the global policy-making context for outer
space and the GSO is the legal regime. Since the 1967 Outer Space
Treaty,[2] outer space has been considered to be 'the province of all
mankind'. It is not subject to claims of national sovereignty (Art. 2).
Thus, claims concerning territorial boundaries and spheres of influence
(if not all power politics – consider the militarization of space, SDI,
Krasnoyarsk, ASAT, etc.) are removed as causes of conflict. There are
always rough edges to any such general assertions, however, and one
concerns the GSO.[3]

In 1976, the Equatorial countries claimed sovereignty over those

Table 8.1   Wavelengths of the electromagnetic spectrum

	Wavelength (cm)	Frequency (sec^{-1})	Photon energy (eV)
Cosmic ray photons	3×10^{-22}	10^{32}	4×10^{17}
	3×10^{-20}	10^{30}	4×10^{15}
	3×10^{-18}	10^{28}	4×10^{13}
	3×10^{-16}	10^{26}	4×10^{11}
	3×10^{-14}	10^{24}	4×10^{9}
	3×10^{-12}	10^{22}	4×10^{7}
Gamma rays	3×10^{-10}	10^{20}	4×10^{5}
X-rays	3×10^{-8}	10^{18}	4×10^{3}
Ultraviolet-visible light	3×10^{-6}	10^{16}	40
Infrared	3×10^{-4}	10^{14}	0.4
Microwaves	3×10^{-2}	10^{12}	4×10^{-3}
Radar	3	10^{10}	4×10^{-5}
UHF, VHF, FM, shortwave, AM	300		10^{8}
radio	3×10^{4}		
	10^{6}		4×10^{-7}
			4×10^{-9}
Longwave radio	3×10^{6}	10^{4}	4×10^{-11}
	3×10^{8}	10^{2}	4×10^{-13}

Source: *Encyclopaedia Britannica*, 6 (1982): 645.

portions of the GSO which were over their territories. This claim was made at a conference in Bogota, Colombia, hence the Bogota Declaration (Galloway, 1979). This claim is still in force but the question is moot because no other countries support it – no other DCs and no other LDCs. Further, it is not supported by scientific evidence as a claim by these countries that the orbit is connected to their territories by the law of gravity is in fact false. We can therefore view this question as interesting, even fascinating, but largely an exercise in symbolic politics, the symbolic politics of the New International Economic Order (NIEO) and the New World Information Order (NWIO).

WARC–ORB '85–'88

The ITU establishes World Administrative Radio Conferences (WARCs) to develop regulations for the radio spectrum. In the case of the GSO, the ITU is also concerned with orbital slots. Less developed

178

Table 8.2   Utilization of radio-frequency spectrum

Very low frequencies (vlf)	Time signals, standard frequencies
— 30 kHz	
Low frequencies (lf)	Fixed, maritime mobile, navigational, radio broadcasting
— 300 kHz	
Medium frequencies (mf)	Land, maritime mobile, radio broadcasting
— 3 MHz	
High frequencies (hf)	Fixed, mobile, maritime and aeronautical mobile, radio broadcasting, amateur
— 30 MHz	
Very high frequencies (vhf)	Fixed, mobile, maritime and aeronautical mobile, amateur, radio and television broadcasting, radio navigation
— 300 MHz	
Ultrahigh frequencies (uhf)	Fixed, mobile, maritime and aeronautical mobile, amateur, television broadcasting, radio location and navigation, meteorological, space communication
— 3 GHz	
Superhigh frequencies (shf)	Fixed, mobile, radio location and navigation, space and satellite communication
— 30 GHz	

Source: *Encyclopaedia Britannica*, 15 (1982): 425.

countries have viewed the frequency space and slots on the GSO as 'limited natural resources' in light of Art. 33 of the ITU Convention.[4] In previous articles I have argued that neither the frequency space nor the GSO are limited in the sense of being depletable natural resources. They are more like public goods provided not by governments or by international organizations but by nature. They cannot be used up (Galloway, 1987). Nevertheless, there can be 'crowding out' and 'noise' can exist. Thus, coordination is required.

The 1979 WARC in Geneva called for a WARC to guarantee equitable access to the GSO and the frequency bands allocated to space services. The first space WARC was held in 1985 and the second in 1988. The basic issue in these conferences was between an a priori planning approach favored by certain LDCs and the more flexible approach favored by the developed countries which favor market-based forces and see many problems being solved by technological innovations.

At the 1985 conference, it was decided that whatever shape planning might take, it would be limited to the Fixed-Satellite Service (FSS). Other services, such as Mobile, Meteorological, Earth Research, Space Research and Radionavigation Services, were so little used or had so small potential impact on the GSO that they did not require planning at that time (Doyle, 1987: 18).

The planning for FSS would guarantee each country at least one slot in a predetermined orbital arc. The plan would last at least ten years but in order to delete a government from its position the party would have to agree. As Stephen Doyle writes, 'This provision may prove to be very undesirable, because its effect is to give nations permanent rights to orbital claims' (Doyle, 1987: 16). On the other hand, LDCs argue that DCs with 10 per cent of the world's population have control of 90 per cent of the frequency spectrum (McPhail, 1987: 127). They think that first come, first served does not take into account scarcity and thus becomes inequitable over time. Freedom is a principle of equity for the powerful but is labeled 'technological imperialism' or 'free trade imperialism' by the weak. The weak see equity as equality, but this rigid equality is not efficient and thus limits growth for all over time. Isn't this inequitable and foolish? What is the solution? Is a synthesis possible?

Another aspect of the LDC concern is not based on scarcity, but cost. Latecomers will have to use higher frequency bands than the 6 gigahertz uplink and 4 gigahertz downlink C Band, which have been in use for the longest time and whose propagation characteristics are best for use by communications satellites. Why should not the poorer countries receive these most optimal conventional bands rather than 'expansion bands'? Under ITU regulations, there is protection of existing services. This makes sense in terms of efficiency, but over the long run does a level playing field result? One can see the basis for competing views and the worries about how the ITU, a functional and technical organization, is being politicized.

On the other hand the results of SPACE WARC '85 showed a return to consensus based on the imperative that if one wants to communicate at all one needs to cooperate or at least coordinate with others. The leader of the consensus was Indonesia, an LDC with its own domestic satellite system, Palapa. The consensus was based on 'a dual planning approach of an allotment plan and improved procedures' (Smith, 1985: 18). The details were left to be worked out in the 1988 conference which determined the regulatory regime for the GSO orbit/spectrum resource for the foreseeable future.

Even in the era of demands for a New World Information Order, less developed states with a majority at the ITU did not press for majority voting. Consensus was the hallmark of the process of global policy-making. The lesson is that it takes two or more to communicate (there are 166 member countries in the ITU) and, if you want to play the game, you have to recognize that it is not a zero-sum game. The game is being played 24 hours a day, 365 days a year on the basis of mutual coordination and adjustment.

The second session of the WARC meeting in Geneva in 1988 started off with the eleven planning principles agreed to in 1985 (Doyle, 1989: 15). These are:

1. guarantee of access and equitability
2. sharing with other services
3. reservation of resources
4. technical aspects of special geographic situations
5. consideration of existing systems
6. provisions for multi-administration systems
7. flexibility to accommodate unforeseen needs
8. planning solutions adopted to circumstances
9. efficiency in orbit and spectrum use
10. provisions for multiservice and multiband networks
11. administrative costs controlled.

It was agreed that a priori planning would occur only in the Fixed

Satellite Service (FSS) and in these frequencies – 4500–4800 MHz and 300 MHz to be selected in the band – 6425–7075 MHz and 10.70–10.95 GHz, 11.20–11.45 GHz and 12.75–13.25 GHz. Each country would also receive a predetermined arc on the GSO. Supplementing this fixed planning would be improved procedures for other frequency bands (Doyle, 1989: 16).

Between the WARC–ORB '85 and WARC–ORB '88, a great many computer studies were done in connection with establishing efficient plans in line with the eleven principles listed above. The use of the computer resulted in technical solutions to dividing the frequency space which make the perceived politicization of the ITU seem remote from everyday reality. As Stephen Doyle writes about the revision in the Radio Regulations, 'the technical nature of the language and the changes becomes so arcane that only the most dedicated electrical engineer specializing in radio/satellite system operation could be comfortable' (Doyle, 1989: 17).

An arc allotment plan was established as well. Each nation will get at least one orbital slot and 800 MHz of usable band width. There is also sufficient flexibility in the plan so as to allow multi-administration systems such as INTELSAT and INMARSAT to be served. The plan will last for 20 years, from March 16, 1990 to March 16, 2010. During this period, multilateral planning meetings will continue working to refine the revisions to the Radio Regulations. Initial perceptions of a growing scarcity before 1985 on the part of countries like India and Indonesia gave way to a more enlightened accommodation, recognizing that the zero-sum aspects of the problem were aggravated by images of national sovereignty in an increasingly interdependent and integrated world.

The major work of WARC–ORB '88 concerned the FSS, but the conference also adopted Feeder Links for the Broadcast Satellite Service (BSS) in ITU Regions 1 and 3. In addition, other matters were considered such as sound broadcasting and bands for high definition television (HDTV), but no decisions were reached.

The outcome of the WARC–ORB '85–'88 conferences gives us reasons for optimism – not pessimism – in looking at global policy issue arenas where there is a premium put on cooperation and coordination if any communication is to occur at all. With a world political economy which reflects not only interdependence between nations but integration among services and global industries, a priority is placed on mutual accommodation. A positive solution is made possible in this case by the following three major factors – the long history of ITU functional successes since 1865, including its support by the great powers and its universality of membership; the fact that, while there are problems with scarcity, the GSO and the electromagnetic spectrum are not non-renewable natural resources like oil that can be permanently endangered by conflicts of interest (it must be remembered that the perception of scarcity involves only one of the seventeen space services); and the highly technical nature of decision-making on the Radio Regulations which gives prominence to rational technical solutions and which deters symbolic politics and the high politics of balance of power confrontations.

WHICH ACTORS ARE COMPETING AND COOPERATING?

While there is consensus-building within the ITU, there is also competition. Who is competing for access to the GSO and the radio spectrum? On the one hand, it seems to be 166 nation-states. DCs want access based on laissez-faire and LDCs demand access based on authoritative planning. This is a dominant perspective. The game, though, is a non-zero-sum one and, as mentioned above, there is a push for solutions based on consensus because without agreement no one wins; everyone's voice is jammed.

Another perspective, equally valid, is that nation-states are not in conflict. Rather, particular commercial interests within and beyond state boundaries want frequencies and orbital arcs for their industrial segments. There are sixteen such services: aeronautical mobile satellite, amateur broadcasting satellite, earth exploration satellite, fixed satellite, maritime mobile satellite, inter-satellite, meteorological satellite, mobile satellite, radionavigation satellite, space operation, space research, standard frequency and time signal satellite, aeronautical radionavigation satellite, land mobile satellite, maritime radionavigation satellite and radiodetermination satellite. Interests within states can pressure their governments to fight for certain assignments, but interests can form worldwide associations and transnational subcultures to fight for allocation to services. Thus astronomers organize for frequency space for space research, maritime interests for maritime research, and so on. Before there can be allotments to countries and assignments within countries, there must be allocation to services. Further, international organizations such as INTELSAT and INMARSAT have observer status at the SPACE WARCs and are crucially interested in outcomes which will enable them to compete with other technologies such as fiber optics (Galloway, 1987). If one examines the ITU's list of 534 geostationary space stations for 1988, one sees that a great many LDCs have domestic satellites – e.g., Mexico, Brazil, India, Indonesia, Pakistan and Thailand, and that a great many LDCs as well as DCs are served by multi-administration systems – e.g., INTELSAT, INMARSAT, ARABSAT and EUTEL-SAT.

A very important point is that these organizations, which use so much of the GSO and frequency space so efficiently, contain both DCs and LDCs. INTELSAT has 114 members which are owners of the satellites in proportion to their use of the system. INMARSAT has 44 members. INTELSAT is a cost-sharing cooperative. The fees charged to each nation are means by which costs are apportioned according to relative use. INTELSAT is not an international venture based on seeking authoritative allocations by a priori planning and it is not wedded to undiluted free market principles (cf. Krasner, 1985). Rather it is a synthesis of both in the sense that ownership is related to a market-based principle of use but ownership gives privileges of access. And actually non-owners have equitable access to the system as well which serves more than 150 countries with 640 earth stations. There is no competition between LDC and DC members of INTELSAT on fulfilling its function to provide commercial telecommunications ser-vices to the world market.

A further point of note is that there is competition to INTELSAT and that INTELSAT and its competitors are becoming more competi-tive, which can lead to greater efficiencies in intersecting domestic, regional and world markets. INTELSAT provides not only global but domestic traffic capabilities through providing transponders to nations for domestic service. Other regional and global organizations are INTERSPUTNIK, EUTELSAT, ARABSAT, INMARSAT and ANIK. Even private organizations provide competition – e.g., PANAMSAT. But the question of private or public ownership is not as important as how these communications satellite organizations com-pete and cooperate in global market-places with themselves and with other technologies – most importantly, fiber optic cables. They com-pete in terms of providing the best price for the best service, but in the end they cooperate or coordinate in terms of consensus-building at the ITU WARCs *vis-à-vis* orbit slot arcs and frequency allocations.

CONCLUSIONS

One way of viewing global policy-making is that it is made by states in international bodies such as the United Nations. Another level of analysis would see the actors not as states (which have often failed in their responsibilities and, indeed in their policies individually and collectively, are causes of the problems individual citizens of these states face as world citizens – e.g., the arms race, pollution of the oceans, acid rain, depletion of the ozone layer, the greenhouse effect) but as grassroots groups and movements and even much-maligned MNCs, if they are operating in their enlightened self-interest rather than their bottom line selfish interests. Also, we should mention functional international organizations such as the ITU which may supersede and transcend private state interests in working towards consensus. The international civil servants in these organizations may act autonomously. In fact, they are obligated to do so by the ITU Convention which requires members of the International Frequency Registration Board to serve 'not as representing their respective countries, or a region, but as custodians of an inter-national public trust'. The framers foresaw that the public good of a state is often the private bad of the world community. For instance, defense, usually seen as a public or collective good from the point of view of a single nation, can be seen as a public bad from the point of view of mankind as a whole. To make positive global public policy requires, then, a new theory of public goods at the world level. It is in this context that the idea of 'international commons' have come into vogue and the concepts of the common heritage of mankind and the province of all mankind have entered space law.

There are three causes of world public goods and bads which global policy-making must address. One cause is nature itself. For instance, the GSO and the frequency space are provided by the laws of nature. Second, world public goods are provided by states acting rationally and collectively in their own common interest. Examples are in providing safeguards on civilian atomic energy through the IAEA and protecting species such as whales against extinction.

A third world public good is provided by private actors such as MNCs and national public actors. By competing in the market-place to sell services and products, the public good is provided through Adam Smith's invisible hand. World public bads can also be produced at all three levels. Nature can disrupt the radio frequency spectrum through solar activity. States acting collectively can produce public goods, but also produce bads as in the case of prohibiting the trade in cocaine and then driving up its price and unintentionally contributing to organized crime. Third, the market can produce negative externalities in terms of pollution.

A theory of actors must combine several disciplines in the natural sciences and the social sciences. Global policy-making must not be reduced to the collective acts of government officials. Non-government actors can influence world policy-making on their own and through capturing governments or parts of governments. Governments are not usually unified rational actors. The best theory to use to explain this at the level of the world political economy is a synthesis of Adam Smith and James Madison's thinking. Smith sees the necessity for a division of labor **between nations and between the factors of production** in order to produce wealth. This division of labor is encouraged by man's basic nature and the drive to 'truck, barter and exchange'. The production of wealth is encouraged if there is a large market. Logically, then, the greater the market – the more national domestic markets become world markets – the more we see the wealth not only of nations but of the world.

Madison, in *Federalist*, 10 (1787–8), sees the necessity for factions given human nature and the assumption of freedom. If we have many factions based on the unequal and diverse sources of property, then no one faction will dominate. This all takes place in a large commercial republic. If by the force of economic and political logic we extend this large commercial republic beyond one nation to a group of nations and then the world we will see the evolution of David Mitrany's functionalism (Mitrany, 1966). To a certain extent this has already occurred.

Policy-making to deal with the GSO frequency resource does take place with many factions or services represented by states, within states and beyond states. Multinational corporations often act as worldwide interest groups (Galloway, 1971) and thus are not represented best as home and host country ventures but as having a 'global reach' (Barnet and Muller, 1974) where 'sovereignty is at bay' (Vernon, 1971). Certainly sovereignty is at bay in the GSO and we see not only one world market but one planetary political–economic–technological market-place. The New Information Society may be a media lab (Brand, 1987) for transcending nationalism and giving birth to humankind.

Notes

1. Indeed, we may call our age the age of ages: the space age, the nuclear age, the computer age, etc.!
2. Officially entitled 'Treaty on Principles Governing the Activities of States in the Exploration and Use of Outer Space, Including the Moon and Other Celestial Bodies' (October 10, 1987). 18 U.S.T. 2410; T.I.A.S. 6347; 610 U.N.T.S. 205.
3. Two more are the identification of the exact spot where air space ends and outer space begins (air space is subject to national sovereignty) and the concept of the Common Heritage of Mankind (CHM) which is part of law insofar as the Moon Agreement is concerned. The Moon Agreement was opened for signature on December 18, 1979 and entered into force on July 11, 1984. Art. 11 provides that 'the moon and its natural resources are the common heritage of mankind'.
4. Art. 33, 131.2. states, 'In using frequency bands for space radio services, members shall bear in mind that radio frequencies and the geostationary satellite orbit are limited natural resources, that they must be used efficiently and economically so that countries or groups of countries may have equitable access to both in conformity with the provisions of the radio regulations according to their needs and the technical facilities at their disposal'.

References

Barnet, Richard J. and Muller, Ronald E. (1974)   *Global Reach: The Power of the Multinational Corporations* (New York: Simon & Schuster).

Brand, Stewart (1987)   *The Media Lab: Inventing the Future at MIT* (New York: Viking).

Clarke, Arthur C. (1984)   'The Space Station: Its Radio Applications' (May 1945); reprinted in *Ascent to Orbit: A Scientific Autobiography The Technical Writings of Arthur C. Clarke* (New York: John Wiley & Sons): 57–8.

Codding, George and Rutkowski, A. M. (1982)   *The ITU in a Changing World* (Dedham: Artech).

Demac, Donna A. (ed.) (1986)   *Tracing New Orbits: Cooperation & Competition in Global Satellite Development* (New York: Columbia University Press).

Dizard, Wilson P., Jr (1985)   *The Coming Information Age: An Overview of Technology, Economics and Politics* (New York: Longman) 2nd edn.

Doyle, Stephen E. (1987)   'Regulating the Geostationary Orbit: ITU's WARC–ORB '85–'88', *Journal of Space Law*, 15 (1): 1–23.

Doyle, Stephen E. (1989)   'Space Law and the Geostationary Orbit: The ITU's WARC–ORB '85–'88 Concluded', *Journal of Space Law*, 17 (1): 13–21.

Dougan, Diana Lady (1988)   'New Telecommunications Services: Let's Not Stack the Deck Against Them', United States Department of State Bureau of Public Affairs, speech of February 3.

Galloway, Jonathan F. (1971)   'Multinational Enterprises as Worldwide Interest Groups', *Politics & Society*, 2 (1) (November): 1–20.

Galloway, Jonathan F. (1972) *The Politics and Technology of Satellite Communications* (Lexington, Mass.: Lexington Books).

Galloway, Jonathan F. (1979) 'The Current Status of the Controversy over the Geostationary Orbit', *Proceedings of the Twenty-First Colloquium on the Law of Outer Space*, Mortimer D. Schwartz (ed.) (Littleton: Fred B. Rothman & Co.): 22–7.

Galloway, Jonathan F. (1987) 'INTELSAT's Markets and the New Competitors', *International Journal*, XLII (2) (Spring): 256–75.

International Telecommunication Union (ITU) (1989) 'Twenty-Eighth Report by the International Telecommunication Union on Telecommunication and the Peaceful Uses of Outer Space', booklet 37 (Geneva: ITU).

Krasner, Stephen F. (1985) *Structural Conflict: The Third World Against Global Liberalism* (Berkeley: University of California Press).

Leive, David M. (1970) *International Telecommunications and International Law: The Regulation of the Radio Spectrum* (Dobbs Ferry: Oceana).

McPhail, Thomas L. (1987) *Electronic Colonialism: The Future of International Broadcasting and Communication* (Newbury Park: Sage) revised 2nd edn.

McPhail, Thomas L. and Brenda McPhail (1987) 'The International Politics of Telecommunications: Resolving the North–South Dilemma', *International Journal*, XLII (2) (Spring): 289–319.

Mitrany, David (1966) *A Working Peace System* (Chicago: Quadrangle Books).

Smith, Milton L. (1984) *SPACE WARC 1985 – Legal Issues and Implications* (Montreal: Institute of Air and Space Law thesis, McGill University).

Smith, Milton L. (1985) 'Space WARC 1985 – Round One Ends', *The Air and Space Lawyer*, 2 (4) (Summer/Fall): 1; 16–18.

Soroos, Marvin S. (1986) *Beyond Sovereignty: The Challenge of Global Policy* (Columbia: University of South Carolina Press) Chapter 10.

United Nations, Outer Space Affairs Division (1980) 'On The Efficient Use of the Geostationary Satellite Orbit', (Paris) (October).

Vernon, Raymond (1971) *Sovereignty at Bay: The Multinational Spread of U.S. Enterprises* (New York: Basic Books).

9 The Atmosphere as an International Common Property Resource

Marvin S. Soroos

INTRODUCTION

The atmosphere is a thin, transparent layer of air enveloping the Earth, which sets it apart from other planets that are inhospitable to all forms of life. Not only is the atmosphere the source of oxygen, nitrogen, and other elements that are critical to the existence of the millions of species of plants and animals, but it also moderates the climate to which they have adapted and filters intense forms of solar radiation that would be destructive to life.

Mankind has used the atmosphere as a convenient medium for disposing of huge quantities of gaseous and particulate wastes, especially since the advent of the industrial revolution two centuries ago. These polluting activities have taken a heavy toll on the environment, but until recently the impact was usually localized around urban areas and industries or smelters that were major emitters or toxic pollutants. In recent years, however, scientific evidence has been mounting that pollution emissions and other human practices, such as large-scale forest clearing and land cultivation, are not only contaminating the atmosphere, but are also bringing about significant changes in the way it functions that could have substantial consequences for the earth's inhabitants. Man has also been developing impressive techniques for intentionally modifying weather conditions toward both peaceful and hostile ends.[1]

This chapter looks at human-induced changes to the atmosphere as a global policy problem. Even though it is an unconventional resource, the atmosphere has the attributes of a 'global common property resource', as do the oceans, the seabed, outer space, and the electromagnetic spectrum, and thus has been subject to a pattern of overuse and misuse portrayed by Garrett Hardin (1968) in his famous essay on 'the tragedy of the commons'.[2] Rather than surveying all anthropogenic influences on the atmosphere, the focus here is on three major phenomena that have recently alarmed scientists and policy-makers: first, acid deposition associated with transboundary air pollution; second, warming of the lower atmosphere due to what is known as the 'greenhouse effect'; and, third, the depletion of the stratospheric ozone layer. Some of the issues that arise in addressing these problems are pertinent to other human impacts on the atmosphere, including the widespread dispersal of radioactive pollutants from nuclear accidents, such as the Chernobyl disaster. They are also applicable to efforts to modify weather intentionally, such as to increase precipitation, prevent hail, or reduce the intensity of hurricanes, which could have impacts far beyond the targeted geographical area.

The second part of the chapter looks at the challenge of limiting further damage to the atmosphere. A growing number of international institutions have a concern with at least one of the major threats to the atmosphere. They, along with national governments and non-governmental organizations, have undertaken ambitious scientific programs to increase the base of knowledge on these problems by monitoring changes in the atmosphere and investigating the complex causes of them. Ultimately, however, **international policies** are needed that will manage the human impact on the atmosphere which are adaptable to common property resources. Several principles of international customary law have some applicability to the problem, especially those dealing with the responsibilities states have for activities under their jurisdiction that can damage the environment of other states. Nevertheless, it has been necessary to negotiate treaties that address the atmospheric problems more directly by setting forth rules on the emission of pollutants that apply to states. Finally, consideration is given to several economic and political factors that complicate the task of reaching an international consensus on measures that will effectively ameliorate the human impact on the atmosphere.

THE PROBLEM OF ACID DEPOSITION

Of the three major threats to the global atmosphere, acid deposition has had the most immediate and readily observable consequences. Acid deposition is a more appropriate term for what is commonly known as 'acid rain' because the acidic moisture may reach the ground as rain, snow, mist, fog, frost, or dew. These forms of acid precipitation occur when oxides of sulphur or oxygen are emitted into the atmosphere where they undergo a chemical transformation in the presence of sunlight and water droplets to form dilute solutions of sulphuric and nitric acid that precipitate to the earth. Acid forming pollutants may also gravitate to the ground in a dry form where they combine with surface moisture.[3]

While sulphur and nitrogen oxides enter the atmosphere from natural sources such as volcanos, human activities account for 90 per cent of the quantity of these substances in the air of the industrialized regions of the Northern Hemisphere (Barnaby, 1988: 160). Sulphur oxides have been the predominant factor in acid precipitation since the early twentieth century, but from 1960 the proportion attributable to nitrogen oxides has been increasing rapidly (WRI/IIED, 1986: 169). The principal anthropogenic source of sulphur oxide in the atmosphere is the burning of fossil fuels containing sulphur, especially in coal fired power-generating plants, smelters, and heavy industry. The same sources are responsible for over half of the emissions of nitrogen oxides, but another significant source is the internal combustion engines of motorized vehicles (ReVelle and ReVelle, 1988: 478).

Acid deposition is an important part of the problem of long-range transport of air pollution, known as LRTAP, which has arisen in industrialized regions with the advent of tall smokestacks designed to remedy localized pollution by dispersing contaminants over a larger area. Swedish soil scientist Svante Odén was among the first to call attention to the spread of acid rain in the European region. Using data from a network of atmospheric monitoring systems in Western Europe begun by Sweden in 1952, Oden by 1968 was able to demonstrate a link between the acid precipitation thought to be responsible for the decline of fish populations in lakes throughout Scandinavia and the emission of large amounts of sulphur dioxide and nitrogen oxides in the United Kingdom and Central Europe (see O'Sullivan, 1985: 14). Foreign sources currently account for approximately 90 per cent of sulphur pollutants in Norway and Switzerland, more than 80 per cent in Sweden and Austria, and more than 70 per cent in the Netherlands (cited in O'Sullivan, 1985: 18). Canada complains that the United States is responsible for at least half of the pollutants causing acid precipitation in its Eastern provinces (Lewis and Davis, 1986: 21).

Emissions of sulphur oxides in Europe rose by 50 per cent between 1955 and 1970, which were reflected in a 2.5 per cent average annual increase in sulphate concentrations in precipitation recorded at a network of 120 sites around the region (WRI/IIED, 1986: 169). Since then, emissions and atmospheric concentrations of sulphur have leveled off and even declined in parts of the region and improvements in air quality have been noted, especially where stringent controls on atmospheric pollution have been imposed. Likewise, concentrations of atmospheric nitrate doubled through much of Europe between the late 1950s and the early 1970s. During the 1970s, emissions from stationary sources were stable, but those from vehicles continued to increase. In Northern and Western Europe, North America, and Japan, overall nitrogen oxide emissions have been stable to lower since 1979, with the sharpest reductions occurring where catalytic converters are required on automobiles (WRI/IIED, 1986: 165). Unfortunately, comparable long-term data on air pollution in North America is sparse by comparison to that for Europe. The only American site where records date back more than 20 years is Hubbard Brook, New Hampshire (WRI/IIED, 1986: 169).

Air pollutants originating in the heavily industrialized regions of the Soviet Union, Europe, and North America are transported thousands of kilometers to the north by seasonal wind currents where they form what is known as 'Arctic haze'. The haze, which is thickest in the late winter from Alaska to Scandinavia, was first monitored in the 1970s by atmospheric scientists who had come to the Alaskan Arctic to study the composition of what they mistakenly assumed would be pristine air (see Rahn, 1984; Heintzenberg, 1989). It is feared that acid deposition resulting from sulphates in the haze will have a particularly serious impact on the fragile fauna and flora of the Arctic (Søybe, 1989: 14).

Acidic precipitation is also being observed in industrialized regions of Third World countries, such as China, Brazil, Nigeria, and South Africa, but the consequences have generally been confined to areas near the sources of pollution and thus has not yet been a significant transboundary phenomenon. China is of particular concern, having passed the Soviet Union as the world's largest producer of coal, much of which is high in sulphur content. Precipitation in some regions of China has had an acid content that is as high as that recorded in the eastern United States, which has taken a heavy toll on Chinese forests especially in the southern provinces of Sichuan and Guizhow (Zhao and Sun, 1986: 3; Li, 1987: 7). China's plans to draw upon its huge reserves to double coal consumption by the year 2000 along with rapidly increasing vehicular traffic portends even more severe damage unless substantial investments are made in emission control (Brown and Flavin, 1988: 12).

Acid deposition has many apparent consequences, some of which are still not adequately understood. Throughout Europe and in other industrialized regions, acid precipitation is causing noticeable damage to stone statues, monuments, and structures, including artifacts of earlier civilizations. It is also corroding metal surfaces, such as steel in railroad tracks and bridges. Pipes that carry acidic water are also subject to corrosion, exposing human population to lead and other toxic metals. Along with ozone, acid precipitation has been found to damage or retard the growth of agricultural crops. When absorbed by the soil, it leaches nutrients and unlocks chemical bonds releasing minerals that are toxic to plants (see McCormick, 1985). But it is the apparent link between acid deposition and the disappearance of aquatic life and the devastation of forests over large areas of North America and Europe that has provoked the greatest concern.

The impact of acid rain on lakes is most pronounced where the bedrock is comprised of igneous or metamorphic rock as opposed to sedimentary rock that dissolves in water runoff, thus injecting minerals into lakes that neutralize acids. The most widespread damage to aquatic life in fresh-water lakes has taken place in eastern North America and Scandinavia. Canadian officials complain that 14,000 lakes in eastern Canada are acid dead as are 13 salmon-bearing rivers in Nova Scotia (Frances, 1987: 11). In Sweden 15,000 lakes have been severely acidified by air pollution, including 1,800 which are virtually lifeless (see McCormick, 1985). Recently, it has been confirmed that acid precipitation is also a primary factor in the death of marine life along the east coast of the United States (Shabecoff, 1988: 1; 9).

Damage to forests, or what is known as *waldsterben* – the German term for 'forest death', has recently become the most ominous environmental consequence of acid precipitation. The first signs of forest damage were observed on Western German white fir in the early 1970s. At the time, these signs were not considered extraordinary because isolated episodes of forest decline attributable to droughts, insects, and other natural causes had been observed in Europe for 250 years. By the end of the 1970s foresters realized that they were confronted with a broader and more complicated problem when an unfamiliar pattern of symptoms of forest death was observed in stands of Norway spruce and Scotch pine and eventually spread to eleven major species of conifers and broad-leafed species. Forest death has also occurred over large areas of North America, but the symptoms differ from those observed in Europe and only conifers have been seriously affected thus far (see WRI/IIED, 1986: 203–26).

The forest-death phenomenon spread dramatically during the early 1980s. Only 8 per cent of West German forests were affected in 1982, but the figure shot up to 34 per cent in 1983 and to 50 per cent in 1984 (Hinrichsen, 1986: 23). One-fifth of the forests in 19 European countries were affected by 1986, with the Netherlands, Switzerland, and West Germany reporting damage to more than 50 per cent of their forests (see Brown and Flavin, 1988: 14–15). Recent figures indicate the forest death problem in West Germany is leveling off, but it continues to spread in most of Europe (see WRI/IIED, 1987: 156).

The causes of *waldsterben* is still a puzzle to scientists, who have been sorting through the effects of scores of potential contributing factors. It is apparent that it is not the result of a single cause, such as acid precipitation, but an entire syndrome of interacting factors. Furthermore, forest death seems to be caused by a different set of factors in Europe than in North America. High levels of acid deposition are present in all afflicted regions. Damage is generally greatest at higher elevations that are frequently shrouded in fogs that have a high acid content. Other pollutants such as ozone also appear to adversely affect forests (ReVelle and ReVelle, 1988: 500–1). The problem of isolating the impact of pollutants is complicated by the tendency for dying trees in afflicted areas to succumb to natural secondary stress factors, such as insects, fungi, or severe climatic conditions – drought, wind, or cold – which healthy trees could be expected to ward off (WRI/IIED, 1986: 208).

THE PROBLEM OF GLOBAL CLIMATE CHANGE

The atmosphere is a major determinant of weather and climate both because it converts short-wave solar energy into longer, infrared waves that warm the surface air, but also because it functions like a greenhouse in retarding the radiation of heat from the earth. This heat would otherwise be lost to outer space and night-time temperatures would plunge dramatically. Paradoxically, oxygen and nitrogen, which together comprise 98 per cent of the atmospheric gases, absorb very little solar radiation. Rather it is carbon dioxide, which naturally comprises only 0.03 per cent of air, along with traces of several other 'greenhouse' gases, that account for most of the warming of the lower atmosphere (Wagner, 1978: 5–6). Abnormally cold periods such as the ice ages have been attributed to naturally occurring reductions of these greenhouse gases.

The heat absorbing qualities of atmospheric carbon dioxide were initially detected in 1896 by Swedish scientist Svante Arrhenius, who went on to calculate the impact a doubling of carbon dioxide would have on surface air temperatures (Kellogg, 1987: 115). Systematic data on atmospheric carbon dioxide dates back only to the late 1950s, when scientists began taking regular readings at Mauna Loa Observatory in Hawaii and at the South Pole in conjunction with the International Geophysical Year. Global networks of atmospheric and weather reporting stations on land and sea along with orbiting satellites now provide much more comprehensive data on current concentrations of greenhouse gases in the atmosphere and global climatic conditions. Long-term historical trends in the concentration of atmospheric gases have been plotted by sampling air locked in glacial ice.

There is now conclusive evidence that atmospheric concentrations of carbon dioxide (CO_2) have risen substantially over the past two centuries. CO_2 levels were in the range of 250–275 parts per million (ppm) prior to the industrial revolution (Kellogg, 1987: 119). Levels of CO_2 recorded at Mauna Loa reached 315 ppm by 1958 and 349 by 1985, an increase over pre-industrial levels of more than 25 per cent (WRI/IIED, 1986: 174–5). This increase can be attributed in large part to a ten-fold increase in the consumption of energy during the twentieth century, most of which was produced by burning fossil fuels in the industrialized countries (Koomanoff, 1985: v–vi). The large-scale cutting and burning of forests, especially in tropical regions, is also believed to be a major factor in the rising CO_2 content of the atmosphere.

Increasing attention has been given lately to the impact that other greenhouse gases, such as nitrogen oxide, ozone, and CFCs, may have on climate. Of particular concern is methane, which is released where bacteria decomposes plant material, as in the rumens of sheep and cattle. Atmospheric concentrations of methane have been growing an average of 1 per cent a year over the past decade (Blake and Rowland, 1988: 1129). If this increase continues, the impact of these other greenhouse gases on the global climate may be as much as that of CO_2 by the early twenty-first century. By 2030 the combined impact of the greenhouse gases may be the equivalent of a doubling of pre-industrial levels of CO_2 (WRI/IIED, 1986: 174).

It is more difficult to gauge the effect of increased atmospheric concentrations of greenhouse gases on climate because of naturally occurring variations in the weather. Moreover, the warming of the atmosphere may be delayed for a decade or more by the heat absorbing capacity of the oceans as well as of the land and its vegetation. The warming that has taken place since 1850 is believed to be on the order of 1° centigrade. It has also been observed that the five warmest years globally have occurred during the past decade (Hansen, 1989: 36). The doubling of greenhouse gases projected for 2030 is forecast to cause a rise in average surface temperatures in the range from 1.5 to 4.5° centigrade, a change that could be sudden rather than gradual (UNEP/WMO/ICSU, 1986: 2; Broecker, 1987: 123). By comparison, natural fluctuations are believed to have been no more than 1 or 2° celcius over the past 10,000 years (UNEP, undated: 5).

Predictions of a potentially broad range of the consequences of global warming are more tentative. While agriculture operations in some northern areas such as Scandinavia may benefit from a longer growing season (Ashuvud, 1986: 2), it is feared that hotter and drier conditions would dramatically reduce production in many of the key food-growing regions of the world, such as the North American grain belt, the Soviet Ukraine, and north China. A 1.5 to 4.5° centigrade increase in temperatures could cause sea levels to rise by 20 to 140 cm due to thermal expansion and a more rapid melting of glacial ice in the polar regions and mid-latitude mountain ranges. A rise of 1 meter or more would inundate low-lying areas where many major cities are located, destroy coastal marshes, erode shorelines, and increase the salinity of rivers, bays, and aquifers. A rise of only 50 cm would displace 16 per cent of Egypt's population (WRI/IIED, 1988/89: 174). Changing temperatures and rainfall would also have a major destructive impact on vegetation that has adapted to specific climate and soil conditions.

THE OZONE DEPLETION PROBLEM

While the greenhouse effect is a phenomenon confined primarily to the troposphere, the lowest level of the atmosphere that extends to an altitude of six miles, the problem of ozone depletion is taking place in the next level, the stratosphere, which extends upward to 30 miles above the earth's surface. In this zone a thin, fragile concentration of naturally occurring ozone, amounting to just a few parts per million of the atmosphere, absorbs 99 per cent of the incoming ultraviolet radiation from the sun. Two scientists reported in 1974 that families of industrially produced chemicals, in particular chlorofluorocarbons (CFCs), can be linked to a diminishing of the stratospheric ozone layer (Molina and Rowland, 1974). CFCs, which also contribute to the greenhouse effect, are highly stable molecules that drift slowly upward to the stratosphere where intense solar radiation breaks down their tight chemical bonds, releasing highly active chlorine atoms that destroy ozone molecules by gobbling up one of their three oxygen atoms.

CFCs were first produced in 1928 and since then have become a major industry. Under the better known trade name Freon, CFCs have been used extensively as coolants in refrigeration and air conditioning systems. They have also been used as the propellant in aerosol sprays, although this type of use has declined substantially after being banned in the United States in 1978, which then accounted for nearly one-third of aerosol use, as well as in Canada and Scandinavia (Crawford, 1986: 927). Other applications include rigid foam packaging, flexible foam for furniture and automobile seats, dry-cleaning fluids, insulation, and solvents in the electronic industry. Halogens, which have also been linked to ozone depletion, are used widely in fire extinguishers. These substances are preferred for these uses because of their chemical stability, efficiency, low toxicity, and low cost of production.

Initial projections of a sizeable loss of ozone made during the late 1970s were revised downward in the early 1980s to the point of being almost inconsequential. The resulting sense of relief soon ended when it was reported that ozone levels had been dropping dramatically over Antarctica during the spring season, leaving what has become known as an 'ozone hole'. Low concentrations of ozone were first detected in this region more than two decades ago by the British Antarctic Survey. The phenomenon was initially attributed to the unique meteorological conditions of the region until the mid-1980s when October readings from British land stations as well as from the American Nimbus 7 satellite indicated a precipitous drop in annual ozone readings. By 1985 ozone concentrations were 40 per cent below the average from 1957 to 1973, with most of the drop taking place since 1979. Furthermore, scientific evidence is now quite conclusive that CFCs were largely responsible for the decline (Rowland, 1987: 54–6; Brasseur, 1987: 40). There is also now evidence of a similar ozone hole in the Arctic region (Kerr, 1988b: 1144–5).

Alarm over the Antarctic ozone hole prompted the United States National Aeronautics and Space Administration (NASA) in collaboration with other national and international agencies to create the Ozone Trends Panel for a stepped up monitoring of the ozone levels. A report released in March 1988 indicated that ozone concentrations over the Antarctic region in 1987 had dropped to 50 per cent of original levels and that the hole was persisting later into the year. It was also reported that ozone concentrations were dropping elsewhere, but inversely with distance from the poles. At the latitudes between New Orleans to Fairbanks, Alaska, the reduction ranged from 1.7 to 3.0 per cent from 1969 to 1986.[4] Surprisingly, the reduction in ozone concentrations over Antarctica was only 15 per cent in 1988, but in 1989 the ozone hole matched the record reduction recorded for 1987 (Cowen, 1989: 7).

The consequences of a continuing depletion of stratospheric ozone cannot be predicted with any degree of precision. Many species of plant and animal life may be damaged, if not killed off by the higher doses of ultraviolet radiation that would reach the biosphere. Aquatic species at the larvae stage may be especially vulnerable. It has been estimated that the increased radiation resulting from each 1 per cent reduction in the ozone layer may lead to a 10 per cent increase in human skin cancers (Kerr, 1988a: 1491).

THE INSTITUTIONAL NETWORK

In Hardin's mythical village (see n. 2), a town council may be needed to formulate and implement a strategy for preventing overgrazing of the common pasture. In the case of the planet's atmosphere, the corresponding governing structures are a complex array of international governmental organizations (IGOs). Unlike a town council or a national government, however, most IGOs lack the authority to impose rules, but must induce the willing cooperation of sovereign states. Some IGOs address environmental problems exclusively; others as part of a wider mission. Some have a global, or universal, membership, others are limited in some way, most frequently to the states of a region. Possessing few financial resources of their own, international agencies commonly coordinate their activities with other IGOs and international non-governmental organizations (INGOs), as well as national governmental bodies and private associations.

Several specialized agencies of the United Nations system have missions related to the condition of the atmosphere. The three most centrally involved are the World Meteorological Organization (WMO), the United Nations Educational, Scientific and Cultural Organization (UNESCO), and the United Nations Environment Programme (UNEP). WMO's primary function is to facilitate not only weather forecasting by providing current information on weather worldwide, but also to sponsor research on the causes of weather and long-term climate change. WMO has its origin in the International Meteorological Congress of 1853, which agreed to standardize reporting of weather conditions from sea-based stations. Coordination of weather reporting continued under the International Meteorology Organization, which was established in 1873. The organization was reconstituted and given its current name in 1951 (Davies, 1972: 327; Cain, 1983: 80). Founded in 1946, UNESCO's principal role in regard to the atmosphere has been to facilitate scientific research by linking scientific organizations throughout the world which have relevant expertise and by promoting major cooperative projects among them. The Inter-Governmental Oceanographic Commission (IOC) was established as off-shoot of UNESCO in 1960 to advance research on oceans, including their impact on the atmosphere.

Since its establishment in 1972 following the United Nations Conference on the Human Environment in Stockholm, UNEP has coordinated the diverse environmental initiatives of the other specialized agencies and promoted a holistic perspective on the global environment. Over the past decade UNEP's Coordinating Committee on the Ozone Layer (CCOL) has produced a series of reports on the condition of the ozone shield. UNEP has not limited its role to investigating problems, but has also sponsored international negotiations on regulations that will limit further degradation of the environment. The Nairobi-based agency has been especially successful in stimulating national governments to institute environmental programs. It also enters into a number of joint projects with both IGOs and INGOs. UNEP has worked with the World Health Organization (WHO) on the impact that higher dosages of ultraviolet radiation would have on rates of skin cancer and the International Civil Aviation Organization (ICAO) on the threat to the ozone layer posed by pollutants from aircraft, especially supersonic types. UNEP has a joint project with WMO and the Food and Agricultural Organization (FAO) on the ramifications that a global warming trend may have for agriculture throughout the world.[5]

The more limited geographical ranges of the problem of acidic deposition and other forms of transboundary air pollutants have prompted regional responses, especially among the developed countries where the problem is most pronounced. During the 1970s the Organization for Economic Cooperation and Development (OECD), which is comprised of the Western industrialized countries (including Japan, Australia, and New Zealand), has sponsored research on the subject and adopted principles pertaining to transboundary pollution. The Final Act of the Conference on Security and Cooperation in Europe in

Helsinki in 1975 listed the environment as one of a number of potential subjects for cooperation between East and West. Thus, the United Nations Economic Commission for Europe (ECE), as the only available organization that encompasses both Eastern and Western Europe and North America as well, was chosen to become the principal arena for treaty negotiations on long-range, transboundary air pollution among the developed countries (Tollan, 1985: 616; see also Wetstone and Rosencranz, 1984). The Commission of the European Community (CEC) has also become increasingly active in the environmental realm. It has adopted standards on air quality and transboundary pollution that are binding on the membership of the Community (see Burchi, 1985). The Council of Mutual Economic Assistance (CMEA) plays a corresponding role in the Soviet bloc, but has not gone as far in addressing the problem of air pollution.

The International Council of Scientific Unions (ICSU) is the most notable of the many INGOs involved in global policy-making on the atmosphere. Established in 1931 to encourage international scientific activity for the benefit of mankind, ICSU is an umbrella organization comprised of scientific academies and research councils from 71 countries, as well as 20 international scientific unions (WRI/IIED, 1987: 178). ICSU has mobilized numerous scientific research efforts on the natural systems of the planet and is frequently called upon to provide expertise that informs global policies, and even to co-sponsor environmental projects along with UNEP and other specialized agencies. Much of the scientific exploration coordinated by the ICSU is undertaken by the interdisciplinary committees it has organized, such as the Scientific Committee on Problems of the Environment (SCOPE), which investigates the general impact of humans on the natural environment (Caldwell, 1984: 98). Other ICSU committees working on problems related to the atmosphere include the Scientific Committee on Ocean Research (SCOR), the Scientific Committee on Antarctic Research (SCAR), and the Committee on Climatic Change and the Ocean (CCCO). The International Institute of Applied Systems Analysis (IIASA), the International Federation of Institutes of Advanced Studies (IFIAS), the World Resources Institute (WRI), and the World Watch Institute are also prominent among the INGOs that either contribute scientific knowledge on atmosphere problems or disseminate information and mobilizing support for national and international policies that will address them.

Problems related to the atmosphere have also been taken up by many national organizations and agencies, including an unusually large number of federal agencies in the United States. The Environmental Protection Agency (EPA) is involved in research and policy-making on a wide range of environmental problems, including atmospheric pollutants. The Department of Energy (DOE), which has at times worked at cross-purposes with EPA, is especially concerned with the relationship between the production of energy and the problems of climate change and acid precipitation. The National Aeronautics and Space Administration (NASA), through its Earth Systems Science project, monitors the interactions of the atmosphere, oceans, and terrestrial systems using both satellites and ground stations. Likewise, the National Center for Atmospheric Research (NCAR) is even more exclusively charged with research on the atmosphere, as is the National Oceanic and Atmospheric Administration (NOAA). The National Science Foundation (NSF) has sought funding for an initiative on Global Ecosystems that will support research aimed at illuminating the relationships between earth systems. The Office of Science and Technology Policy (OSTP) has undertaken a review of the wide-ranging research taking place in the earth sciences (see Malone, 1986). Outside of governmental bureaucracy, the National Academy of Sciences has encouraged support for a concerted effort among scientists to learn about earth systems and the human impact on them.

EXPANDING THE BASE OF SCIENTIFIC KNOWLEDGE

Rational decisions on environmental policies presuppose reliable and pertinent information on the magnitude of human activities and the consequences that follow from them. The village council in Hardin's story (see n. 2) might make use of time-series data on the numbers of cattle that were grazed and the corresponding condition of the pasture, as it deliberates on how many cattle to allow on the commons. Weather records over the same period could be helpful in determining the degree to which the observed depletion of the grasses was caused by overgrazing as opposed to natural fluctuations in temperature and rainfall. Similarly, an effective international response to contemporary problems such as the greenhouse effect and ozone depletion requires knowledge of the complex dynamics of the atmosphere and interrelated systems, namely the oceans, biosphere, and glaciers and polar ice, as well as the impact of human activities on them.

Development of such a base of knowledge entails systematic monitoring of the condition of the atmosphere, oceans, and glaciers using standard procedures at locations throughout the world. The data collected can be entered into computer models that simulate natural systems, which can be used to forecast future conditions and to gain insights into causes and consequences of observed changes. These endeavors have been facilitated by new generations of large, high-speed computers and state-of-the-art telecommunication networks. Nevertheless, global monitoring is a formidable undertaking in view of the sheer size of the planet, much of which is uninhabited, and the difficulties encountered in arranging for precise, standardized observations from countries of primative scientific means. Even more challenging is the task of understanding the dynamic and highly complex interaction between the sun and the Earth's natural system, and the impact of a wide variety of human activities on them.

IGOs and INGOs, as well as national institutions, have done much to provide the scientific knowledge upon which global policy on the atmosphere can be based. The first major international initiative aimed at understanding the planet's natural systems was the eighteen-month International Geophysical Year (IGY) of 1957–8, which was sponsored jointly by the WMO and ICSU. The project was timed to coincide with a period of unusually strong solar activity and the first launchings of orbitting satellites by the Soviet Union and United States. Scientists from 66 nations participated in the effort, using the latest innovations in instrumentation to learn more about the properties of space, the weather, the oceans, and the frigid zones (see Atwood, 1959).

The ostensible success of the IGY encouraged further international scientific cooperation. The WMO, in partnership with the ICSU, initiated the World Weather Watch (WWW), which has grown into a worldwide network of reporting stations on land and sea that provides meteorological data daily to national weather services and other international atmospheric research programs (Davies, 1972: 329). WMO and the ICSU also collaborate on the Global Environmental Research Programme (GARP), instituted in 1967, which investigates large-scale patterns of air circulation and the effects of the oceans, as well as human activities, on the global climate (Caldwell, 1984: 94–5). The Background Air Pollution Monitoring Network (BAPMoN), another WMO program that was initiated in 1970 and is now jointly sponsored with UNEP, collects data on air pollutants at 'baseline' stations located in isolated regions in 95 countries where the air is less polluted than in urban regions (UNEP, 1987: 25).

UNEP has considerably expanded and coordinated the environmental monitoring efforts of IGOs, INGOs, and national governments through its Worldwatch Program. A principal component of this program is the Global Environmental Monitoring System (GEMS), which surveys trends on numerous variables pertaining to climate, transboundary pollution, terrestrial renewable national resources, and oceans, many of which have some bearing on the condition of the atmosphere. Thus far, as many as 142 nations and 30,000 scientists and technicians have participated in at least one GEMS activity (UNEP, 1987c: 25).

UNEP joined with WMO and ICSU in sponsoring the World Climate Program (WCP), an outgrowth of the International Climate Conference held in 1979. A major conference on the extent of global climate change as well as its causes and consequences was held in Villach, Austria, in 1985 (see UNEP/WMO/ICSU, 1986). The condition of the oceans is monitored by the Integrated Global Ocean Station System (IGOSS), a cooperative venture of WMO and UNESCO's IOC, using automated buoys that collect and transmit information useful for studying the relationship between the oceans and the atmosphere (Caldwell, 1984: 241). In 1988, UNEP and WMO jointly established the Intergovernmental Panel on Climate Change (IPCC), which is seeking to draw together the knowledge of more than 1,000 experts from 60 countries to inform international efforts to address the global warming problem.

Mounting concern about the effects of human activities on the global environment prompted the ICSU, which in the 1950s had sponsored the IGY, to launch another ambitious scientific effort called the International Geosphere–Biosphere Programme (IGBP) in 1986. Projected to be the biggest research project undertaken by organized science, IGBP would last for 10–20 years with the objective of accumulating knowledge on the total earth system, including the interactions between the atmosphere, hydrosphere, lithosphere, and ecosphere, as a way of understanding more fully the probable magnitude of human-induced changes over the next one hundred years (see Malone, 1986). A complementary effort among social scientists called the Human Dimensions of Global Change Programme (HDGCP) is being organized by the United Nations University (UNU), the International Social Science Council (ISSC), and the International Federation of Institutes of Advanced Study (IFIAS) (see Price, 1989).

THE ATMOSPHERE AS A COMMON PROPERTY RESOURCE

Global monitoring and simulation models of the atmosphere do nothing in and of themselves to ameliorate the problems elaborated upon in the first part of this chapter. International policy-makers must face the more formidable challenge of instituting a management scheme that reduces human activities that are altering the atmosphere. The options available to them are limited by physical attributes of the atmosphere, which conform to the three basic criteria of a 'common property resource' (see Wijkman, 1982: 511). First, the resource is subject to 'joint use', which implies that several users can not only derive benefits from it, but can also diminish its value to others. Second, it is not feasible to divide the resource into sections that could be assigned to individual users. Third, it is not practical to exclude unauthorized users from the resource (Oakerson, 1986: 15–17).

The atmosphere is subject to joint use in that emissions of multiple polluters can be absorbed up to a point, beyond which the cumulative effects begin seriously to disrupt planetary ecosystems. Furthermore, while what is known as 'air space' has, in a legal sense, been divided into sections that coincide with the boundaries of the states that can potentially develop the capacity to ward off encroachers, the gases that comprise air itself are continually circulating and intermingling and thus cannot be contained within boundaries. Finally, short of military occupation, it is not possible for states physically to prevent actors in other sovereign states from emitting wastes into the atmosphere that will drift across international borders or to undertake landuse projects that will have an impact on regional or global climatic patterns.

Several legal principles pertaining to ownership and user privileges have been applied to domains or resources that are beyond the territorial jurisdictions of states, such as the oceans and seabed, Antarctica and other uninhabited territories, the atmosphere, and outer space. The status of *res nullius* presumes that such a domain is not owned presently, but that all or part of it is subject to exclusive claims by states that will make use of it. *Res communis* also presumes a domain is currently unowned, but prohibits the staking of any exclusive claims in the future. All states are permitted to make use of the commons to the extent that they do not unduly interfere with the legitimate activities of others. A third alternative, *res publica* vests ownership with the community of states as a whole, which is entitled to establish rules regarding use of the domain by states or even to authorize use by a community enterprise. In the case of the oceans, the principle of the 'freedom of the seas' incorporates the assumptions of *res communis*, while the contending 'common heritage of man' and the establishment of an international public enterprise for mining the deep seabed are applications of *res publica* (see Christy and Scott, 1965: 6–7). As with most international common property resources, the atmosphere has traditionally been governed by the *res communis* doctrine and states accordingly have taken for granted the right to use it as a sink for their pollutants.

While being more suitable for common property resources, the *res communis* arrangement is susceptible to the overuse and even permanent destruction of a resource, for the reasons that the pasture in Hardin's village is overgrazed (see n. 2). In the case of the atmosphere, the 'tragedy' results not from what is taken out of the resource domain, but what is put into it. Actors throughout the world have been permitted to use the atmosphere as a sink for pollutants rather than absorb the much higher costs of disposing of them in other ways. By their calculations, the immediate benefits from emitting pollutants into the atmosphere outweigh the harmful environmental consequences of these activities, which they will eventually share with the larger community. Likewise, forests have been cleared and grassland plowed up for immediate private or national gain with little concern for how these activities may accelerate global warming.

Several strategies are theoretical possibilities for preventing destructive overuse of a commonly used resource. In Hardin's analogy, a village council could retain the commons system, but set and enforce limits on the number of cattle the herdsmen could graze. Alternatively, the village council could discard the commons arrangement and divide the pasture into fenced plots assigned to individual herdsmen, who would then not only enjoy the profits but also absorb all of the environmental costs from overgrazing their portion of the pasture. Finally, the council could buy the cattle from the herdsmen and manage them as a community herd within environmental limits. The profits would be distributed to the villagers according to an agreed-upon formula (see Soroos, 1988).

The only viable approach for alleviating the disruptive impact of human activities on the atmosphere is for regional or global groupings of states to agree upon international regulations that limit or prohibit the activities that are causing the conditions of concern to scientists. The alternative of partitioning the resource into private sections assigned to states would be impractical in the case of the atmosphere because of the continual movement of air across national boundaries.

It would also not be feasible for an international institution to take control over all operations that pollute the atmosphere in view of the enormous number and diversity of polluting activities and the long-standing freedom that states have had to use the atmosphere at their whim.

APPLICABLE PRINCIPLES OF INTERNATIONAL CUSTOMARY LAW

Several of customary norms of state behavior, which is the traditional source of international law, are applicable to the problem of regulating human activities that affect the atmosphere. International customary law does not originate in a written document but in the **practice of a large number of states over a long period of time**. However, interpretations of it are found in the writings of legal authorities, decisions of international tribunals, resolutions adopted by international bodies, and attempts to codify them, most notably by the International Law Commission. International customary law is generally considered to be binding on all states.[6] This section briefly considers two sets of conflicting norms relevant to the problem of preserving the environment: first, the prerogatives of state sovereignty vs the responsibilities of states for damage beyond their borders and, second, the freedom to use common property and shared resources is the mandate of equitable sharing.

The doctrine of state sovereignty, one of the cornerstones of the international legal order, recognizes the state as the supreme decision-making authority and enforcer of rules within its territory. In its purist, laissez-faire interpretation, sovereignty would imply a right of a state to permit polluting activities on its territory without regard to consequences beyond its borders, such as the occurrence of acid precipitation. Similarly, a state would be within its rights to undertake large-scale clearing of tropical forests despite warnings about the impact such operations would have planet's CO_2 balance. While sovereignty has generally not been viewed in such an absolute way, states traditionally have acknowledged few restrictions on what they have permitted to take place within their borders even if significant damage to the environment is caused elsewhere (Springer, 1983: 130).

There has been a growing realization, however, that states must assume some responsibility for the external consequences of what takes place within their jurisdiction or control. Widely referred to as the principle of 'good neighborliness', this doctrine can be traced to the Roman law maxim of *sic utere tuo ut alienum non laedas* (use your own property so as not to injure that of another) (Schneider, 1979: 142). The applicability of this principle to transboundary air pollution is illustrated by the celebrated Trail Smelter arbitration (1941) in which the United States complained that fumes from a smelter in British Columbia damaged orchards across the border in the state of Washington. A special international tribunal ruled in favor of the United States on grounds that 'no state has the right to use or permit the use of its territory in such a manner as to cause injury by fumes in or to the territory of another or the properties or persons therein, when the case is of serious consequence or the injury is established by clear and convincing evidence' (International Court of Justice, 1949: 1905). Article 21 of the Declaration adopted at the Stockholm conference of 1972 is also frequently cited as an expression of the principle of good neighborliness.

States have in accordance with the Charter of the UN and the principles of international law, the sovereign right to exploit their own resources pursuant to their own environmental policies, and the responsibility to ensure that activities within their jurisdiction or control do not cause damage to the environment of other States or of areas beyond the limits of national jurisdiction (UN Conference on the Human Environment, 1972).

A state victimized by activities taking place in another state may invoke the principle of liability, arguing that harm to its territory perpetrated by foreign actors is an infringement upon its property rights. The responsible party may be called upon to pay compensation for the damages and, to the extent possible, to re-establish the conditions that would have existed had the incident not occurred. The Trail Smelter arbitration directed Canada to pay compensation to the United States for damages caused by the pollution originating in its territory. Likewise, the United States paid Japan $2 million in 1954 to compensate fishermen exposed to fallout from a nuclear test in the Pacific. Article 22 of the Stockholm Declaration of 1972 encourages states to 'cooperate to further develop the international law regarding liability and compensation for the victims of pollution and other environmental damage caused by activities beyond their jurisdiction' (UN Conference on the Human Environment, 1982). International thinking about the conditions under which liability can be claimed has been changing to the benefit of victims. The traditional presumption that liability must involve a wrongful behavior committed intentionally or out of negligence is giving way to the notion of **strict** liability, which does not assume these conditions, and even **absolute** liability, which does not even excuse a state for damage resulting from an 'act of God' in the case of operations that are inherently risky and could have catastrophic results (see Weis, 1978).

States are assuming a growing set of obligations to countries that might be adversely affected by projects that are being planned. They have a 'duty to inform' other states of danger or harm that may emanate from areas within their jurisdictions. Such information should be provided in a timely fashion with sufficient detail to allow the potential victims to minimize the resulting damage.[7] The Soviet Union's failure promptly to warn of the radiation hazard caused by the Chernobyl accident in 1986 is an apparent breach of this duty to inform, although in this case the threat was from an accident rather than a proposed project. The 'duty to consult' suggests that states should go a step further and allow states that may be harmed by a project to express their concerns about it. Recommendation 70 adopted at the 1972 Stockholm conference suggests that this 'duty to consult' applies to those whose activities may have an appreciable effect on the climate beyond their borders. Consultations may occasionally persuade a state to abort a potentially harmful activity, especially if the environmental consequences had not been fully anticipated or there is a desire to minimize political conflict with states that oppose it. A further step would be to require the 'prior approval' of potentially affected states. Aside from certain regional groupings, the community of states has been reluctant to recognize this more stringent requirement, which could become a major infringement of their sovereignty (Springer, 1983: 146–52).

International customary law also offers some guidance on the use of resources that are shared by a group of states, such as river systems, aquifers, or radiowaves, or of areas that are beyond the jurisdiction of states, such as the oceans, the seabed, and outer space. It could be argued that air is a shared resource like water in that it flows across national boundaries, or that it is like outer space in being an international commons. But here again, conflicting principles of customary law must be reconciled.

There is, on the one hand, a long-standing presumption that states have a right to make generally unrestricted use of shared or common resources. Under the 'freedom of the sea doctrine', a basic tenet of international ocean law for centuries, states were allowed to help themselves to the bounty of the living resources as well as dump their wastes with few if any limitations (see Anand, 1983). Similar freedoms applied to launching satellites into orbit in outer space and the use of airwaves for radio transmissions (see Soroos, 1982). Likewise, it has been generally assumed that states could make use of the atmosphere to dispose of gaseous or particulate wastes.

These freedoms can be tolerated as long as the shared resources or international commons were vast enough that users did not interfere with one another. As the demands on these resources intensified to the point that serious conflicts arise between users, it becomes necessary to adopt rules that impinge on the traditional freedoms they have exercised. In the case of river systems where downstream states have been at the mercy of those upstream, arrangements have been worked out in accordance with the principle of 'equity' or 'equitable shares' (see Goldie, 1985). Under this principle, down-wind states could similarly argue that the usefulness of an airshed is significantly compromised by the pollution emissions of up-wind countries (Van Lier, 1980: 114). Application of the equitable share principle is more complicated in the case of the atmosphere, however, because wind directions are variable whereas stream flows flow through down-channels.

The tenets of international customary law that have been cited in this section are more applicable to the problem of acid deposition than they are to conditions of global warming and ozone depletion. The acid-related damage to buildings and statues and more importantly to fresh-water lakes and forests can be readily observed, and to some extent quantified. Much is known about the sources of the pollutants and the chemical transformations that they undergo as they are transported by the atmosphere. Nevertheless, because pollutants from neighboring countries intermingle, it is difficult if not impossible conclusively to demonstrate that the pollutants from a specific country are responsible for specific damage in others. Moreover, the death of lakes and forests is a complex process that involves the interaction of many factors that are still not fully understood, making it all the more difficult to establish liability. Thus, the circumstances involving acid rain are not nearly as clear-cut as they were for the Trail Smelter arbitration. Climate change and depletion of the ozone layer are problems that are unlikely to have serious manifestations for decades, although several scientists attribute the hot, dry summer of 1988 in North America and elsewhere to the 'greenhouse effect'. Even if the consequences of these tendencies become more tangible, the link between these damages and pollution from specific countries will be even more tenuous than in the case of acidic precipitation.

Aside from these specific problems, it is unlikely that customary law will ever be an adequate basis for managing use of the atmosphere. The general nature of its principles are an advantage in that they can be applied flexibly to a wide range of situations, but their vagueness and lack of specificity also allows states to be evasive when it comes to taking the action that would be necessary to ameliorate the problems. Moreover, because it based on norms of behavior that have been observed over time, customary law tends to legitimize continuity of behavior, rather than being an instrument that can be used to mandate the rather abrupt changes in what is expected of states that may be needed to prevent substantial changes to the atmosphere.

THE ATMOSPHERE IN INTERNATIONAL TREATY LAW

In view of the limitations of customary law, more effort is being invested in negotiating treaties that spell out specific expectations of states that sign and ratify them. Nevertheless, international treaty law on the atmosphere is still at a primitive stage of development, especially compared to that which has been negotiated to protect the marine environment. Of 140 multilateral treaties that have been adopted to address international environmental problems, 36 focus primarily on pollution of the oceans or specific regional seas (UNEP, 1989). By contrast, only a few treaties address the condition of the atmosphere, and because they address narrowly defined problems, many of the human activities that are altering the global atmosphere and climate remain to be addressed.

Two treaties prohibit certain military uses of the atmosphere. The 1963 Treaty Banning Nuclear Weapon Tests in the Atmosphere, in Outer Space and Under Water, which had 117 parties by 1989, was a response to mounting scientific evidence that radioactive fallout from extensive atmospheric testing by a few nuclear weapons states posed a serious danger to human health. Since then, the United States, the Soviet Union, and the United Kingdom have conducted their testing underground. However, France and China refused to accept the treaty and continued to conduct atmospheric tests in the atmosphere. The French discontinued their atmospheric testing program in 1974 in the face of vigorous protests from the states near their South Pacific test site, as well as from more distant states such as Chile and Peru, which experienced sharp increases in radioactivity following test explosions. Australia and New Zealand brought the issue before the International Court of Justice, but the case became moot when the French announced an end to their atmospheric testing program. China has also ceased testing nuclear explosives in the atmosphere.

The impact of warfare on the environment became a divisive issue at the Stockholm Conference in 1972, when the host country sharply criticized the United States for committing 'ecocide' – the deliberate destruction or alteration of an environment as a military tactic – in fighting the Vietnam War. The Convention on the Prohibition of Military or Any Other Hostile Use of Environmental Modification Techniques was signed four years later and by 1989 had 50 ratifiers, including the United States and the Soviet Union. The convention prohibits the hostile use of a wide range of environmental modification techniques against other parties including those that would alter the atmosphere, such as cloud-seeding operations. Allegations of violations are to be directed to the Security Council if substantiated by a Consultative Committee of Experts. A significant limitation of the convention is its failure to address environmental damage that is merely an unintended side effect of a military operation, such as the 'nuclear winter' phenomenon that it is feared would result from an all-out nuclear war.[8] Nor does the convention address weather modification projects undertaken for expressly peaceful purposes.

Negotiations taking place in the United Nations Economic Commission for Europe (ECE) led in 1979 to the adoption of the Convention on Long-Range Transboundary Air Pollution, which called upon the parties 'to limit and as far as possible, gradually reduce and prevent air pollution', including that of long-range variety. The convention is essentially a declaration of general objectives and a call for international cooperation in monitoring pollution levels and devising strategies for reducing emissions. It obligates no abatement methods, nor does it mandate any specific reductions in emissions. Moreover, the convention is regional in scope, being limited to the membership of the ECE. The 28 parties to the convention do, however, account for two-thirds of the significant forms of anthropogenic atmospheric pollution (Sand, 1987: 28).

The alarming spread of the forest death syndrome in central Europe during the early 1980s prompted efforts to put teeth into the 1979 ECE convention. With West Germany – one of the states most resistant to a strong treaty just a few years previously – playing an instrumental role, a protocol was added in 1985 that obligates participating states to reduce total national emissions or transboundary fluxes of sulphur 30 per cent below their 1980 levels by 1993. The protocol was initially signed by 21 countries, which comprise what is known as the '30 per cent Club'. Noting scientific uncertainty, the United States, United Kingdom, and Poland have not yet accepted the protocol. Ten states were already in compliance with the protocol by 1986; five of which are committed to cutting sulphur emissions by 50 per cent of 1980 levels by the mid-1990s; four others have set an even higher goal of a two-thirds reduction. It has been more difficult to reach agreement on limiting emissions of nitrogen oxides. In 1988 a protocol on nitrogen oxides was added to the 1979 ECE convention, which provides that emission levels after 1994 should not exceed those of 1987 (see Ågren, 1989).

UNEP has been engineering a parallel response to the ozone depletion problem, but on a global scale. The Convention for the Protection of the Ozone Layer, adopted in Vienna in 1985, parallels the 1979 ECE convention in calling for an international research effort on the severity of the problem and its causes and for unspecified strategies for reducing ozone-attacking emissions (see Sand, 1985). Two years later, a stronger agreement was negotiated in Montreal in the face of compelling new evidence about the growth of the 'ozone hole' over Antarctica. The Montreal protocol would almost immediately freeze production of CFCs and halons at 1986 levels, followed by a reduction of 30 per cent by 1993 and an additional 20 per cent by 1998. Trade in CFCs or halons with non-party states is prohibited, but rules remain to be established on trade in products that contain or were produced with these substances. Less developed countries are given an additional ten years to comply in view of their development plans and much lower level of CFC production and consumption (UNEP, 1987a: 1–2). The Convention came into force on January 1, 1989, only fifteen months after adoption. The ratification vote in the United States Senate was 83–0.

These few treaties are only the first steps toward limiting or preventing further adverse changes to the atmosphere and climate. Thus far, the most significant progress has been made in setting goals for reductions of transboundary air pollution responsible for acidic pollution in the European region and the global emissions of CFCs and halons that are attacking the stratospheric ozone layer. Nevertheless, some environmental NGOs have been critical of these targets for not going far enough. Representatives of 22 European groups meeting in Lida, Sweden, in September 1987 called for a 90 per cent reduction in sulphur emissions in the region (Ågren, 1987: 16). Frustrated by what they perceived to be the weakness of the 1988 ECE protocol nitrous oxides, twelve European states issued a declaration calling for a 30 per cent reduction in emissions by 1998, using the level of any year from 1980 to 1986 as a base for calculations (Ågren, 1989). Finally, reacting to new scientific evidence regarding the ozone depletion problem, 81 countries and the ECE meeting in Helsinki in May 1989 unanimously adopted a declaration calling for a total phaseout of CFCs by the year 2000 and of other ozone depleting substances as soon as possible.

Negotiations on rules that would limit the emission of carbon dioxide and gases that contribute to global warming are to begin in late 1990 in conjunction with the issuing of a report by the IPCC and the convening of the Second World Climate Conference in Geneva in November. A 'framework' treaty is anticipated by 1992, with protocols limiting emissions of specific gases to be adopted later. It remains to be seen if other causes of climate change will be addressed, such as the destruction of forests and other land uses.

The conventions on transboundary air pollution and protection of the ozone layer are promising precedents for additional international regulations that will be needed. They are notable for establishing goals for a reduction of specified types of pollutants by a certain date, and thus are examples of **result-oriented**, as opposed to **conduct-oriented**, policies. The Montreal convention on the ozone layer is also significant for demonstrating a willingness of states to make economic sacrifices in response to less than conclusive warnings of scientists of a problem that as yet has few tangible manifestations. It is also encouraging that Du Pont Chemical Company, the world's leading producer of CFCs, has announced a phase out of its production of them by the year 2000 in favor of developing environmentally benign substitutes (Goldstein, 1988). Given the delayed impact of many atmospheric pollutants on the environment, it is important that additional steps such as these be taken to avert problems long before severe symptoms can be observed.

THE POLITICS OF MANAGING THE ATMOSPHERE

Sovereign states have had considerable difficulty in agreeing upon strategies for limiting the impact of their activities on the atmosphere. While across-the-board reductions have the virtues of simplicity and consistency of standards, questions of **equity** inevitably arise. For example, should states that have a historically low level of pollution emissions be expected to achieve the same percentage reduction as those that have been heavy polluters? Thus, despite being a heavy net importer of acid-forming, transboundary air pollutants, Norway resisted making a commitment to an international agreement specifying a 30 per cent reduction in nitrogen oxides in view of its almost complete reliance on hydroelectric power and consequently low level of NOx emissions (Dilworth, 1988). Less developed states, which have a history of low pollution emissions, may argue that 'it's now our turn to pollute' in order to industrialize and achieve a standard of living closer to those being enjoyed in the highly developed countries.

A second question of equity arises in regard to states that have previously taken steps to control emissions. Should they be expected to achieve the same future reductions as less environmentally responsible states that have yet to take any action to address the problem? In the negotiations on the protocol on NOx emissions, the United States argued that it was only fair that it should be compensated for the substantial reductions it had achieved as a result of being a pioneer in requiring catalytic converters on automobiles.

Poorer countries, including those that perceive a need for preserving the atmosphere, may simply lack the financial resources and the technologies necessary to comply with international standards, or consider the costs to be too heavy a burden to absorb given what appear to be more pressing priorities. Thus, Poland and several of its Eastern European neighbors, which are heavy recipients of trans-boundary pollutants and thus would benefit from stronger international regulations, have been unable to make a reciprocating commitment to reduce their own emissions substantially for lack of sufficient hard currencies to import pollution abatement technologies (Rosencranz, 1986: 47–8).

Equity and economic considerations are not the only reasons why some states have not seen it in their interests to agree to percentage reductions, or any other type of restriction on polluting activities. Among the least cooperative states on the acid deposition problem are up-wind states in an airshed, such as the United Kingdom and the United States, which contribute more to the problem on other countries than they are the victims of pollution originating elsewhere (Rosencranz, 1986: 48–9). In the case of the greenhouse effect, some states may perceive that they have little to lose or may even be net gainers from a global warming, and thus have less incentive to contribute to a global solution to the problem. States without large coastal populations will not have to cope with a rise in sea levels; in some areas agriculture may benefit from a longer growing season or increased rain (Kellogg, 1987: 125). Finally, some states elect to play the free-rider role if they perceive that the severity of the atmospheric problems is being ameliorated sufficiently by the unilateral restraint of others. The unilateral decision of the United States in 1978 to ban the use of CFCs in most consumer goods perhaps lessened the sense of urgency for similar actions in other countries (Ember *et al.*, 1986: 49).

States that are persistent resisters on international regulations on air pollution can undermine the willingness of other states to fulfill the commitments they have made. The international community has little leverage for bringing sovereign states into the fold. Political pressure such as that brought to bear on the United States by Canadian leaders may have some effect if it is perceived that a continuing failure to live up to international norms on air pollution will cause considerable discord in otherwise friendly and constructive relations between states. The economic incentives for certain polluting activities can be reduced by trade embargoes on polluting substances or the products created with them. For example, the United States, Soviet Union, and China, with 90 per cent of known coal reserves, might consider curtailing exports of coal to countries that do not responsibly control emissions (Rose *et al.*, 1984: 56). Additional pressure could be placed on deviant states by farther-reaching sanctions, a model being a United States' law dictating that states violating international rules pertaining to the conservation of whales and other marine mammals should lose 50 per cent of the fishing rights they have previously enjoyed in the American 200-mile exclusive fishery zone.

States that lack the economic resources to comply with international standards must be dealt with in other ways. To bring them into a treaty framework, it may be necessary to grant them certain concessions. The Montreal protocol on the ozone problem allows developing states a ten-year grace period for accomplishing CFC reductions and specifies that they are to be granted access to substitutes for the CFCs and halons causing the problem. Even then, richer victims of the pollution may have no other recourse but to assume a disproportionate share of the cost of reducing emissions, such as by subsidizing the transfer of abatement technologies. In making decisions on loans, international lending agencies, including the World Bank, have increasingly been taking environmental impacts into account, although not to the degree to which environmentally oriented NGOs would have preferred. Offers of debt relief can also be used as leverage for environmentally responsible projects, a strategy that has already been financed on a small scale by NGOs.

ASSESSMENT AND PROSPECTS

The three atmospheric problems highlighted in this chapter – acid deposition, global warming, and depletion of the ozone layer – are recent additions to the environmental agenda of the world community, and it is only in the last few years that the seriousness and magnitude of these problems has become apparent. Only the acid deposition problem has readily observable manifestations that demonstrate the need for a prompt international policy response. Global warming and ozone depletion would seem to be more serious threats to the well-being of mankind, but it will be decades before there will be significant tangible consequences. However, because of the considerable lag between the release of the pollutants and their effects, preventive measures must be undertaken in response to the warnings of the scientific community, which after earlier disagreements is becoming increasingly unified in its assessment of the severity of the greenhouse and ozone problems. Nevertheless, it is tempting for governments besieged with a multitude of more immediate problems to procrastinate on confronting these future environmental problems, which they can at least hope will not be as serious as was originally feared.

In view of these ominous possibilities resulting from human use of the skies as a sink for pollutants, it is imperative that the atmosphere be managed as a global common property resource, as has been done for the oceans and outer space. The problems are too complex and too large geographically to be treated simply as incidents of transboundary damage that can be resolved by general principles of international customary law, such as state responsibility, strict liability, good neigh-borliness, and the duty to inform. Internationally agreed upon standards are needed that pertain to emissions of the polluting substances which are of particular concern and, in the case of global warming, the other practices that compound the problem, such as large-scale clearing of tropical forests. The 1985 ECE protocol calling for reductions in emissions of sulphur dioxide and the 1987 Montreal Convention that mandates similar reductions in the manufacture of CFCs and halons are promising examples of the types of international regulations that are needed to avert these problems, but it appears they do not go far enough in view of new scientific evidence that the problems are more severe than had been previously believed.

The global warming problem will be especially challenging to address not only because the consequences are difficult to anticipate but also, more significantly, because a major reduction in emissions of

CO_2 will require basic changes in the energy policies of all states. Nuclear power has not proved to be a suitable substitute for fossil fuels, as was once hoped. Thus, conservation may be the most promising strategy for reducing CO_2 emissions. There are limits, however, to what can be achieved without major sacrifices, especially in view of the continuing rapid growth in the world's population and the ambitions of Third World countries to industrialize and achieve the energy-intensive life styles of 'modern' societies. It will also be difficult to persuade states that are desperately in need of import revenue and agricultural land to forgo the harvesting or clearing of tropical forests for the benefit of the world as a whole. The question also remains as to whether the problem has already reached the point that even major sacrifices would have only a marginal impact in retarding climate changes. If so, there may be no alternative but to invest heavily in strategies for anticipating and adapting to the inevitable climate changes.

Notes

1. Stephen H. Schneider (1976) was one of the first to call attention to the relationship between human activities and the atmosphere. See also Schneider (1989) for a more recent discussion of this subject.
2. In his essay, Hardin tells the story of a mythical English village in which the resident herdsmen keep adding privately owned cattle to a commonly owned pasture to the point of its destruction, figuring that as individuals they would personally gain more from each additional head of cattle than lose from their share of the resulting increase in the cost of overgrazing.
3. For further information on the phenomenon of acid deposition, see Likens *et al.* (1979) and ReVelle and ReVelle (1988: 493–9).
4. This report is summarized by Kerr (1988a: 1490).
5. For a more detailed description of the United Nations institutional network as it pertains to atmospheric and environmental problems, see Cain (1983) and Caldwell (1984: 87–100).
6. For a concise description of customary law and other sources of international law, see Akehurst (1982: 1–42). See also Nardin (1983).
7. The duty to inform is included in the Principles Concerning Transfrontier Pollution adopted by the OECD in 1974.
8. For a recent, non-technical collection of articles on the potential environmental implications of nuclear war, see the July 1988 issue of *Environment*.

References

Ågren, Christer (1987) 'Drastic Emission Cuts Essential', *Acid Magazine* (November 1): 16–17.

Ågren, Christer (1989) 'ECE Convention: Now a Protocol for Nitrogen', *Acid News* (1) (February): 8–9.

Akehurst, Michael (1982) *A Modern Introduction to International Law* (London: George Allen & Unwin) 4th edn.

Anand, R. P. (1983) *Origin and Development of the Law of the Sea* (Boston: Martinus Nijhoff Publishers).

Ashuvud, J. (1986) 'Impacts of the Greenhouse Effect: Sweden as a Case Study', *Ambio*, 15 (4): 252–3.

Atwood, Wallace W., Jr (1959) 'The International Geophysical Year in Retrospect', *Department of State Bulletin*, 40 (11) (May 11): 682–9.

Barnaby, Frank (1988) 'Acid Rain: UK Policies', *Ambio*, 17 (2): 160–2.

Blake, Donald R. and Rowland, F. Sherwood (1988) 'Continuing Worldwide Increase in Tropospheric Methane', *Science*, 239 (4844) (March 4): 1129–31.

Brown, Lester R. and Flavin, Christopher (1988) 'The Earth's Vital Signs', *The State of the World 1988* (New York: W. W. Norton): 1–21.

Brasseur, Guy (1987) 'The Endangered Ozone Layer', *Environment*, 29 (1) (January/February): 6–11; 39–45.

Broecker, Wallace S. (1987) 'Unpleasant Surprises in the Greenhouse?', *Nature*, 328 (July 9): 123–6.

Burchi, Stefano (1985) 'Shared Natural Resources in the European Economic Community Legislation', *Natural Resources Journal*, 25 (3) (July): 635–49.

Cain, Melinda L. (1983) 'Carbon Dioxide and the Climate: Monitoring and a Search for Understanding', in Kay, David A. and Jacobson, Harold K. (eds), *Environmental Protection: the International Dimension* (Totawa, NJ: Allanheld, Osmun & Co.): 75–100.

Caldwell, Lynton K. (1984) *International Environmental Policy: Emergence and Dimensions* (Durham, NC: Duke University Press).

Christy, Francis T., Jr and Scott, Anthony (1965) *The Common Wealth in Ocean Fisheries: Some Problems of Growth and Economic Allocation* (Baltimore: Johns Hopkins Press).

Cowen, Robert C. (1989) 'Scientists Puzzle over Antarctica's Ozone Hole', *Christian Science Monitor* (November 7): 7.

Crawford, Mark (1986) 'United States Floats Proposal to Help Prevent Global Ozone Depletion', *Science*, 234 (November 21): 927–9.

Davies, David A. (1972) 'The Role of the WMO in Environmental Issues', *International Organization*, 26 (2): 327–36.

Dilworth, Craig (1988) 'NOx Talks Losing Momentum', *Acid Magazine*, 6 (March).

Ember, Lois R., Layman, Patricia L., Lepkowski, Wil and Zurer, Pamela S. (1986) 'Response to Global Warming', *Chemical & Engineering News*, 64 (November 24): 14–64.

Francis, David R. (1987) 'Canada Acts on Acid Rain, Looks to US', *Christian Science Monitor* (April 6): 11.

Goldie, L. F. E. (1985) 'Equity and the International Management of Transboundary Resources', *Natural Resources Journal*, 25 (3): 665–99.

Goldstein, Bruce E. (1988) 'Dupont to Abandon CFCs', *World Watch*, 1 (3) (May/June): 6–7.

Hansen, James E. (1989) 'The Greenhouse Effect: Impacts on Current Global Temperature and Regional Heat Waves', in Abrahamson, Dean E. (ed.), *The Challenge of Global Warming* (Washington, DC: Island Press): 35–43.

218   *Atmosphere as an International Common Property Resource*

Hardin, Garrett (1968)   'The Tragedy of the Commons', *Science*, 162 (3859): 1243–8.
Heintzenberg, Jt. (1989)   'Arctic Haze: Air Pollution in Polar Regions', *Ambio*, 18 (1): 50–5.
Hinrichsen, Don (1986)   'Waldsterben: Forest Death Syndrome', *The Amicus Journal*, 7 (Spring): 23–7.
International Court of Justice (1949)   US/Canada Trail Smelter Arbitration, 19411 Registry Reports of International Arbitration Awards, 3: 1905.
Kellogg, William W. (1987)   'Mankind's Impact on Climate: the Evolution of Awareness', *Climatic Change*, 10 (2): 113–36.
Kerr, Richard A. (1988a)   'Stratospheric Ozone is Decreasing', *Science*, 239 (March 25): 1489–91.
Kerr, Richard A. (1988b)   'Evidence of Arctic Ozone Destruction', *Science*, 240 (May 27): 1144–5.
Koomanoff, Frederick A. (1985)   'Forward', in McCracken, Michael C. and Luther, Frederick M., *Detecting the Climatic Effects of Increased Carbon Dioxide* (Washington, DC: US Department of Energy): v–vii.
Lewis, Drew and Davis, William (1986)   'Joint Report of the Special Envoys on Acid Rain' (January).
Likens, Gene E., Wright, Richard F., Galloway, James N. and Butler, Thomas J. (1979)   'Acid Rain', *Scientific American*, 241 (4): 39–47.
Malone, Thomas F. (1986)   'Mission to the Planet Earth: Integrating Studies of Global Change', *Environment*, 28 (8) (October): 6–11; 39–41.
McCormick, John (1985)   *Acid Earth* (Washington, DC: International Institute for Environment and Development).
Molina, M. J. and Rowland, F. S. (1974)   'Stratospheric Sink for Chlorofluoromethanes: Chlorine Atom-Catalysed Destruction of Ozone', *Science*, 249: 810–12.
Nardin, Terry (1983)   *Law, Morality, and the Relations of States* (Princeton, NJ: Princeton University Press).
Oakerson, Ronald (1986)   'A Model for the Analysis of Common Property Problems', in National Research Council (ed.), *Proceedings of the Conference on Common Property Resource Management* (Washington, DC: National Academy Press): 13–31.
O'Sullivan, Dermot A. (1985)   'European Concern About Acid Rain is Growing', *Chemical and Engineering News* (January 28): 12–18.
Price, Martin (1989)   'Global Change: Defining the Ill-Defined', *Environment*, 31 (8) (October): 18–22; 42–4.
Rahn, Kenneth A. (1984)   'Who's Polluting the Arctic?', *Natural History*, 93 (5): 30–8.
ReVelle, Penelope and ReVelle, Charles (1988)   *The Environment: Issues and Choices for Society* (Boston: Jones & Bartlett Publishers).
Rose, David J., Miller, Marvin M. and Agnew, Carson (1984)   'Reducing the Problem of Global Warming', *Technology Review* (May–June).
Rosencranz, Armin (1986)   'The Acid Rain Controversy in Europe and North America: A Political Analysis', *Ambio*, 15 (1): 47–51.
Rowland, F. Sherwood (1987)   'Can We Close the Ozone Hole?', *Technology Review*, 90 (6) (August–September): 51–8.
Sand, Peter H. (1985)   'Protecting the Ozone Layer: The Vienna Convention is Adopted', *Environment*, 27 (5) (June): 19–20; 40–3.

Sand, Peter (1987) 'Air Pollution in Europe: International Policy Responses', *Environment*, 29 (10) (December): 16–29.

Schneider, Jan (1979) *World Public Order of the Environment: Towards an International Ecological Law and Organization* (Toronto: University of Toronto Press).

Schneider, Stephen H. (1976) *The Genesis Strategy: Climate and Global Survival* (New York: Plenum Press).

Schneider, Stephen H. (1989) *Global Warming: Are We Entering the Greenhouse Century?* (San Francisco, CA: Sierra Club Books).

Shabecoff, Philip (1988) 'Study Finds Wider Risk of Acid Rain', *Raleigh News and Observer* (April 25): 1; 9.

Soroos, Marvin S. (1982) 'The Commons in the Sky: the Radio Spectrum and Geosynchronous Orbit as Issues in Global Policy', *International Organization*, 36 (3) (Summer): 665–77.

Soroos, Marvin S. (1988) 'The Tragedy of the Commons in Global Perspective', in Kegley, Charles E. and Wittkopf, Eugene R. (eds), *The Global Agenda: Issues and Perspectives* (New York: Random House, 1988) 2nd edn: 345–57.

Søbye, Helen K. (1989) 'Arctic Nature Under Threat', *Acid News*, (1) (February): 14–15.

Springer, Allen L. (1983) *The International Law of Pollution: Protecting the Global Environment in a World of Sovereign States* (Westport, Conn.: Quorum Books).

Tollan, Arne (1985) 'The Convention on Long-range Transboundary Air Pollution', *Journal of World Trade Law*, 19 (November–December): 615–21.

United Nations Conference on the Human Environment (1972) *Final Documents* (Stockholm) (June 5–16) 1 UN GAOR, UN Doc/Conf. 48/14.

United Nations Environment Programme (UNEP) (1987a) 'A Global Agreement to Save Earth's Protective Ozone Layer', *UNEP: North America News*, 2 (5) (October) ISSN 0258–5146.

United Nations Environment Programme (UNEP) (1987b) *Register of International Treaties and Other Agreements in the Field of the Environment* (Nairobi, Kenya) (May 1) (UNEP/GC/Information/11/Rev.1/Supplement 1).

United Nations Environment Programme (UNEP) (1987c) *UNEP Profile* (Nairobi, Kenya: UNEP).

United Nations Environment Programme (UNEP) (1988) 'Climate Change Cannot Be Prevented', *UNEP North American News*, 3 (2): 1–2, ISSN 0258–5146.

United Nations Environment Programme (UNEP) (1989) *Register of International Treaties and Other Agreements in the Field of the Environment* (Nairobi, Kenya) (May) (UNEP/GC/Inf.2).

United Nations Environment Programme (UNEP) (undated) 'The Changing Atmosphere', UNEP Environment Brief, 1.

United Nations Environment Programme, World Meteorological Organization, and International Council of Scientific Unions (UNEP/WMO/ICSU) (1986) 'Report of the International Conference on the Assessment of the Role of Carbon Dioxide and of Other Greenhouse Gases in Climate Variations and Associated Impacts' (Villach, Austria) (October 9–15, 1985) WMO, 661.

Van Lier, Irene H. (1980) *Acid Rain and International Law* (Alpen Aan Den Rijn, the Netherlands: Sijthoff & Noordhoff).

Wagner, Richard H. (1978) *Environment and Man* (New York: W. W. Norton) 3rd edn.

Weiss, Edith Brown (1978) 'International Liability for Weather Modification', *Climate Change*, 1 (3): 267–90.

Wetstone, Gregory and Rosencranz, Armin (1984) 'Transboundary Air Pollution: The Search for an International Response', *Harvard Environmental Law Review*, 8 (1): 89–138.

Wijkman, Per Magnas (1982) 'Managing the Global Commons', *International Organization*, 36 (3) (Summer): 511–36.

World Resources Institute/International Institute for Environment and Development (WRI/IIED) (1986) *World Resources 1986: An Assessment of the Resource Base that Supports the Global Economy* (New York: Basic Books).

World Resources Institute/International Institute for Environment and Development (WRI/IIED) (1987) *World Resources 1987: An Assessment of the Resource Base that Supports the Global Economy* (New York: Basic Books).

World Resources Institute/International Institute for Environment and Development (WRI/IIED) (1988/89) *World Resources 1988–89* (New York: Basic Books).

Young, Patrick (1986) 'Warming Earth Expected to Create Varied Problems', *Raleigh News and Observer* (November 30).

Zhao, Dianwu and Sun, Bozen (1986) 'Air Pollution and Acid Rain in China', *Ambio*, 15 (1): 2–5.

10 Towards a Western Counter-terrorist Policy

James E. Winkates[1]

There is substantial consensus on key characteristics and trends in the pattern of international terrorism since 1985–6, the peak period of incidents and casualties. The intent of this chapter is to initiate an examination of what is the likely policy future for a concerted, if not wholly consensual, effort among the European and US components of the Group of Seven (G-7) for anti- and counter-terrorist actions.

THE 1980s TERRORIST ENVIRONMENT

In retrospect, 1985 proved to be a watershed year for terrorist violence worldwide. There were more attacks than in any year in the decade of the 1980s, with numerous dramatic incidents including the Air India explosion, the *Achille Lauro* affair, the Rome and Vienna airport massacres, the TWA 847 incident, and two major restaurant bombings in Rome and just outside Madrid.

Unlike earlier years, terrorist violence in 1985 erupted out of the Middle East and spilled over repeatedly into the Western European environment. Perhaps only because governmental and military security had been tightened on the continent did Western Europe, as a venue for terror, slip to second place in the number of international terrorist incidents in 1985, as illustrated in Figure 10.1.[2]

While there appeared to be no worldwide pattern of terrorist behavior at this time, it became clear that the European landmass had become a primary battlefield for terrorist attacks. In 1985, 782 international terrorist incidents took place – a 30 per cent increase over 1984. Fully one-third of these attacks resulted in casualties, with more than 800 killed and 1,200 wounded. Nearly 28 per cent of the incidents occurred in Western Europe and the region suffered 60 per cent of the lethal attacks.[3]

Moreover, the target set for terrorist attacks had begun to change away from public, official, and diplomatic sites and personnel to private

221

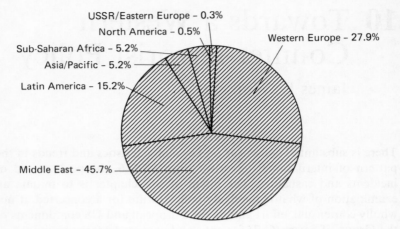

USSR/Eastern Europe – 0.3%
North America – 0.5%
Sub-Saharan Africa – 5.2%
Asia/Pacific – 5.2%
Latin America – 15.2%
Middle East – 45.7%
Western Europe – 27.9%

Figure 10.1   Geographical distribution of international terrorist incidents, 1985

parties and business targets. Relatedly, the modes of terrorist violence increasingly centered on arson, bombings, and kidnappings, with the dominant victim set being random targets. Most significantly, the rise and impact of state-sponsored terrorism became very evident. In 1985, one-third of all international terrorist incidents that were attributed to state-sponsored terrorism occurred in Western Europe.[4] Arguably, the governmental machinery in both Western Europe and the United States began to emerge from a rather lethargic posture to one of proactive, if not focused, initiatives to stem the rising tide of terrorism on their domestic doorsteps.

At the macro level, too, the global environment – both structures and processes – were then and are still changing in content and direction suggesting even more persistent terrorist violence. Western Europe likely will remain a premier locational target, and both US and Western European citizenry are victims of choice.

The US debacle in Vietnam and the Soviet failure in Afghanistan in 1989 only ratified for the world public the demise of superpower control of world affairs. The center had been fractured, though certainly not demolished. What these cataclysmic politico–military events did reveal, inevitably, was the desuetude of – or at least the greatly diminished utility and reliance upon – formal alliance systems. The growth of international terrorism, and its sub-set of state-sponsored terrorist violence, offered no viable rationale or rallying point for alliance reaction. Whereas alliances served well to thwart, or at least to deter, nuclear and conventional attack, and at the same time soothe the perceived or real inferiority complexes of nation-states, they served little purpose in combatting low-level and terrorist violence. The spectrum of conflict had shifted and its center of gravity dropped to violence modes that were not easily amenable either to superpower or alliance responses.

Moreover, as both superpowers and terrorist support states increasingly recognized this change, the incidence of low-intensity violence has increased, certainly a key component of which is terrorism. Combat on the streets of Beirut now more characterizes conflict than does conventional warfare. Such conflict remains inherently cheap for the perpetrators, with inexpensive tactical weaponry, state-supported havens for training, governmental disbursements for expenses, semi-permeable borders still easily crossed, and an ample supply of repressed minority and irredentist groups to do their bidding. The complex urban infrastructures of the industrialized nations, which offer excellent communications and logistics facilities, serve as fertile operational areas with many discrete safe houses in pluralistic neighborhoods.[5]

Throughout the decade of the 1970s, by far the most pronounced and chronic terrorist violence was directed toward Israel. The United States, then and now, remained largely immune from terrorist attacks within its borders. The foremost US concern in the decade was the unscheduled diversion of eastern seaboard flights to Havana – a diversion that became so frequent it achieved a sort of gallows humor among passengers travelling to Florida. Cuba quickly tired of the characters who sought free entry and ultimately signed an accord with the US government that ensured the prompt return of hijacked planes and passengers, often the next day. In point of fact, not until the wake of the Black September massacre at the Munich Olympics did President Nixon establish the first cabinet-level committee and companion working group to combat terrorism.[6]

With the exception of Great Britain, and that mostly due to IRA violence against British soldiers stationed in Northern Ireland, Western Europe did not encounter a great deal of terrorist violence in the 1970s either. Until the 1972 Lod Airport and Munich attacks, only an estimated 250 people worldwide were killed as a direct result of international terrorism between 1968 and 1972.[7] During this period of the 1970s, several continental European nations, notably France and Italy, harbored and even provided safe haven to international terrorist groups.

In the decade of the 1980s, however, the focus of terrorist attacks clearly was directed at Western European and US targets. The growth and success of Arab–Palestinian terrorist violence, sometimes in collusion with domestic terrorist organizations indigenous to European nations, accounted for the new emphasis. Reportedly, from 1980 to mid-1986, 78 per cent of all terrorist attacks perpetrated by Arab or PLO-related groups took place in but 7 countries: United Kingdom, France, Spain, Italy, West Germany, Greece, and Cyprus. A total of 259 terrorist incidents were counted in this period.[8] Interestingly, the record also shows that since 1973, the Abu Nidal group executed 70 per cent of its attacks in Western Europe and that roughly 95 per cent of Libyan-directed attacks since 1980 have taken place in Western Europe.[9]

As acknowledged at an international conference hosted by the Jaffee Center for Strategic Studies at Tel-Aviv University in 1979, 'the West has generally failed in responding to the challenge of political terrorism, some local successes notwithstanding'. Further, 'All it has managed to do so far, and with only partial success, is limit the physical damage done by terrorists'.[10] During the decade of the 1970s and into the mid-1980s, no serious effort emerged between Western European governments and the United States to act jointly or in concert against the threat of terrorism to their societies.

Before examining what later transpired to bring about a more proactive posture, one must recognize the criticality of national perceptions on terrorist violence, at least insofar as the trans-Atlantic national cultures are concerned. One who has worked very closely in forging and coordinating US anti-terrorist policy with that of key Western European nations, Geoffrey Levitt of the US Department of State, has related how very different cross-national perspectives are on the terrorism issue, and why. He views the US perspective on international terrorism as unique in several respects. Unlike the European democracies, none of whom have been spared terrorism on their soil, the United States has not been seized of repeated terrorist violence at home. Bombings, arson, hostage seizures, and high citizen risk have at times been commonplace in Western European cities in the 1980s. Consequently, for Europeans international terrorism has been a domestic security problem of major magnitude, not simply a foreign policy issue. Additionally, European governments share a quite different relationship with the nations of the Middle East than does the United States. More geographic proximity, important trade ties and, with the exception of the United Kingdom, energy dependency, together with long-standing historical, cultural, and even social ties, comprise key influences in Western European policy-making. Notwithstanding these considerable differences, the near-titanic US support of Israel in and of itself prompts a very weighty policy distance between Washington and European capitals.[11]

But the milieu of US–Euro relations on the terrorist threat perhaps has been even more colored by the conviction in much of Western Europe, especially among elite public opinion and for many years, that the United States too often acts before it thinks and certainly before it consults adequately with its European allies. The aggressive tenor of the Republican Party campaign preceding the 1980 presidential election, and the ardor of political rhetoric on the use of force to solve problems, as evidenced in President Reagan's repeated reference in his first term to 'the evil empire', certainly made European publics and some governments uncomfortable. Indeed, as this perception was widely shared, and perhaps less so as time proceeded, the heavy-handed image remained even within the United States. As Eric Willenz of the Carnegie Endowment for International Peace asserted, 'In essence, U.S. policy ... seems unduly stultified by its proneness to seek a military solution for the highly differentiated and indirect threats which terrorism presents'.[12] Given these obviously divergent perspectives what, then, would account for the burgeoning policy congruence that began to occur by 1986 among the G-7 on governmental actions against terrorist threats?

THE G-7: PLAYERS AND PATTERNS OF INTERACTION

The Summit Seven or G-7 have met annually since 1975, invariably concluding with a joint declaration or communiqué.[13] The seven include Japan and the major Western democracies: the United Kingdom, France, Germany, Italy, Canada, and the United States. From the outset of the Seven economic summits, terrorism was not considered a major agenda item for the meetings; because of terrorist attacks or threats, however, it became an action item each year. At the initial Bonn Summit, for example, Chancellor Schmidt read the joint statement, which stipulated consensus on terminating air services to those states refusing to prosecute or to extradite hijackers. The purpose of summits, certainly, is not to respond to terrorist violence. Yet in the decade of the 1970s, terrorist hijacking became epidemic. The seven heads of state and heads of government could ill afford not to address this seething concern.

At each successive summit, one dimension of the terrorist threat or another penetrated those high-level discussions. In Tokyo (1979), they concluded a joint statement on hijacking. In Venice (1980) the joint statement emphasized action against the taking of hostages. In Ottawa (1981) the Seven focused on the hijacking of a Pakistani International Airlines flight, and the alleged culprits who sought safe haven in Afghanistan. The London summit (1984) initiated international governmental cooperation among police and other security organizations, for exchange of intelligence and technical expertise. Steps were also taken to review the transfer of weapons to states known to support terrorists, to limit the size of diplomatic missions under the Vienna Convention, and to inform other states when alleged terrorists were expelled from national jurisdiction.

The telstar G-7 meeting, however, proved to be the Tokyo Summit (1986), following the violent terrorist attacks on land, sea, and air of late 1985 and in the immediate wake of the April 1986 US punitive raid on Libya. International terrorism was condemned in all forms, to include those who sponsor and support violence. Never before had the industrialized democracies gone on record in unison to avow that 'Terrorism has no justification'. For the first time, Libya was cited as a prime violator of the norms of custom and law in sponsoring terrorist attacks. The Tokyo summit statement most clearly signaled G-7 consensus on combatting terrorism and offered a common frame of reference for individual governments to pursue active anti- and counter-terrorist policies on a broad front. To be sure and with some degree of difference, the Seven had by now blocked out political, diplomatic, economic, and security measures against the terrorist cancer launched decidedly on Western societies.

The Venice summit (1987) reconfirmed the earlier summit postures on international terrorism, the values of international law in state behavior, and the utility of international organizations, both general and functional, in resolving terrorist violence. Special note was made of their joint commitment to the 'no concessions' policy to terrorists or to their sponsors and to extradite or bring to trial perpetrators of terrorist acts.

Aside from the occasional rhetoric of the Reagan Administration about the importance and sometime utility of general purpose international organizations like the United Nations (UN), during the 1980s Washington saw the UN only in terms of damage limitation. Turtle Bay was viewed at best as an onerous, unwieldy, ideologically unkind arena for policy projection and bridge-building. The United States could, and occasionally did, plead its policy case in New York but too often made little effort, especially in the one nation–one vote General Assembly. Similarly, outside of NATO, regional organizations were too locality-based for broad initiatives to counter the growth of international terrorism. Moreover, the functional international organizations that had responsibility for aspects of anti-terrorism defenses – ICAO, ITU, and IMO, for example – were too politically disparate to ensure that very significant measures could be adopted. Other organizations with democratic membership – NATO and OECD – were prohibited by their charters or were disinclined to open up new areas of responsibilities for official action. The 1986 Vice President's Task Force on Combatting Terrorism *Public Report*, in fact, noted that 'the best multilateral forum for the discussion of terrorism to be the industrialized democracies which constitute the Summit Seven'.[14] Consequently, by late 1985 or early 1986, Washington had determined that the G-7 would be its primary vehicle, outside of the US governmental bureaucracy, to launch its anti-terrorism initiatives. As one high US policy advisor has argued, however, 'Washington ... turned to the Summit Seven, almost by default ... to work out collective measures'.[15]

The rationale for why the other six members of G-7 seized the terrorism initiative within that organization is more problematic. The cascading frequency of terrorist attacks in Western Europe during this period gives considerable credence to William Waugh's emphasis on the connection between perception and policy reaction. In short, '**how one responds**, depends a great deal on **where one sits**'. This time-tested adage applies well in this instance. He argues that when terrorism moves from 'spilling over' into an area to the persistent, if irregular, attack on domestic targets in that state, those governments are more likely to respond overtly and directly.[16]

A second explanation turns on an economic issue of major importance to much of Europe – the rise in booking cancellations to the traditional summer tourist meccas as the incidence of terrorist attacks occurred with seemingly devastating frequency during 1985. Large numbers of travelers simply stayed away by the summer of 1986. Despite substantial package discounts (in some cases 50 per cent) and reassuring official and private pronouncements, a large percentage of US summer vacationers bought into the 'Travel America' campaign of the US Department of Commerce that summer.[17] After all, Libya lay just the other side of the water from the beaches and playgrounds of Southern Europe.

There is also a very plausible third explanation, namely the personal chemistry of three heads of state or government. Reagan, Thatcher, and Kohl (elected in October 1982) got on well, sharing a like-minded conservative public philosophy. Reagan and Thatcher, especially, had a personal bent for tough policy positions and were inclined to want to take some action against the terrorist carnage. In Britain's Falklands crisis, Reagan not only supported the British possession in the conflict but provided technical support to the British campaign. Thatcher returned the favor in allowing UK bases to be used to launch the US air attack against Libya in April 1986.

The other four G-7 members – Canada, Japan, France, and Italy – were also generally supportive of stronger measures. Once the Progressive Conservatives, under Mulroney, won control of parliament in September 1984, Canada joined the US, UK, and Germany in a stable coalition favoring additional public pressure on the sources of terrorism. Despite the fact that the Japanese Red Army posed one of the most lethal terrorist threats at this time, their operations were all conducted outside of the Japanese state. Tokyo tended to follow the US lead on the terrorist issue, at least insofar as diplomatic instruments were employed. While low key on the issue of international terrorism generally, the large number of Japanese business interests worldwide, their externally-oriented tourist trade, their total energy dependency, and the sizeable fleet of Japanese supertankers plying routes to the Persian Gulf undoubtedly make Tokyo aware, too, of its vulnerability to attacks.

The French case is more complex. Paris had denied overfight rights to US planes en route to Benghazi and Tripoli only three weeks before the Tokyo summit in 1986. Yet the French announced prior to the opening of the summit, it was prepared to support a vigorous counter-terrorism posture if major Western members were prepared to do so. The French statement followed immediately a meeting between the French and British prime ministers. Certainly, the new French position on the issue paralleled the official stance of conservative Prime Minister Jacques Chirac, who had pressed for more international cooperation on counter-terrorism.[18] Interestingly, and perhaps due to the wide publicity achieved by the release of the Tokyo summit statement, both France and Japan almost immediately made it clear that their joint declaration was discretionary only and that their governments retained the right to decide for themselves how to proceed on terrorism in the future.[19] Later, in early 1987, several G-7 members – reportedly concerned over the US naval buildup in the Eastern Mediterranean and any potential for US miitary action against terrorist havens in Lebanon – even declined to meet at the request of the United States.[20]

The last G-7 member to be discussed, Italy, had been subject in 1980–1 to dramatic terrorist violence, including the assassination of a former prime minister, the kidnapping of US General Dozier, and finally, the embarrassment of the *Achille Lauro* piracy. Rome already had achieved considerable success in buying vital terrorist intelligence information with guarantees of amnesty and monetary rewards. The summit postures coincided well with ongoing Italian government policy. So for different reasons, including changes of government, the G-7 became progressively more consensual on raising the ante against the threatening tide of terrorism.

Particularly during the early Reagan Administration, the United States kept the terrorism issue hot in the media and at one point then Secretary of State Alexander Haig accused the USSR of virtually controlling all international terrorism. The US intelligence community, after extensive efforts, was unable to corroborate the Secretary's claim. This Haig allegation, however, well illustrated the emotional strength of the issue for the government. In retrospect, it is not inconceivable that at least several of the European members of the Seven believed that the G-7 might serve as a useful forum to influence US actions and verbiage on the terrorism issue, perhaps even to defuse possible US responses, political or military, that appeared overly aggressive for European taste. Perhaps related to the Gorbachev *perestroika* campaign and the many *glasnost'* initiatives to which the United States was reacting, by 1988 there was no further official mention of Soviet direction of international terrorism. US Ambassador at Large for Counter-terrorism, L. Paul Bremer III, in recounting the deaths of American citizens at the hands of terrorists (7 in 1987 vs. 38 in 1985), listed only Libya, North Korea, South Yemen, Cuba, and Syria as terrorist sponsors.[21] One could conclude perhaps that, at least from a European perspective, the more flamboyant US rhetoric on terrorism had been curbed and that American policy appeared to be more balanced than in the early 1980s.

The very nature of the G-7 suggests some distinct advantages and disadvantages as a policy vehicle, both from a theoretical and a country perspective. Certainly the group represents the highest levels of government in the seven nations. All are either heads of state or heads of government. The annual meetings are both informal and reportedly candid. Except for any resulting end of summit statements or communiqués, there are no formal minutes or written record of the negotiations among the Seven.

Unlike other high-level, international organizations, no charter or mandate governs the jurisdictional or geographic breadth of the G-7's discussions. Structurally, they are all democracies, with freely-elected governments, necessarily responsive to a large degree to their respective publics, and all share concerns and problems with events beyond their immediate sovereign jurisdictions. Oddly enough, it was then President Valéry Giscard d'Estang of France who suggested the G-7 organization in 1975, when they met at Rambouillet – the same location at which former President de Gaulle vetoed British entry into the Common Market in 1963.

The early and dominant focus of the G-7 on global economic issues has been broadened to embrace virtually any issue or problem of importance to the world's leading industrial democracies. As time passed, the initial and informal ambience has devolved into a considerably more preparatory agenda and structured assemblage. The essence of the G-7 utility, however, derives from its very limited membership, the lack of a constitution or confining bylaws, and its regular meeting schedule. In general, if the G-7 becomes seized of an issue and comes to some substantial consensus, when the leaders return to their capitols some followup actions are virtually assured.

On the other hand, the G-7 virtues are also its disadvantages. It has no permanent staff to prepare position papers, to coordinate policy, to follow up on agreed-upon actions, and of course has only the historical memory of the oldest sitting head of state or government. Its single annual meeting, moreover, means the G-7 inevitably may be slow in responding to an acute international crisis.

Importantly, the very exclusivity of the group acknowledges its limited decision-making range. On issues related to terrorism, for example, the absence of Spain, Belgium, Holland, Greece, and Turkey is surely a limiting factor. As Levitt relates, 'Clearly the United States and its major allies do not formulate their responses to state-supported terrorism in a political vacuum. Western counter-terrorism cooperation is but one link in the complex web of relationships among the industrialized democracies'.[22]

At the same time, many actions are taken more easily in the G-7 that relate to broader European considerations than what might be possible in the European Community (EC) organizations, NATO, the Council of Europe, or the OECD. At the time of the Tokyo summit in May 1986, for instance, if Greece were represented, most assuredly the G-7 would not have found consensus on targeting Libya with governmental sanctions. At that very time, the EC desire for stronger policy curbs against Qaddafi was blocked by Athens.[23]

The issue of overlapping organizational memberships, all of which possess different charters, jurisdictions, and multinational norms, as well as political weights in the larger global fabric, can engender difficulties for states wishing to demonstrate both consistency in policy application and to protect sovereign flexibiity in decision-making. The late 1988 test ruling of the European Court of Human Rights against the United Kingdom is a case in point. The Court held that a law allowing terrorist suspects to be held up to a week without charges violates the European Convention on Human Rights, to which Britain is a signatory.[24] The United Kingdom had agreed that European Court rulings on the convention were binding. Therefore, the 1984 detention without charge of alleged terrorists breached the human rights convention. Britain has chosen not to comply with the ruling.

It cannot have gone unnoticed in Washington either that European nations which have multiple organizational memberships can effectively exclude the United States from direct political participation on an issue by simply shifting the debate arena to a wholly European forum. That approach, less likely on international terrorist issues, is nevertheless a potential political trump card for Western European states. While unstated, the measured US enthusiasm for the G-7 forum may well reflect this reality. Pointedly, bridge-building efforts to ensure mutual exchange of views between the G-7 and the EC ensued in 1986 with stepped-up liaison between US and EC counter-terrorism officials. That formalized cooperation was further extended with the May 1987 meeting of G-7 and EC cabinet level officials.[25]

PUBLIC OPINION AMONG THE G-7 NATIONS ON TERRORIST RESPONSE[26]

The peak period of terrorist attacks on US and Western European population and facilities, as we should recall, occurred in 1985–6. At this time public attention among these national electorates reached a similarly high level of acute concern. In early 1986 an independent European polling organization conducted a cross-national, face-to-face survey of European views on terrorism. This survey coincided with a *New York Times*/CBS News telephone poll completed at approximately the same time asking about US governmental responses to terrorism.[27] The results of the two polls appear in Figures 10.2 and 10.3.

As depicted in Figure 10.2, all four national response groups indicated that their governments should be doing more to protect their citizenry against international terrorism. While Great Britain showed

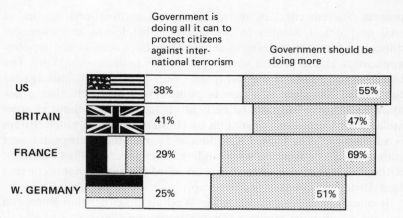

Figure 10.2   Taking action against terrorism

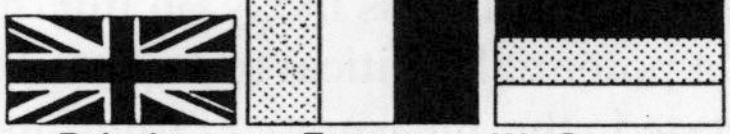

	Britain (%)	France (%)	W. Germany (%)
Steps that would curb international terrorism			
Military action against terrorists	29	22	22
Much stricter airport security	63	69	65
Military action against governments that support terrorists	15	16	12
Economic sanctions against governments that support terrorists	34	48	39
Pressure on Israel to make concessions to the Palestinians	16	20	15
Government can do nothing	9	7	5
Don't know/no answer	9	9	17
US military action against terrorists every time an attack affected Americans . . .			
. . . would reduce international terrorism	17	27	22
. . . would make things worse	64	45	45
US is getting overexcited about terrorism	41	21	19

Figure 10.3   European views on terrorism

only a distinct plurality of those queried favoring more governmental action, respondents in the United States, France, and West Germany in the majority wanted more governmental response. Interestingly, and perhaps somewhat unexpectedly, both West German and French respondents voiced the most disenchantment with the posture of their respective governments.

In Figure 10.3, the European survey asked respondents what steps they favored in curbing international terrorism. Some distinct, transnational preferences are clearly evident. Two-thirds of the British, French, and West German respondents favored much stricter airport security. One-third to nearly half of those questioned desired economic sanctions against states supporting terrorism. Nearly one-fifth sought more pressure on Israel, closest US ally in the Middle East, to make concessions to the Palestinians.

Perhaps most significant were the percentage responses on those questions asking for views on military action. A limited range from a low of 22 per cent (France and West Germany) to a high of 29 per cent (Great Britain) favored military action at all against terrorists. Then, only half of those wishing any military action recommended military responses against governments supporting terrorism (Britain 15 per cent; France 16 per cent; West Germany 12 per cent).

With the April 1986 military raid against Libya only a few months into the future, the European respondents clearly opposed any US military action against terrorists, concluding that any such action would be counter-productive (Britain 64 per cent; France 45 per cent; and West Germany 45 per cent). Most suggestive of differing, and not unsympathetic, cross-national perspectives are the responses to the final question in the European survey. When asked if the United States was getting overexcited about terrorism, an overwhelming majority in France and West Germany thought not (21 per cent and 19 per cent respectively), while 41 per cent in the British sample did feel so.

Assuming these survey responses are representative of national opinion in that time window, and there is no reason to believe otherwise, the only Western European government to aid US military action against Libya – Great Britain – ran most against its domestic public opinion on that issue. At the same time, France, which denied US overflight rights for the raid, and West Germany which was not asked for a priori support nor gave it after the fact, would appear to have had more latitude based on their domestic public opinion, in sanctioning military response to the Libyan threat. In both Paris and Bonn, however, US military action still remained unpopular.

As one European politician remarked shortly after the Libya raid,

frequently, the Europeans have been too satisfied with mere declarations which have been politically ineffectual while leaving the U.S.
alone in its struggle against international terrorism ... If we Europeans do not want to follow the Americans for reasons of our own,
we must develop political initiatives.[28]

A year after the Libya raid, there was wide acknowledgment in Western
Europe that the US military action galvanized those nations to
intensify their own anti-terrorism efforts and to coordinate police
operations across state borders.[29] While Europeans seemed to plumb
the depths of America's outrage on the terrorism issue, the raid also
had a corrosive effect on US–European relations and on US leadership
in the counter-terrorist agenda. Europeans, reportedly, viewed the raid
as one more 'example of the Reagan Administration's inclination to go
it alone in foreign affairs'.[30] The overselling of the US Strategic Defense
Initiative (SDI), the US posture at the Reykjavik summit in October
1986, and the earlier American effort to derail the Soviet natural gas
pipeline to Europe, together with its 'machoism' on terrorism generally,
put public and policy distance between the European nations in G-7
and the United States. Instead of following the US lead, Western
European nations, in and out of G-7, initiated their own forms of
cooperation, often bilaterally.

European public and governmental opinion, however, became most
disillusioned over the surfacing of the Iran–Contra affair. Former
Italian Prime Minister Spadolini, for example, observed in early 1987
that 'the affair has seriously damaged the West's anti-terrorism efforts'
particularly in the Middle East and in the moderate Arab governments.[31] There has always been a conviction, and perhaps it is even a
growing conviction, in Western Europe that it must take command of
its own destiny as a full and equal player with its American brethren on
the key policy questions central to trans-Atlantic survival and prosperity. That trend most certainly has been set in the economic realm as the
EEC looks to full integration beginning in 1992. The conjunction of
European public and governmental perceptions of the failings and
skewed interests of the United States have prompted Western European nations to move out with increasing confidence in forging more
genuinely European positions on terrorist responses. Those successes
have been well related elsewhere.[32]

Although the European record of firm policy, increased intergovernmental cooperation, and consistent action remains far from perfect, the pattern is most encouraging. Stepped-up police work, stiffer penalties, and cross-national cooperation is on the rise, resulting in diminished terrorist activity in Western Europe as a whole.[33]

France and Spain now work jointly to contain Basque terrorist activity on their common border, with a degree of cooperation perhaps unprecedented.[34] The French coastguard seized and confiscated the largest cache of missiles, guns, and ammunition ever destined for the IRA. Convicted *Accion Directe* terrorists received long prison terms in a Paris court. Belgium infiltrated its domestic Fighting Communist Cells and arrested the entire terrorist leadership. German courts convicted Abbas Ali Hamadei on kidnapping and other charges even while Bonn refused to extradite Hamadei's younger brother to the United States for his role in the TWA 847 hijacking. German customs apprehended the older brother, because the customs agent became suspicious at the Frankfurt airport. When German authorities examined Hamadei's belongings, they found multiple names and addresses of Lebanese residents in Paris. The French police, provided with the information, arrested seven terrorists within days.

Special anti-terrorist task forces – Cobra in Great Britain and Uclat in France – devote full time to counter-terrorism activity. English courts convicted Nezar Hindawi, who attempted to blow up an El Al aircraft. A French judge sentenced Lebanese terrorist Georges Abdallah to life imprisonment.[35]

In Italy, which had an early record of successful anti-terrorist actions, more than 1,000 people were sentenced between 1970 and 1980, often to long prison terms, for politically-inspired criminal offences. The Italian-style political tactics have resulted in four kinds of anti-terrorist penalties depending on the degree of cooperation evident in those terrorists who are or may be apprehended by authorities. There are the 'repented' (those who confess and provide information); the 'disassociated' (those who gave up the terrorist struggle, but did not offer information); the 'detached' (those who still believe, but think the cause is futile); and the 'hard core' (those still on the run and the most dangerous).[36] Once the most terrorism-ridden nation, Italy now serves as something of a counter-terrorism model.[37] As pointed out by Paul Wilkinson, specialist on European terrorism at the University of Aberdeen, Scotland, 'For all Europe's mistakes and errors . . . it is the area with the most regional cooperation, the most sharing of police information'.[38] According to Wilkinson, while 50 per cent of all world terrorist incidents took place in Europe several years ago, in 1987 the percentage fell to 20 per cent with only 168 incidents in the entire region. Supportive public opinion, intergovernmental trust and cooperation, and uniquely European national remedies account for the vast improvement.

THE MATRIX OF FUTURE G-7 RESPONSES TO TERRORISM

Based on the principles and practices of the annual G-7 meetings since 1975, it is possible to construct a simple matrix of national policy comparisons on the 7-nation response to international terrorism. Table 10.1 depicts these policy postures.

As can be readily seen, there is substantial policy consensus among the European G-7 members on all policy actions short of the use of military force. All four European members (France, Germany, Italy, and the UK) adhere to the 1977 European Convention on the Suppression of Terrorism (ECST), permit 'hot pursuit' across their national borders, and employ restrictions on diplomatic personnel and on the issuance and renewal of visas. All but Italy would invoke economic sanctions. The two former major colonial powers, France and the UK, also have anti-terrorist foreign assistance programs in place.

Most significantly, all seven members cooperate transnationally on the exchange of intelligence information, and will prosecute or extradite alleged terrorists apprehended within their sovereign jurisdictions. All are on record, as well, as prohibiting concessions to terrorists. There have been, and will be, exceptions to these principles.

With respect to the use of military instruments to deter, defend against, or punish international or state-supported terrorists, there is considerably more disparity in views and policy. Moreover, proclaimed postures may not, nor have they been, necessarily consistent with national practice. Canada, France, and the United States are characterized as strongly supportive of military measures, with the UK in a moderate to strong policy posture. In reality and under given circumstances, constrained by the general tenor of domestic and world public opinion, particularly when hostages are taken, those governments may resort to rescue or raid using national armed forces. Three nations – Germany, the UK, and the United States – have had established for some time military units in place, trained, and deployable for counterterrorist missions. Two such units, Germany's GSG9 and Britain's Special Air Service (SAS), possess almost legendary reputations because of their past prowess of success in unique hostage situations.

The US Delta Force, newest of the three, has not yet enjoyed the tactical successes of its European counterparts.

While Rome's overt objection to the use of force has been very consistent in recent years, it is also more consonant with the context of Italian domestic, partisan politics and traditions. So, Rome's position is well accepted and understood even within the G-7. The Bonn government, however, exemplifies some policy/practice contradictions if one recalls the successful German hostage rescue in Mogadishu, Somalia a few years ago. Certainly German reticence on the use of force in part can be understood given the several German hostages still held by terrorists in Lebanon. But it is less simple than that. Prior to the US raid on Libya, the Bonn government remained dissatisfied with the US 'proof' that Libya was the culprit in the bombing of the West German discothèque, and their doubts lingered well after the raid.[39] As to Japan, there is little likelihood that Tokyo would deploy its Self-Defense Force outside the Japanese islands given the constitutional prohibition on external force and the deep and long-standing cultural inhibitions on such deployment. Internally, however, it may be quite a different matter since the Japanese authorities are very well trained in riot control and in the passive use of military contingents.

How, then, does past practice suggest a future course of action for Western counter-terrorist policy? The 1988 G-7 summit in Toronto, Canada, and its final declaration, is suggestive in looking to the future. The text again emphasized the resounding G-7 'condemnation of terrorism in all its forms, including the taking of hostages', expressed support for the continued work of ICAO, and concluded with the statement,

> We reaffirm our determination to continue the fight against terrorism through the application of [the] rule of law, the policy of no concessions to terrorists and their sponsors, and international coope-ration.[40]

The endorsed focus is preferably for a legal, political, and mutually cooperative course of action. As Levitt has suggested, four main themes have emerged from the G-7 discussions on terrorism: consensus, credibility, clarity, and consistency.[41] Policy will be characterized by persistence, patience, firmness, and pursuit of a political atmosphere that allows successive prohibitions against terrorist violence to become more accepted as examples of legitimate state behavior.

Inevitably, the pressures of politics and economics will invade and

Table 10.1 G-7 national terrorist policy comparisons[1]

Policy	Canada	France	Germany	Italy	UK[2]	US[2] (Japan)[3]
Extradition	Bilateral	ECST	ECST	ECST	ECST	Bilateral
Economic Sanctions[a]	Moderate	Moderate	Moderate	Reluctant[b]	Moderate[c]	Favors[d]
Concessions[e]	No	No	No	No	No	No
Anti-terrorist Assistance Program[f]	Yes	Yes	No	No	Yes	Yes
Pursuit Across Borders (EEC)[g]	No	Yes	Yes[h]	Yes	Yes	No
Intelligence Cooperation[i]	Yes	Yes	Yes	Yes	Yes	Yes
Diplomatic/Visa/ Immigration	Yes[j]	Yes[k]	Yes[l]	Yes[m]	Yes[n]	Yes[o]
Military[p]	Strong[q]	Strong[r]	Ambivalent[s]	Reluctant[t]	Strong/ Moderate[u]	Strong[v]
Prosecution/ Detention	Strict[w]	Strict[x]	Strict[y]	Strict[z]	Strict[aa]	Strict[bb]

Notes
1. This comparison was constructed by Colonel Gaines.
2. Also signatories to US–UK Supplemental Extradition Treaty.
3. Except where it concerns oil, Japan generally supports the US (*The New York Times*, December 30, 1985): A1).

Sources

a   *The Financial Times* (March 29, 1986), Sect. 1: 46; *The Times* (London) (June 4, 1988): 2.

b   Karin Santoro *et al.*, 'Italian Attitudes and Responses to Terrorism', *Terrorism*, 4 (1987): 289.

c   *The Times* (London) (April 27, 1987): 2.

d   *The Christian Science Monitor* (March 27, 1987): A12.

e   Paul L. Bremer III, 'U.S. Antiterrorism Assistance Program', *Department of State Bulletin* (June 1988): 63.

f   Bremer, 'U.S. Antiterrorism'.

g   *El Pais* (May 30, 1987): 16.

h   *Hamburg Deutsche Presse-Agentur* (December 5, 1986).

i   Great Britain, Foreign and Commonwealth Office, *International Terrorism: The European Response* (London) (June 1986): 2; Paul L. Bremer III, 'U.S. Policy and Proposed Legislation', *Department of State Bulletin* (January 1988): 44.

j   *The Windsor Star* (July 31, 1988): A1, A4.

k   *The Financial Times* (March 29, 1986), Sect. 1: 46; Great Britain, Foreign and Commonwealth Office, *International Terrorism*: 1.

l   Great Britain, Foreign and Commonwealth Office, *International Terrorism*.

m   Great Britain, Foreign and Commonwealth Office, *International Terrorism*: 2.

n   Great Britain, Foreign and Commonwealth Office, *International Reaction to Terrorism* (London) (January 1986).

o   Paul L. Bremer III, 'Counterterrorism Strategies and Programs', *Terrorism*, 4 (1987): 337ff.

p   Robert Oakley, 'International Terrorism', *Foreign Affairs*, 3 (1986): 619; *The New York Times* (April 14, 1987): A8.

q   *Time* (March 28, 1986): 16.

r   *The Financial Times* (March 29, 1986) Sect. 1: 46; *The Christian Science Monitor* (September 23, 1986): 32.

s   *The Washington Post* (April 17, 1986): A22.

t   Santoro *et al.*, 'Italian Attitudes': 289.

u   *The New York Times* (June 15, 1988): A1.

v   *The New York Times* (April 14, 1987): A8.

w   *The Sun* (Vancouver) (December 12, 1986): A7.

x   *The Christian Science Monitor* (July 24, 1987): 137.

y   *The Christian Science Monitor* (March 27, 1987): A12.

z   *The Christian Science Monitor* (March 27, 1987): A12.

aa *The Montgomery Advertiser* (October 21, 1988): A1; A14.

bb Dante B. Fascell, 'Combatting International Terrorism: The Role of Congress', *Georgia Journal of International and Comparative Law* (Winter 1986): 659.

perhaps peremptorily disengage the consensus, subtract from the clarity, put in doubt the credibility, or negate the consistency. But the pattern appears set. The G-7 typifies that 'sort of creeping institutionalization'[42] that acknowledges and activates a collective body of norms, in this case against terrorist activity.

Interestingly for future researchers, is the question of whether the G-7 informal organization might be useful for multilateral action on issues other than economics and terrorism. Given the select membership of seven heads of state or government, could the issues of brain drain, refugees, environmental pollution, and other transnational problems of concern to these governments also be addressed with some success? Agreement on these and other issues among this key Seven could augur positively for more unified positions and action plans at other international fora. The vehicle of international coalition-building, like its domestic counterpart, stemming from consensus on issue imperatives, would seem to offer fertile soil for social science researchers.

Notes

1. This manuscript represents only the author's view and does not purport to represent official opinion of the Air War College, Air University, or the Department of the Air Force.
2. United States Department of State, *Patterns of Global Terrorism: 1985* (October 1986): 2.
3. *Patterns of Global Terrorism*: 3–4.
4. *Patterns of Global Terrorism*: 2.
5. For more on this line of argument, see James E. Winkates, 'The Terrorism Environment', *Quarterly Journal of Ideology*, 11 (3) (1987): 9ff.
6. 'President Nixon Establishes Cabinet Committee to Combat Terrorism', *Department of State Bulletin* (October 23, 1972: 475–80. For the most complete and detailed treatment of the origin, evolution, and policy considerations of US anti- and counter-terrorist initiatives through the Reagan Administration, See Marc A. Celmer, *Terrorism, U.S. Strategy, and Reagan Policies* (Westport, CN: Greenwood Press, 1987).
7. Central Intelligence Agency, *International Terrorism in 1979* (National Foreign Assessment Center, 1980): iv.
8. R. G. Sawhney, 'International Terrorism: Focus on Western Europe', *Strategic Analysis* (January 1987): 1161.
9. Sawhney, 'International Terrorism': 1160.
10. Ariel Merari (ed.), *On Terrorism and Combatting Terrorism*, proceedings of an international seminar (Tel Aviv, 1979) (Frederick, Md: University Publications of America, 1985): x.

11. Geoffrey M. Levitt, 'The Western Response to State-Supported Terrorism', *Terrorism*, 11 (1988): 55–66.
12. Eric Willenz, 'U.S. Policy on Terrorism; In Search of an Answer', *Terrorism*, 9 (1987): 238.
13. The G-7 declarations and statements on terrorism can be found in toto through 1987 in Geoffrey M. Levitt, *Democracies Against Terror; The Western Response to State-Supported Terrorism* (New York: Praeger Publishers, 1988).
14. *Public Report of the Vice President's Task Force On Combatting Terrorism* (Washington, DC: US Government Printing Office, February 1986): 12.
15. Levitt, 'The Western Response': 56.
16. William L. Waugh, Jr, *International Terrorism: How Nations Respond to Terrorists* (Chapel Hill, NC: Documentary Publications, 1982): 210–12; later expanded in 'Informing Policy and Administration: A Comparative Perspective on Terrorism', *International Journal of Public Administration* (December 1988).
17. Winkates, 'The Terrorism Environment': 5. The natural connection between terrorism and tourism is explored more fully in Linda Richter and William L. Waugh, Jr, 'Tourism and Terrorism as Logical Companions', *Tourism Management* (December 1986): 230ff.
18. *The Times* (London) (April 5, 1986): 6; *The Times* (London) (April 28, 1986): 5.
19. *Facts on File*, 46 (May 9, 1986): 329.
20. *The Times* (London) (February 6, 1987): 6.
21. John M. Broder, 'Terrorism Still Rising, U.S. Expert Says', *Los Angeles Times* (September 28, 1988): 5.
22. Levitt, *Democracies Against Terror*: 93.
23. *The Times* (London) (April 18, 1986): 8.
24. *The Montgomery Advertiser and Alabama Journal* (December 26, 1988): 5A.
25. Levitt, *Democracies Against Terror*: 97.
26. The author gratefully acknowledges the research assistance, in this section especially, of Colonel George P. Gaines, USAF, who prepared his major research project at the Air War College (1989) on this subject, and which was completed with the author serving as research advisor.
27. *The New York Times* (March 9, 1986): A1.
28. George J. Church, 'Hitting the Source', *Time* (April 28, 1986): 16.
29. James M. Markham, 'Europe's Anti-Terrorism Tied to U.S. Libya Raids', *The New York Times* (April 14, 1987): A8.
30. *The New York Times* (April 14, 1987).
31. *The New York Times* (January 6, 1987): A13.
32. See, for example, Great Britain, Foreign and Commonwealth Office, *International Terrorism: The European Response* (London: June 1986); Levitt, *Democracies Against Terror*; Sawhney, 'International Terrorism': 1159–69; and Ekkehart Muller-Rappard, 'The European Response to International Terrorism', in M. Cherif Bassiouni (ed.), *Legal Responses to International Terrorism* (Dordrecht: Martinus Nijhoff, 1988): 385–417.

33.   William Echikson, 'Euro-Terrorism on the Run', *The Christian Science Monitor* (March 8, 1988): 1.
34.   Personal interviews with senior French and Spanish officers (February 1989).
35.   Echikson, 'Euro-Terrorism': 1.
36.   *The Manchester Guardian Weekly* (January 31, 1988).
37.   William Echikson, 'Italian Terrorism Plummets', *The Christian Science Monitor* (March 27, 1987): 1.
38.   Echikson, 'Euro-Terrorism': 1.
39.   Markham, 'Europe's Anti-Terrorism': A8.
40.   *Weekly Compilation of Presidential Documents*, 24 (23) (June 13, 1988): 822.
41.   Levitt, *Democracies Against Terror*: 97ff.
42.   Levitt, 'The Western Response to State-Supported Terrorism': 57.

11 International Crime Policy and Efficient Resource Allocation

Scott McKinney

THEORETICAL DISCUSSION

From this economist's point of view, the interesting question about international legal relations is the impact that they have on the **resources that individual nations allocate to police and law enforcement activities**. How do these relations affect the overall level of expenditures for these activities? How do they influence the way these expenditures are used? How do the level chosen and the uses decided upon compare to the optimal level and the optimal uses? In this chapter I will explore these and related questions using a general model developed to analyze the influence of interjurisdictional interactions on resource allocation. The model takes into account both direct interactions between the police and legal institutions of one nation and those of another, and indirect interactions that take place through the impact that these institutions have on criminal activity and its distribution across nations.

My approach will be to begin by developing the model, making clear the assumptions on which it rests. I will then use the model to analyze the impact of various types of international interactions and to compare these impacts to a concept of optimality widely used in the economic literature. This analysis will enable me to discuss the influence of cooperation and to evaluate it. In the second section of the chapter I will present the results of some studies that have investigated the influence of interjurisdictional interaction in a number of contexts in order to suggest the importance of these interactions and of cooperation. Finally, I will bring the results of these studies to bear on the issue of international legal relations.

The model that I will be using to address these questions is based on mainstream micro-economic analysis as it has been applied in the area of public finance or public sector economics. We make rather strong

243

assumptions about the rationality of government decision-making in applying this analysis, but it has proved to be extremely fruitful in interpreting, modeling, and predicting jurisdictional behavior. This approach has been widely used to analyze the influence of 'brain drains' on the level of public education expenditures chosen by governments, of crime spillovers from one community to another on the level of police expenditures in those communities, of military alliances on the military expenditures of the allies. A good number of these studies have found that these interactions between jurisdictions – drains, spillovers, alliances, and so on – have significant effects on the level of expenditures in these jurisdictions.

Following the path broken by these studies, I assume that each jurisdiction has a decision-making process that involves the comparison of the benefits and costs resulting from any change in police and law enforcement expenditures, and that as a result of the frequent application of this process the jurisdiction's expenditures tend toward an efficient level.[1] There are two important questions that can be asked about this process and its outcome. The first is how reflective the decision-makers' evaluations are of those of their fellow citizens; this question will not be investigated here. The second is whether these decision-makers take into account **externalities** – that is, benefits and costs to citizens of other jurisdictions – when they choose a level of expenditures. I will assume initially that they do not; in this case the efficient outcome toward which they tend is efficient only from the point of view of that jurisdiction, and not necessarily from the point of view of all the interacting jurisdictions taken together. Subsequently I will consider the influence of institutions that facilitate international cooperation and thus perhaps result in these externalities being taken into account.

I assume that police and law enforcement expenditures in a given jurisdiction are effective in reducing crime in that jurisdiction, both by encouraging people to abandon criminal activity altogether and by diverting some criminal activity to other jurisdictions. This effectiveness is the source of a number of externalities that I will explicitly take into account in this model. The first, the crime diversions or spillovers already mentioned, arise when rational and mobile criminals decide that the heightened risk of getting caught and convicted in the more active jurisdiction makes it worthwhile to shift their activities to another jurisdiction. For example, when Colombia cracked down on drug production and trafficking in 1984, these activities simply popped up in the bordering countries of Venezuela, Brazil, Ecuador, and

Panama.[2] Interestingly, a part of these crime spillovers are also **internal costs** and should be taken into account by the more active jurisdiction's decision-makers. Given the extent of international travel in today's world, a country with many of its citizens abroad at any time for tourism, education, and business cannot produce crime spillovers with impunity. For example, the United States cannot support the war against drug traffickers in Bolivia and Peru secure in the knowledge that no US citizens will be killed.

The second externality included in the model, an external benefit, is the obverse of the internal cost just mentioned. The lower crime rate in the more active jurisdiction is a benefit to foreigners in the country. As long as tourism is an important source of revenue for many countries these benefits may not be undervalued by the decision-makers; but under different circumstances, such as when the foreigners are unwelcome immigrants to begin with, these benefits might not be considered at all in deciding how much to spend on police protection.

The third externality arises from the globalization of criminal activity and the existence of international criminal organizations. Centralized command of criminal activity and the international movement of illegal goods means that criminal activity in one country is not independent of that in another. As a result, effective police action in one country may reduce crime in another if an organization is crippled or a supply line destroyed. This interdependence is behind the efforts of the United States to control the flow of drugs into the country by supporting police, military, and legal activities in Latin America and the Caribbean. Activities aimed at the drug trade carried out by countries other than the US with their own funds generate external benefits for the US to the extent that they actually achieve their goal.

It might also be argued that the US generates external costs for other countries in the Western Hemisphere by choosing to fight its drug wars on foreign soil (and, indeed, by providing a market for cocaine in the first place). This is a variation of the first type of externality in the sense that US actions create costs for citizens of other countries, but differs from it because it is not the displacement of the crime but the relocation of the police activity that creates the costs.

Before moving on to discuss cooperation and its impact on resource allocation, I want to develop a framework for evaluating the influence of externalities and to briefly explore the implications of the model I have been developing within this framework. This framework is built around two benchmarks, two identifiable patterns of resource allocation. The first is the pattern that results when a nation looks out only for its own narrow interests – that is, ignores the externalities. The second is the pattern that would result if the externalities were fully taken into account. This is a Pareto-optimal level of output (or, more precisely, a Pareto-improvement) – that is, a level of output that is better than the first because all the countries are better off, or because the benefits to those countries that are better off are more than sufficient to compensate those countries that are worse off. The presumed superiority of this pattern is based on the argument that, given the rational behavior of the decision-makers, the greater the circle of people whose interests are taken into account the more opportunities for mutually beneficial resource reallocation can be explored. This is not to suggest that there won't be times when the interests of the different nations won't be at odds, but simply that if there are methods available for negotiation and compensation, then mutually beneficial arrangements can be made.

As long as the benefits and costs of police and law enforcement activities vary in consistent ways with the level, externalities have predictable effects on how the internally efficient level of these activities differs from the optimal. I will make the standard assumption of this literature, based on the law of diminishing returns, that the marginal or additional benefit of one more unit of the activity – one more police officer, for example – will fall as more and more units are used. Conversely, the marginal or additional cost will rise as more units are used. Consider first a situation where there are external benefits such as a reduced flow of drugs into the United States because of Colombian police actions against the Medellin mafia. This model suggests that the level of police activity that is efficient from Colombia's point of view will be lower than the optimal level. The difference between Colombia's likely choice and the optimal level is made up of police activity with benefits that outweigh costs only if the external benefits are taken into account. Now consider a situation where there are external costs such as violence in South America as a result of US-funded operations against cocaine-refining facilities. This model suggests that the US will be interested in carrying out more of these operations than is optimal, with the difference being made up of operations with benefits that outweigh costs only when the external costs are ignored.

Not only do externalities influence the behavior of the jurisdictions generating them, they also influence the behavior of jurisdictions **receiving them**. A jurisdiction that receives the external benefits of a certain activity carried out by a neighbor is likely to reduce its own level of that activity and reallocate some of those resources to other functions. To use the example of action against the Medellin mafia, the more the US does in this area the less Colombia may feel called upon to do. This is often referred to as Colombia 'free-riding' on US police and law enforcement activities – that is, enjoying the external benefits of US activity and in some sense not doing its part. This reaction on Colombia's part is the first in a possible series of reactions between the two countries. The US can respond in at least two ways. The first is that it might simply increase its level of activity in response to Colombia's reduction, in an attempt to increase the joint US–Colombian level to what the US considers an optimal level. Clearly, at this point Colombia may decrease its activity once again, and so on. Some economists[3] have argued that this sort of interaction takes place in NATO with the result that the larger members of the alliance spend a larger proportion of their GDP on defense. The second possible US response is a strategic one:[4] seeing where the first pattern of response leads, the US might decrease its attacks on the drug traffickers in the hope that Colombia will respond by increasing its attacks. Colombia may respond as hoped, or it may also behave strategically. In any case, as long as either of the countries behaves strategically, there will be a tendency for the campaign against the Medellin mafia to be pursued half-heartedly both because of the behavior of the producer of the external benefits discussed above and because of the behavior of the recipient just discussed.

In the face of the resource misallocations expected to result from the presence of externalities, what improvements might cooperation achieve? I will concentrate on two major types of effects that cooperation among nations can have on the level and effectiveness of police and law enforcement activities. The first of these effects, and one that I will discuss only briefly because it is less central to my argument, is the **efficiency effect**. This is the lower cost of particular activities assumed here to result from the cooperative use of facilities and information. Nations can shift procedures such as sophisticated forensic analyses to the more efficient or advanced agency, for example. They can achieve economies of scale in activities such as information storage and retrieval, where economies of scale are lower costs per unit of the activity achieved by carrying out many units of the activity.[5] Nations might also increase their effectiveness by sharing information and coordinating their actions against criminal activity, such as is done through the US DEA in the case of drug trafficking.[6]

These reduced costs of achieving a given goal are clearly an advantage to the countries involved, but it is less clear exactly how the countries will respond to the opportunities presented. One possibility, of course, is that the savings will be used for other functions. Alternatively, we can think of a fixed amount of money being allocated to this function, so that more activities will be possible at this lower cost per unit. Using a standard micro-economic analysis of the situation, I would argue that the country will respond on the basis of a demand curve for the police or law enforcement function in question, demanding more units of the activity at the lower cost per unit. The impact on the total budget for this function will depend on the relative sizes of the change in cost per unit and the number of units demanded. On the basis of my estimate of the response of US metropolitan area police agencies,[7] I would predict that the budget will fall as costs fall but by a smaller percentage; however, this response will certainly vary from country to country and for different functions.

The second effect that cooperation can have is the **internalization effect**. Internalization is the act of including formerly external benefits and costs in the decision of how to allocate resources among different functions, activities, and so on. It can be achieved by shifting the decision-making responsibility to a group whose interests encompass the jurisdictions that produce externalities for one another. The Federal Government, the US Department of Justice, the FBI, as examples, achieve this in the United States, allocating resources with a view to their impact on the whole country rather than simply to one state or one local jurisdiction. As a result they will investigate crimes, such as interstate frauds, where no individual state would find it worthwhile to do so because so many of the benefits would accrue to other states. It is not necessary for the decision-making group to have direct control over an agency in order to internalize externalities. The same goal can be achieved if the group simply has the power to coordinate the activities of various national agencies with a view to the general welfare.

The model that I have developed here suggests that the internalization effect of cooperation will be to move the actual level of police and law enforcement activity toward the optimal level. If external costs loom larger than external benefits in the minds of the new decision-making group, then internalization should lead them to choose a lower level of activity. For example, if the most evident externality is the diversion of drug-related crime from one country to another, shifting the responsibility for allocating police and law enforcement resources from national agencies to an international coordinating committee will reduce the perceived benefits of many police activities. A good portion of the benefits perceived by the national agencies are simply transfers of drug production and trafficking to another country, and these will not be seen as benefits by the international coordinating committee. As a result, this body should choose a lower level of activity.

If, on the other hand, external benefits loom larger, then internalization should lead to a higher level of activity. If the international pay-offs to one country's efforts against international drug cartels are the most evident externalities, major campaigns against these cartels that were previously considered too expensive might make sense once the benefits to all the countries in which the cartel operates are taken into account. The international body can thus be expected to argue for higher levels of activity. In general this model leads us to expect that, as criminal activity becomes more international and more complex in its organization, cooperation among law enforcement agencies becomes more important; to the extent that the latter are less organized internationally than crime organizations, valuable law enforcement activities will remain unrealized.

How do international discovery orders fit into the model I have developed here? I will treat as external benefits any services that the courts of one country give to those of another through the principle of comity. These services fit into the category of benefits to the citizens of one country that result from the actions of another country. They differ from the externalities already discussed in that the interaction between the countries occurs through the **legal structure** rather than through criminal activity. This difference has the consequence of giving the country more control over these externalities. In the case of other types of externalities we have discussed, the level of externalities followed automatically from the level of the activity chosen; in the case of international discovery orders the country or court has some independent control over the extent to which these will be honored.

The model that I have developed here suggests that courts will tend to respond to international discovery orders less than optimally. Satisfying the request of a foreign court requires resources that could be put to the use of the domestic court. A court will be much more willing to grant these requests if it knows it will receive like treatment when it issues an international discovery order, since it can balance the benefits it will receive at some other time against the resources it uses now to respond to another court's discovery order. The principle of comity, in supporting this treatment of international discovery orders, is a first step toward the optimal use of courts' resources. In one sense, comity can be seen as playing the part of an international coordinating committee and internalizing these externalities; following this principle, every court would respond to another's discovery order, regardless of the cumulative impact on its own resources, in pursuit of the common good. However, I doubt that the principle of comity alone can yield this outcome. The court issuing the discovery orders cannot be counted on to take into account its orders' impact on the foreign court's resources, and an overburdened foreign court cannot be counted on to maintain its commitment to the principle.

Simple reliance on the principle of comity or other legal principles is likely to break down when there are substantial differences in the number of orders issued by different courts. Countries that issue few orders but receive many might not find it in their interest to enter into an agreement that requires them to respond. Thus the European Community would find the Brussels Convention on Jurisdiction and the Enforcement of Judgements in Civil and Commercial Matters advantageous, but the US and the UK might not enter into a similar agreement.[8] An overburdened country may resort to blocking legislation and refusal to enforce the judgments of US courts.

· My interpretation of this situation is that the principle of comity is a good foundation for policy, and that suggestions like David Gerber's[9] are valuable extensions, but that an effective policy must address the resource issues as well as legal ones. I have suggested as a response to other externalities a policy of internalization through the creation of a coordinating committee. This prescription is based on the argument that this response will move the allocation of police and law enforcement resources toward the Pareto-optimal. However, more than simple internalization is called for. It is important to keep in mind that a Pareto-optimal allocation of resources is an improvement over the original either because all countries are better off or because the benefits to those countries that are better off are more than sufficient to compensate those countries that are worse off. It seems unlikely to me that a country made worse off, because it is responding to many more international discovery orders than it is issuing, will be satisfied by the knowledge that the group of countries is better off. I think that a realistic solution must attempt to make all the participating countries better off by actually **paying compensation out of the benefits created by the resource reallocation**.

This leads me to think in terms of an international body that would serve two functions. One is to negotiate a set of criteria for international discovery orders and to control the flow of discovery orders by applying these criteria. The second function is to gather funds from the countries involved, probably on the basis of the number of discovery orders issued, and redistribute them with the goal of compensating countries heavily burdened by requests. The creation of this body would provide a forum for a discussion of the valid uses of discovery orders. If this discussion led to agreement, it would give courts issuing orders some confidence that, if they followed the guidelines, those orders would not be ignored. Courts asked to respond to an order would have been party to the negotiation of the agreement, would know that the order had been approved by the international body, and would be compensated at least approximately for its use of resources; they should thus be more willing to respond. In this way both legal and resource issues would be dealt with.

EMPIRICAL EVIDENCE

In this section I want to support the theoretical possibilities suggested by my model with some empirical evidence. I will review a number of studies which have estimated the impacts that interjurisdictional inter-action and cooperation have on resource allocation. None of these studies has examined the specific area I have discussed in the previous sections; I am using them to show the importance of spillovers and cooperation in various areas in order to convince the reader that these interactions are worth taking into account in the case of international legal relations.

The first study involves the influence that the migration of educated individuals has on expenditures for education. In 'Geographic Spill-lover Effects and the Allocation of Resources to Education', Burton Weisbrod[10] argues that the education provided by a community yields benefits to the community in general as well as to the individual receiving the education and his or her immediate family. These benefits include a richer cultural and political life, greater economic produc-tivity and higher local tax revenues. To the extent that the individuals receiving the education move to other communities, or those support-ing the education through their taxes do so, those paying for the education do not enjoy the community benefits that result. This problem has bedeviled many communities. The British were at one time concerned about the loss of their scientists. Developing countries have long been concerned about their 'brain drain' to the developed world. Why should a community spend a large portion of its resources educating its young if most of them are going to leave and provide benefits somewhere else?

Weisbrod hypothesizes, first, that a community that loses a larger proportion of its citizens through outmigration will spend less on the education of each student than it would in the absence of that outmigration and, second, that a community which gains citizens through immigration will not as a result spend more on the education of each student. He tests these hypotheses using 1950–8 data on migration and 1960 data on all other variables for the 48 contiguous states. He uses simple regression analysis to estimate the relationship between current expenditures on public education per public school student, on the one hand and, on the other, the percentage change in the population resulting from net outmigration or from net immigration and a number of other important explanatory variables.

There are some problems with the data. For one thing, net rather than gross migration is used, so that a community that is actually losing many of its educated citizens may not be shown as doing so if it is simultaneously gaining many individuals through immigration; nonetheless, the model we are using suggests that in a case like this the incentives to spend on education will be much lower since the relationship between the expenditures and the educational level of the population is weakened by the migration. For another thing, the data are for states while the decision-making unit is the local school district; a school district losing all of its youth to an in-state city will have a smaller incentive to educate them well, but the loss will not show up in the state data being used.

Despite the weaknesses of the data, the analysis finds a significant **negative relationship** between net outmigration and expenditures per public school student. A one percentage point increase in net population outmigration is associated with a 1.1 per cent decrease in public education expenditures per public school student. This result suggests that in the most extreme case, that of Arkansas, the net outmigration of 22 per cent of its population over the 1950–8 period led to a 27 per cent reduction in expenditure per student. These results are consistent with the first hypothesis; the lack of a significant relation between expenditures per student and net immigration is consistent with the second hypothesis. Interpreted in terms of the model we have developed, Weisbrod's study suggests that spillovers have a substantial impact and can lead to serious underprovision of public services.

An example of the influence that negative externalities can have is provided by my own study of crime spillovers and police agency cooperation in US metropolitan areas.[11] The situation in this study is similar to the international one analyzed on pp. 244–9 above, and the categories presented there are based on those used in this study. Police activity is seen as yielding internal benefits to residents of the jurisdiction and external benefits to residents of other jurisdictions who commute in. At the same time, it generates crime spillovers which yield external costs to neighboring jurisdictions and internal costs to residents of the active jurisdiction who commute into other jurisdictions.

My analysis, based on the same assumptions as those presented on pp. 244–6 above, leads me to make the following hypothesis. First, if external benefits are the more significant externalities, a jurisdiction's decision-makers will tend to choose a level of police expenditures lower than the optimal. Under these circumstances, I expect cooperation to have both an **efficiency effect**, which should lower expenditures and increase police protection, and an **internalization effect**, which will tend to increase police protection and, with it, police expenditures; thus cooperation should unambiguously increase police protection but may either increase or decrease expenditures. Second, if external costs are the more significant, decision-makers will choose a level of police expenditures and protection greater than the optimal level. Cooperation should have the same efficiency effect as before, reducing expenditures and increasing protection, and an internalization effect of decreasing both expenditures and protection; as a result cooperation should reduce expenditures, but its impact on police protection is unclear. Finally, the outcomes in those cases where the influence of cooperation is ambiguous can be used to suggest whether the efficiency or the internalization effects are dominant.

I investigate these questions using 1970 data for 80 Standard Metropolitan Statistical Areas (SMSA). Since I am not able to measure externalities directly I use an indicator of potential externalities. I argue that if there is only one agency there can be no spillovers and that as the number of agencies increases the probability increases that both law-abiding individuals and criminals will cross from the jurisdiction of one agency to that of another. Since individuals are more likely to go to nearby jurisdictions than ones farther afield, what is more important than the total number of police agencies is the number nearby. Therefore the density of police agencies is used, that is, the number per 100,000 SMSA residents. Cooperation is measured more directly, since formal working relationships between police agencies can be identified. It is measured by the proportion of the SMSA population that receives police services from two or more agencies on the basis of two forms of cooperation referred to as coordination and alternation.[12]

I develop a model of the determinants of crime rates and of the determinants of the demand for police expenditures, and then estimate the impact that potential spillovers and cooperation have on these variables, holding other determinants constant. Potential externalities are related to higher expenditures and lower crime rates, from which I conclude that negative externalities are more significant than positive ones. A one standard deviation increase in potential externalities is associated with an 8.2 per cent increase in police expenditures according to one estimate, with an insignificant 2.1 per cent increase according to another. It is associated with a decrease in property crimes ranging from 8.3 to 10.2 per cent, a decrease in violent crimes ranging from 10.7 to 11.4 per cent.

An increase of one standard deviation in cooperation is associated with a 6.6 per cent decrease in expenditures according to one estimate, a statistically insignificant 4.5 per cent reduction according to another; this negative impact is what the model predicts, since both the efficiency and the internalization effects will be exerting pressure in this direction. It is associated with a decrease in the violent crime rate variously estimated to be 10.5 and 12.9 per cent; this I interpret to mean that the efficiency effect of cooperation, which tends to reduce crime, outweighs the internalization effect, which would tend to allow a higher crime rate.

The results of the analysis are consistent with the model I developed, conforming to predictions in those instances where a hypothesis could be tested, suggesting the greater significance of negative externalities than of positive and of efficiency effects than of internalization effects in those instances where the data did not allow a hypothesis test. They indicate that the crime spillovers resulting from police activity and the improvements in efficiency resulting from police cooperation are important, and they suggest that it is worth thinking about similar effects in the international sphere.

A third area where there has been a substantial amount of research on the influence that interjurisdictional interactions have on resource allocation has been that of military alliances and international organizations. An early article in this area was Olson and Zeckhauser's 'An Economic Theory of Alliances',[13] which looked at behavior in NATO, in the United Nations and in foreign aid giving. The authors argue that international organizations are formed to serve a common interest, and they choose to analyze this common interest as a public good. As they use this term, a 'public good' has the following characteristics. Nonpurchasers cannot be kept from consuming the good; for example, a country like Switzerland which is not a member of NATO might be protected by NATO nonetheless. Secondly, there is little or no additional cost to extending the benefits of the public good to another country; once NATO's nuclear deterrent is in place, using it to protect one more country may not require any added expenditure.

Treating the members of the alliance as rational and individualistic welfare-maximizers, Olson and Zeckhauser conclude that no member of the alliance will have the incentive to allocate an optimal amount of resources to the common interest of defense, since they will not consider benefits to other members of the alliance in their decision. Each country will provide less than the optimal amount of defense and so the alliance as a whole will provide less than the optimal amount. Furthermore, the level of defense that is provided will be disproportionately provided by the larger members of the alliance. This results from each ally's reaction to receiving the benefits of others' defense expenditures. A nation will take this spill-in into account in deciding how much to spend on defense itself, generally deciding to spend less because of it. The spill-in received by a smaller ally is much larger than the spill-in received by a larger ally, so the former will tend to reduce its expenditures more than the latter, thus shifting the burden to the larger members of the alliance.

Olson and Zeckhauser test the hypothesis that larger countries will devote larger proportions of their national income to public goods. They find a positive and statistically significant rank correlation between a NATO member's national income and the proportion of its national income spent on defense. They find the same for the relation between a UN member's GNP and the proportion of their financial assessment actually contributed. In one of two samples they find a significant positive relation between national income and the proportion spent on foreign aid, but in the second sample the positive relation is not significant. The authors suggest that the mixed results in the last case might be due to the fact that, while there is a common interest in development, there are also special relationships between some developed nations and particular developing countries which would reduce the public good aspect of giving aid.

Olson and Zeckhauser return to the NATO example to suggest a solution to the problem of public good underprovision and disproportionate burdens. They indicate that NATO infrastructure is provided jointly and that the costs are shared according to a negotiated agreement. This contrasts to other elements of defense, where each nation pays fully for what it provides. Because the costs as well as the benefits of the public good are shared, each country finds it in its self-interest to agree to infrastructure expenditures closer to the optimal. Because the shares are negotiated, the process of adjustment that leads to disproportionate burdens does not get under way. Not only do the authors not find a positive relationship between national income and the proportion allocated to infrastructure expenditures, they find a significant **negative one**. The lack of a positive relation is important for two reasons. First, it is consistent with the theoretical interpretation we are giving these results. Second, it suggests that cost-sharing policies are effective ways of dealing with the problems raised by the commonality of interests in alliances.

What conclusions can we draw from these studies that are applicable to the issue of international legal relations? My interpretation is that, particularly in conjunction with numerous other studies, these studies indicate that spillovers have significant effects on the way in which resources are allocated to public goods such as education, police protection and defense. Weisbrod's study, because it has a measure of the spillover (however imperfect), provides fairly clear evidence that positive externalities are associated with lower expenditures, here interpreted as sub-optimal expenditures.

My study, because it has an indicator of potential spillovers rather than a measure of actual spillovers, does not provide evidence that is as clear as Weisbrod's on the impacts of externalities. It does suggest that crime spillovers influence police activity, though it is difficult to guess how international crime spillovers compare with those that occur within a metropolitan area, or how police reactions at the international level compare with those at the local level. It also shows that cooperation helps to both reduce crime and decrease police expenditures. This tells us that at the local level police agencies use cooperation to increase efficiency, and that mere cooperation of still separate agencies does not result in much internalization. On the other hand, the fact that lower potential spillovers, the number of police agencies per 100,000 people, are associated with lower expenditures and higher crime rates suggests that internalization does occur when jurisdictions are merged. In other words, internalization may not be easy to achieve in the international sphere where nations are unwilling to give up their sovereignty.

The Olson and Zeckhauser study indicates that the type of process we see at work at the level of local and state governments also works at the international level. More specifically, it suggests not only how the burden of international undertakings such as the fight against drug cartels might be distributed, but also how the problem of disproportionate burdens might be alleviated through negotiated cost-sharing.

The international nature of much crime demands of police agencies and legal systems a cooperative and equally international response. In the case of the example of drug trafficking that I used extensively on pp. 244–9 above, there is evidence of movement in this direction. The growth of drug abuse in countries besides the US makes control of production and trafficking more of an international public good than it was previously.[14] Cooperation should be more forthcoming than if the drug trade represented simply a source of income and employment for these countries. At the same time, an institutional framework for cooperation is being built. Treaties are being negotiated to facilitate cooperation in law enforcement and the US DEA has begun to serve as a coordinating agency in international criminal matters.[15] These studies suggest that the capabilities created by this framework will be used by the cooperating countries to improve the efficiency of their law enforcement efforts, rather than to internalize spillovers. Internalization must probably wait for the establishment of an international organization with a mandate and a structure to separate the decision-making process from national interests, so that international considerations can drive the allocation of resources used to control international crime.

In the case of international discovery orders, the international body I have proposed to deal with criteria, coordination, and compensation represents a movement toward a cooperative international response to crime. I presume that most countries view the ability to gather evidence abroad as an important weapon in the fight against crime. The incentive to join this international body should be strong as long as membership does not come with a significant burden, and Olson and Zeckhauser's results suggest that payment of compensation should alleviate this problem. I do not think that this proposal represents a transfer of power anywhere near as significant as that suggested at the end of the previous paragraph. Rather than moving decision-making to a higher level, it simply provides a forum for agreement and a mechanism for facilitating that agreement. Nonetheless, it will tend to internalize the external benefits that international discovery orders create by facing the court issuing the order with a cost and giving the court receiving the order access to the resources it needs to respond. Thus the proposed body could do more to move resource use toward the Pareto-optimal than cooperation among metropolitan police agencies seemed to. This is not to say that it will be easy to overcome the differences in legal systems and reach agreement on the legal issues. It is to suggest, rather, that there is an **economic problem** that stands in the way of gaining the cooperation of many countries, and that this problem as well as the legal one must be dealt with before the common interest can be served.

Notes

1.   Used here to mean that level of expenditures that is part of the particular overall allocation of a group's (one jurisdiction or many) limited resources that does the most to achieve the group's goals.

2.   Ethan A. Nadelmann, 'International Drug Trafficking and U.S. Foreign Policy', *The Washington Quarterly* (Fall 1985): 93.

3.   M. Olson and R. Zeckhauser, 'An Economic Theory of Alliances', *Review of Economics and Statistics*, 48 (1966): 266–79.

4.   Scott McKinney, 'Public Good Producers and Spillovers: An Analysis of Duopoly Behavior', *Public Finance Quarterly*, 12 (1984): 97–116.

5.   This differs from the rising marginal costs referred to earlier in that I assume that marginal costs rise when more activities are carried out using a facility of a given size, while here I suggest that for some activities lower costs per unit will result if the size of the facility is increased.

6.   Nadelmann, 'International Drug Trafficking': 100.

7.   Scott McKinney, 'Interjurisdictional Externalities and Cooperation: Effects on Police Expenditures and Crime Rates', *Urban Affairs Quarterly*, 20 (1985): 325–43.

8.   Mark W. Janis, *An Introduction to International Law* (Boston: Little, Brown and Company, 1988): 261.

9.   David J. Gerber, 'International Discovery After Aerospatiale: The Quest for an Analytical Framework', *The American Journal of International Law*, 82 (1988): 521–55.

10.   Burton Weisbrod, 'Geographic Spillover Effects and the Allocation of Resources to Education', in Julius Margolis (ed.), *The Public Economy of Urban Communities* (Baltimore: Johns Hopkins Press, 1965): 192–206.

11.   McKinney, 'Interjurisdictional Externalities'.

12.   **Coordination** indicates that agencies 'interact in the planning of the day-to-day operations of service provision'; **alternation** indicates that different agencies provide the service either to different clientele or areas within the jurisdiction or to the same clientele at different times, Elinor Ostrom, *et al.*, 'Defining and Measuring Structural Variations in Inter-organizational Arrangements', *Publius* (1974): 87–107.

13.   Olson and Zeckhauser, 'An Economic Theory'.

14.   Nadelmann, 'International Drug Trafficking': 96.

15.   Nadelmann, 'International Drug Trafficking': 100.

Bibliography

Adams, John (ed.) (1985) *The Contemporary International Economy: A Reader* (New York, NY: St Martin's Press).

Akehurst, Michael (1982) *A Modern Introduction to International Law* (London: George Allen & Unwin).

Anand, R. P. (1983) *Origin and Development of the Law of the Sea: History of International Law Revisited* (The Hague, the Netherlands: Martinus Nijhoff).

Axelrod, Robert (1984) *The Evolution of Cooperation* (New York: Basic Books).

Baldwin, David (1985) *Economic Statecraft* (Princeton, NJ: Princeton University Press).

Bandow, Doug (1985) *U.S. Aid to the Developing World: A Free Market Agenda* (Washington, DC: The Heritage Foundation).

Barnet, Richard J. and Muller, Ronald E. (1974) *Global Reach: The Power of the Multinational Corporations* (New York: Simon & Schuster).

Basic Agreement of 1986 (1986) (Oslo: Norwegian Federation of Trade Unions and Norwegian Employers' Federation).

Bates, Robert (1981) *Markets and States in Tropical Africa* (Berkeley, CA: University of California Press).

Baum, Warren C. and Tolbert, Stokes M. (1985) *Investing in Development: Lessons in World Bank Experience* (New York: Oxford University Press).

Bennett, A. L. (1988) *International Organizations: Principles and Issues* (Englewood Cliffs, NJ: Prentice-Hall).

Brand, Stewart (1987) *The Media Lab: Inventing the Future at MIT* (New York: Viking).

Brandt Commission (1983) *Common Crisis North South: Cooperation for World Recovery* (Cambridge, MA: MIT Press).

—— (1986) *North–South: A Program for Survival* (Cambridge, MA: MIT Press).

Brown, Lester R. and Flavin, Christopher (1988) *The State of the World 1988* (New York: W. W. Norton).

Browne, William and Hadwiger, Don (eds) (1988) *World Food Policies: Toward Agricultural Interdependence* (Denver: Lynne Reinner).

Brundtland Commission (1987) *Our Common Future* (New York: Oxford University Press).

Bulmer, Charles and Carmichael, John (eds) (1988) *Employment and Labor-Relations Policy* (Lexington, MA: Lexington-Heath).

Caldwell, Lynton K. (1984) *International Environmental Policy: Emergence and Dimensions* (Durham, NC: Duke University Press).

Calista, Donald (ed.) (1986) *Bureaucratic and Governmental Reform* (Greenwich, CT: JAI Press).

Carroll, Owen (1986) *Decision Power with Supersheets* (Homewood, IL: Dow Jones-Irwin).

Celmer, Marc A. (1987) *Terrorism, U.S. Strategy, and Reagan Policies* (Westport, CN: Greenwood Press).

259

Christy, Francis T., Jr and Scott, Anthony (1965)   *The Common Wealth in Ocean Fisheries: Some Problems of Growth and Economic Allocation* (Baltimore: Johns Hopkins Press).

Cingranelli, David (ed.) (1988)   *Human Rights: Theory and Measurement* (London: Macmillan).

Clark, Robert (1985)   *The Future Taking Shape* (Fairfax, VA: George Mason University).

Clarke, Arthur C. (1984)   *Ascent to Orbit: A Scientific Autobiography The Technical Writings of Arthur C. Clarke* (New York: John Wiley).

Codding, George and Rutkowski, A. M. (1982)   *The ITU in a Changing World* (Dedham, MA: Artech).

Cutler, Neal (ed.) (1984)   *Aging and Public Policy* (Urbana, IL: PSO).

D'Amato, A. A. (1971)   *The Concept of Custom in International Law* (Ithica, NY: Cornell University Press).

Davies, Paul and Freedland, Mark (1983)   *Kahn-Freund's Labour and the Law* (London: Stevens).

Demac, Donna A. (ed.) (1986)   *Tracing New Orbits: Cooperation & Competition in Global Satellite Development* (New York: Columbia University Press).

de Soto, Hernando (1989)   *The Other Path* (New York: Harper & Row).

Dizard, Wilson P., Jr (1985)   *The Coming Information Age: An Overview of Technology, Economics and Politics* (New York: Longman).

Downing, Paul and Hanf, Kenneth (eds) (1983)   *International Comparisons in Implementing Pollution Laws* (Amsterdam: Kluwer-Nijhoff).

Evans, Peter *et al.* (1985)   *Bringing the State Back In* (Cambridge, MA: Cambridge University Press).

Falk, R. A. (1975)   *A Study of Future Worlds* (New York: Free Press).

Food and Agriculture Organization (1987)   *Fifth World Food Survey* (Rome: FAO).

Galloway, Jonathan F. (1972)   *The Politics and Technology of Satellite Communications* (Lexington, MA: Lexington Books).

— — (1987)   *International Journal* (Lexington, MA: Lexington Books).

Gardiner, John and Mulkey, Michael (eds) (1975)   *Crime and Criminal Justice: Issues in Public Policy Analysis* (Lexington, MA: Lexington-Heath).

German Yearbook of International Law, (1983) (1984)   (Kiel: University of Kiel).

Goulet, Dennis (1989)   *Incentives for Development: The Key to Equity* (Chico, CA: New Horizons Press).

Groom, A. J. R. and Taylor, Paul (eds) (1975)   *Functionalism: Theory and Practice in International Relations* (New York: Crane, Rusak & Co.).

Gross, Bertram and Pfaller, Alfred (eds) (1987)   *Unemployment: A Global Challenge. Annals of the American Academy of Political and Social Sciences* (Beverly Hills, CA: Sage).

Handelman, J. R. *et al.* (1974)   *Introductory Case Studies for International Relations: Vietnam/The Middle East/Environmental Crisis* (Chicago: Rand McNally).

Heclo, Hugh (1974)   *Modern Social Politics in Britain and Sweden* (New Haven, CT: Yale University Press).

Hilsman, R. (1987)   *The Politics of Policy Making in Defense and Foreign Affairs: Conceptual Models and Bureaucratic Politics* (Englewood Cliffs, NJ: Prentice-Hall).

Holt, Jack (1988)   *Cases and Applications in Lotus 1-2-3* (Homewood, IL: Irwin).

Hwang, Ching-Lai and Yoon, Kwangsun (1981)   *Multiple Attribute Decision Making: Methods and Applications* (New York: Springer-Verlag).

ILO (1968)   *The ILO and Human Rights* (Geneva: UN).

—— (1985)   *Freedom of Association: Digest of Decisions and Principles of the Freedom of Association Committee of the Governing Body of ILO* (Geneva: UN).

—— (1987a)   *Freedom of Association: A Workers' Education Manual* (Geneva: UN).

—— (1987b)   *Report of the Director General* (Geneva: UN).

—— (1988a)   *Human Rights – A Common Responsibility* (Geneva: UN).

—— (1988b)   *Record of Proceedings* (Geneva: UN).

—— (1987c)   *Social Security Protection for Seafarers Including those Serving in Ships Flying Flags other than those of their own Country* (Geneva: UN).

IUF (1981)   *The Coca-Cola-Guatemala Campaign 1979–1981* (Geneva: UN).

Jackson Commission (1969)   *A Study of the Capacity of the United Nations Development System* (Geneva: UN).

Janis, Mark W. (1988)   *An Introduction to International Law* (Boston: Little, Brown and Co.).

Jervis, Robert (1976)   *Perception and Misperception in International Politics* (Princeton, NJ: Princeton University Press).

Kant, Immanuel (1981)   *Kritik der Praktischen Vernunft* (New York: Random House).

Katzenstien, Peter (ed.) (1978)   *Between Power and Plenty: The Foreign Economic Policies of Advanced Industrial States* (Madison, WI: University of Wisconsin).

Kay, David A. and Jacobson, Harold K. (1983)   *Environmental Protection: The International Dimension* (Totawa, NJ: Allanheld, Osmun & Co.).

Kegley, Charles E. and Wittkopf, Eugene R. (1988)   *The Global Agenda: Issues and Perspectives* (New York: Random House).

Kolodziej, Edward and Harkavy, Robert (eds) (1982)   *Security Policies of Developing Countries* (Lexington, MA: Lexington-Heath).

Krasner, Stephen F. (1978)   *Defending the National Interest* (Princeton, NJ: Princeton University Press).

—— (1985)   *Structural Conflict: The Third World Against Global Liberalism* (Berkeley, CA: University of California).

Latin America Bureau (1987)   *Soft Drink – Hard Labour: Guatemalan Workers Take on Coca-Cola* (London: Latin America Bureau Ltd).

Lawrence, Robert and Heisler, Martin (eds) (1980)   *International Energy Policy* (Lexington, MA: Lexington-Heath).

Lazin, Fred *et al.* (1988)   *Developing Areas, Universities, and Public Policy* (London: Macmillan).

Levitt, Geoffrey M. (1988)   *Democracies Against Terror: The Western Response to State-Supported Terrorism* (New York: Praeger).

Lewis, John and Kallab, Valeriana (eds) (1986)   *Development Strategies Reconsidered* (New Brunswick, NJ: Transaction Books).

Lindblom, C. E. (1980)   *The Policy Making Process* (Englewood Cliffs, NJ: Prentice-Hall).

Lopez-Rey, M. (1985)   *A Guide to the U.N. Criminal Policy* (Burlington, VT: Gower).

MacRae, Duncan and Wilde, Janet (1979) *Policy Analysis for Public Decisions* (North Scituate, MA: University Press of America).

Margolis, Julius (ed.) (1965) *The Public Economy of Urban Communities* (Baltimore: Johns Hopkins Press).

Mason, S. and Asher, Robert E. (1973) *The World Bank Since Bretton Woods* (Washington, DC: The Brookings Institution).

McCord, William and McCord, Arline (1986) *Paths to Progress: Bread and Freedom in Developing Societies* (New York: Norton).

McCormick, John (1985) *Acid Earth* (Washington, DC: International Institute for Environment and Development).

McCracken, Michael C. and Luther, Frederick M. (1985) *Detecting the Climatic Effects of Increased Carbon Dioxide* (Washington, DC: US Department of Energy).

McPhail, Thomas L. (1987) *Electronic Colonialism: The Future of International Broadcasting and Communication* (Newbury Park, CA: Sage).

Mitnick, Barry (1980) *The Political Economy of Regulation: Creating, Designing, and Removing Regulatory Forms* (New York: Columbia University Press).

Mitrany, David (1966) *A Working Peace System* (Chicago: Quadrangle Books).

Montgomery, Robert and Marshall, Dale (eds) (1980) *Housing Policy for the 1980s* (Lexington, MA: Lexington-Heath).

Nadel, Mark (ed.) (1983) *Consumer Protection Policy* (Urbana, IL: Policy Studies Review).

Naess, Arne (1962) *Filosofiens historie. II* (Oslo: Universitetsforlaget).

Nagel, S. S. (ed.) (1990) *Global Policy Studies* (London: Macmillan).

Nagel, S. S. (1984) *Public Policy: Goals, Means, and Methods* (New York: St Martin's Press).

Nardin, Terry (1983) *Law, Morality, and the Relations of States* (Princeton, NJ: Princeton University Press).

Olson, Mancur (1968) *The Logic of Collective Action* (New York: Schocken Books).

—— (1982) *The Rise and Decline of Nations: Economic Growth, Stagflation, and Social Rigidities* (New Haven, CT: Yale University Press).

Palley, Marian and Preston, Michael (eds) (1979) *Race, Sex, and Policy Problems* (Lexington, MA: Lexington-Heath).

Paterson, Thomas (1988) *Kennedy's Quest for Victory: American Foreign Policy, 1961–1963* (New York: Oxford University Press).

Pearson Commission (1969) *Partners in Development* (New York: Praeger).

Peters, Tom (1987) *Thriving on Chaos* (New York: Knopf).

Phaup, E. Dwight (1984) *The World Bank: How It Can Serve U.S. Interests* (Washington, DC: The Heritage Foundation).

Quade, Edward (1989) *Analysis for Public Decisions* (Amsterdam, Holland: Elsevier-North Holland).

Reich, Robert (1983) *The Next American Frontier* (New York: Penguin).

—— (1987) *Tales of a New America* (New York: New York Times Books).

Republic of Cyprus, Ministry of Agriculture and Natural Resources (1983) *Southern Conveyor Project* (Nicosia).

ReVelle, Penelope and ReVelle, Charles (1988) *The Environment: Issues and Choices for Society* (Boston, MA: Jones and Bartlett).

Rodgers, Harrell (ed.) (1984)   *Public Policy and Social Institutions* (Greenwich, CT: JAI Press).

Roessner, David (ed.) (1988)   *Government Innovation Policy: Design, Implementation, Evaluation* (London: Macmillan).

Salamon, Lester (ed.) (1989)   *Beyond Privatization: The Tools of Government Action* (Washington, DC: Urban Institute Press).

Schelling, Thomas C. (1960)   *The Strategy of Conflict* (Cambridge, MA: Harvard University Press).

Schneider, Jan (1979)   *World Public Order of the Environment: Towards an International Ecological Law and Organization* (Toronto, Canada: University of Toronto).

Schneider, Stephen H. (1976)   *The Genesis Strategy: Climate and Global Survival* (New York, NY: Plenum Press).

Schneider, Stephen H. and Randi Londer (1984)   *The Coevolution of Life and Climate* (San Francisco, CA: Sierra Club Books).

Schwartz, Mortimer D. (ed.) (1979)   *Proceedings of the Twenty-First Colloquium on the Law of Outer Space* (University of California, Davis: International Astronautical Society).

Sjostedt, Gunnar (1974)   *Integration and 'Actor Capability'. A Survey of the Theories of Regional and Political Integration* (Stockholm, Sweden: Utrikespolitiska).

Smith, Milton L. (1984)   *Space Wars 1985 – Legal Issues and Implications* (Montreal, Canada: McGill University).

Sohn, Louis B. (ed.) (1972)   *Basic Documents of African Regional Organizations* (Dobbs Ferry, NY: Oceana).

Soroos, Marvin (1986)   *Beyond Sovereignty: The Challenge of Global Policy* (Columbia, SC: University of South Carolina Press).

Springer, Allen L. (1983)   *The International Law of Pollution: Protecting the Global Environment in a World of Sovereign States* (Westport, CT: Quorum).

Steinbruner, John D. (ed.) (1989)   *Restructuring American Foreign Policy* (Washington, DC: The Brookings Institution).

Stepan, Alfred (1978)   *The State and Society: Peru in Comparative Perspective* (Princeton, NJ: Princeton University Press).

Stockwell, Edward and Laidlaw, Karen (1981)   *Third World Development: Problems and Prospects* (Chicago, IL: Nelson-Hall).

Straetz, Ralph *et al.* (eds) (1981)   *Critical Issues in Health Policy* (Lexington, MA: Lexington-Heath).

Tessitore, J. and Woolfson, S. (eds) (1989)   *Issues Before the 43rd General Assembly of the United Nations* (Lexington, MA: Lexington Books).

The World Bank and International Finance Corporation (1983)   (Washington, DC: World Bank).

Thompson, Dennis (ed.) (1985)   *The Private Exercise of Public Functions* (Port Washington, NY: Associated Faculty Press).

Thurow, Lester (1981)   *The Zero-Sum Society: Distribution and the Possibilities for Economic Change* (New York: Penguin).

Toffler, Alvin (1980)   *The Third Wave* (New York: Bantam).

Underdal, Arild (1980)   *The Politics of International Fisheries Management: The Case of the Northeast Atlantic* (Oslo: Norwegian University Press).

Union of International Associations (eds) (1987/88)   *New York: Yearbook of International Organizations.*

United Nations (1972) *Final Documents* (Stockholm, Sweden: UN).
—— (1977) *Treaty Series*, vol. 587 (Stockholm, Sweden: UN).
—— (1977) *Treaty Series*, vol. 634 (Stockholm, Sweden: UN).
United Nations Environment Programme (1985) *Register of International Treaties and Other Agreements in the Field of the Environment* (Nairobi, Kenya: UNEP).
—— (1987) *UNEP Profile* (Nairobi, Kenya: UNEP).
van Lier, Irene H. (1980) *Acid Rain and International Law* (Alpen Aan Den Rijn, the Netherlands: Sijthoff & Noordhoff).
Vernon, Raymond (1971) *Sovereignty at Bay: The Multinational Spread of U.S. Enterprises* (New York: Basic Books).
von Glahn, G. (1986) *Law Among Nations: An Introduction to Public International Law* (New York: Macmillan).
Wagner, Richard H. (1978) *Environment and Man* (New York, NY: W. W. Norton).
Wallis, Allen (1983) *Economics and Politics: The Quandary of Foreign Aid* (Washington, DC: Economics and Security).
Walton, R. E. and McKersie, R. B. (1965) *A Behavioral Theory of Labor Negotiations* (New York, NY: McGraw-Hill).
White, Louise (1987) *Creating Opportunities for Change* (Boulder, CO: Lynne Rienner).
Willetts, P. (ed.) (1982) *Pressure Groups in the Global System* (London: Frances Pinter).
Williams, D. (1987) *The Specialized Agencies and the United Nations: the System in Crisis* (New York, NY: St Martin's Press).
Wilson, James Q. (1973) *Political Organizations* (New York: Basic Books).
World Bank Atlas (annual) (Washington, DC: World Bank).
World Resources Institute/International Institute for Environment and Development (1986) *World Resources 1986: An Assessment of the Resource Base that Supports the Global Economy* (New York, NY: Basic Books).
Young, O. R. (1977) *Resource Management at the International Level* (New York, NY: Nichols).
Zeleny, Milan (1982) *Multiple Criteria Decision Making* (New York, NY: McGraw-Hill).

Name Index

Subject Index